NEVER TURN BACK

THE LIFE OF WHITEWATER PIONEER
WALT BLACKADAR

BY

RON WATTERS

GR THE GREAT RIFT PRESS

NEVER TURN BACK
The Life of Whitewater Pioneer Walt Blackadar

Printed in the United States of America

Published by:
The Great Rift Press
1135 East Bonneville Avenue
Pocatello, Idaho 83201

ISBN: 1-877625-02-7 (hardcover)
        1-877625-03-5 (paperbound)
        1-877625-04-3 (library binding)

Library of Congress Catalog Card Number: 94-76564

Every effort has been made to trace the ownership of photographs and
other materials used in this work and to secure permission when
required. In the event that any question arises as to the use of this
material, we will be pleased to make necessary corrections in future
printings. The author wishes to express his sincere thanks to the
following for permission to use the material indicated:

Portions of Walt Blackadar, "Caught Up In A Hell Of White Water,"
from *Sports Illustrated*, August 14, 1972. Copyright © 1972, Time Inc.
All Rights Reserved.

Photographs by Rob Lesser, courtesy of Rob Lesser Photography, Boise,
Idaho. © Rob Lesser.

Photographs from the Summit Films Collection, courtesy of Roger
Brown, © Summit Films, Inc.

Additionally, a special thanks is due to the following photographers:
Bob Bales, Edgar Boyle, James T. Brock, Dr. Dee Crouch, John
Dondero, Jim Garriety, Dr. Kay Swanson, Dick Tero, and Frank "Shorty"
Wilcox. Additional photos came from the collections of Bob Blackadar,
Sue Blackadar, and Nan Bryant.

Cover photo: Alsek River, James T. Brock.
Back cover (upper): Walt Blackadar, © Frank "Shorty" Wilcox.
Back cover (lower): Colorado River, courtesy of Roger Brown.

Second Printing: January, 1995.

Contents

Contents

*Maps of Idaho and Alaska and 16 pages of
photographs appear between pages 120 and 121.*

Never give in, never give in,
never, never, never, never—
in nothing, great or small, large or petty—
never give in . . . .

Sir Winston Spencer Churchill

Prologue
The Portal

THE COLD, grit-filled water rumbled as it ground between the dark polished walls of the gorge. The half-mile-wide river funnelled into the canyon, and the current accelerated as it narrowed to half its width and then to half again and half once more until it stretched only 200 feet from bank to bank.

Insignificant in the midst of the gray river, a white object floated. Squeezed within the thin fiberglass walls of the 13-foot-long craft, a man with a red helmet paddled toward the portal of the gorge. The red helmet and the orange from his life jacket flashed the only warm colors present in the grim grayness. The man himself was dressed all in black, covered by a quarter-inch layer of neoprene to shelter his skin from the sharp biting cold of the river. He dipped the kayak paddle in one side and then on the other, alternating sides, propelling his boat ever nearer to the rumble. The rhythmic motion of his arms was the only human movement for a hundred miles.

A vast scale of inconceivable proportions rose above him, a monstrous scale of the towering icy mountains of the Saint Elias Range, standing like giant transfixed souls shrouded in white; and slipping slowly downward between the white shrouds moved great masses of glacial ice groaning and cracking, flowing toward the river. To his right the glacier snapped, and another house-sized slab of ice slapped against the river and joined him as an unwanted companion while the water raced into the canyon.

It was early in the day on August 25, 1971, when Walt Blackadar entered Turnback Canyon on the Alsek River. He was a doctor from a small town in Idaho. Originally from the East, he moved his family west shortly after the war so he could be near hunting and fishing. Forty-nine years of age, he had only started kayaking four years earlier, yet with each stroke of his paddle he edged nearer to the start of the most difficult stretch of big whitewater ever attempted by anyone. There was something incredible in the fact that he was there in the first place. He wasn't much of an athlete. He had done some wrestling in high school and certainly he was endowed with strong shoulders, but otherwise he wasn't impressively built nor a particularly attractive man, lacking the smooth muscular look of young, fit world champion kayakers. He was short, had a slight paunch and lacked an athlete's endurance. He mostly kept in shape after his long days at his medical office by working on his ranch and doing a little hunting, hardly the kind of fitness program one would expect in preparation for attempting one of the world's great unrun stretches of whitewater.

On top of that, he had little information to go on. Only a few parties had ventured down the river, and when these early explorers had scampered up to the icy edge and peered down upon the furious torrent of water cascading through Turnback Canyon, they quickly understood the danger and arduously carried their boats and equipment around on the glacier. Blackadar had been told that trying to run the canyon was foolish and impossible. So why was he now attempting it?

He had, at least, hedged his bets somewhat before starting.

2

He was adventurous, but not foolish. Five days earlier, he had reconnoitered the canyon from the seat of a single-engine, fixed-wing plane. Carefully looking at the rapids below, he could see that the waves appeared huge, perhaps as high as 20 feet, but he could see nothing that from his experience was virtually impossible. Difficult? Certainly. Exceedingly difficult? Yes, that it most accurately was—and is. He knew that looking at the river from 500 to 800 feet in the air is deceiving. Once a kayaker gets to river level, rapids that appear harmless from above can be death traps. He would cautiously enter the canyon, he had planned, and get out of his boat, scouting here and there, looking at the rapids. If he saw anything too dangerous, he would carry his boat around.

It was a sensible plan, but the normal standards of river running did not apply here. The water raged between the narrow walls of Turnback Canyon with more raw power, more exhausting frigidity, and more frightening turbulence than anything in his experience. Though he didn't fully realize it at the time, the challenge he faced would in time represent the Everest of the whitewater world. It took years of probing Everest with teams of mountaineers before it was climbed, and then more years of team ascents before it was climbed solo. Walt Blackadar was making the first attempt at whitewater's Everest, and he was making the attempt alone.

He reached the point of no return. The current dashed him between the twisting canyon walls. He paddled up over building swells of water. The bow of the kayak rose and fell, rose and fell. Cold icy water splashed over him as he struggled to keep upright. The pace quickened, and his boat, like a mouse tossed between the paws of a cat, reeled from side to side. "I was in a frothy mess that was far worse than I've seen," he wrote. "[It was] like trying to run down a coiled rattler's back, the rattler striking me from all sides .... I skidded and swirled and turned down this narrow line."

He held on, trying to survive the powerful grip of the river. Busy with the business of survival, he had little time to reflect why he was there. He had mentioned in his diary of the trip that he got depressed watching patients with incurable diseases and that he wasn't getting any younger. He refused to retire from his manhood into what Steinbeck called "a kind of spiritual and physical semi-invalidism." Invalidism. It was a chilling word to Blackadar. He wanted nothing to do with it. In his work, he had seen it all too frequently. And he had seen its menacing shadow descend upon his father. He wondered why his father couldn't fight back. "A kind of second childhood," said Steinbeck, "falls on so many men. They trade their violence for the promise of a small increase of life span." Blackadar held fast to his violence like a miser; no, more like a boxer fighting his way out of a corner, but he had picked some place to stage his fight.

Perhaps he really didn't know why he was there. He knew, simply, that he must try. And try he must, for he was in for the ride of his life. Powerful whirlpools, back-rushing walls of water and vicious holes lay in his path below. He hadn't even begun to face the full fury of the river. If he faltered—or even if he did everything right, but had bad luck—the current could tear him from his boat and he would die. Conrad put it aptly: "An elemental force is ruthlessly frank." To survive the forces of Turnback he must not leave the protection of his boat. Indeed, in his own words, he was "caught up in a hell of whitewater."

Elemental forces had always captivated him. He found a certain sensual pleasure and heightened sense of self-mastery from paddling a canoe across a stormy, white-capped lake, stalking an elk in a snowstorm, or maneuvering a raft over a waterfall. He was motivated by the problem and risk posed by an obstacle and was stimulated by surmounting it, the tougher and more physical the effort, the better. His attempt on Turnback Canyon was an extension of this need to test himself, to arouse his sensibilities, carried to an extreme. In a sense, Blackadar's run of Turnback Canyon is a metaphor for his own life. Even the word "Turnback" is so accurately representative of what he sought to overcome that a Hollywood script writer couldn't have thought of a better appellation. There could be no turning back for Blackadar. The powerful motivating forces which brought him to face the treacherous waters of Turnback Canyon are the same which drove him relentlessly through his life.

And except for one raw, trying day when youth swirled past his reach, he never looked back, he never turned back.

I

Salmon City

SALMON CITY. In a name, the West is embodied. Wilderness. Wild rivers. Plentiful fish and game. The rich struggle of life and nature.

Situated along the banks of the Salmon River, the town began as a collection of canvas tents which sprang up where miners paused, on their rush to the newest gold discoveries, before crossing the Salmon River and making a tiring climb up to the mining camps in the mountains. The nearby gold petered out, but the town grew, quickly turning into a dusty, cow town with liveries, blacksmiths, saloons, and a red-light district. It was a gate to the nearby wilderness: cattle moved in and out of town from remote mountain pastures. Salmon packers guided hunters and fishermen to the bounty of central Idaho. And Captain Guleke and other river pilots started their river trips here to take prospectors on a one-way ride down the rapids of the Salmon, the River of No Return.

By the time the two world wars had ended, the dusty cow town had become more civilized. The red-light district was gone. Main Street was "oiled." Gradually, the valley had been ranched and the Indians moved to the Fort Hall Reservation to the south. Roads had been pushed into the surrounding mountains, but much of the wilderness to the west and north of town remained.

Salmon City. It had a ring to it. It was just the place that the young Dr. Walter Lloyd Blackadar had been looking for. He claimed that he had driven 20,000 miles in the summer of 1949 searching for the "best place to live in the U.S.A." The search began by placing an ad in the American Medical Association journal announcing his desire to work as a family doctor in an established practice in a locale with good hunting and fishing. Eastern medical friends warned him that his announcement lacked the serious, determined tone fitting a young professional fresh from Dartmouth and Columbia. But a handful of established physicians—from Michigan, Oregon, Washington and Salmon, Idaho—found the AMA ad serious enough to reply.

One of those replying was Dr. J. L. Mulder, one of the four medical doctors practicing in Salmon. Mulder told the young doctor of plentiful game, terrific salmon, steelhead and trout fishing and an abundance of primitive, untouched country nearby. That in itself was enough, but Mulder held another ace. Construction would begin soon on the city's first hospital, where Blackadar could conduct general surgery. The new 18-by-18-foot surgical room with a static resistant floor would be outfitted with an advanced hydraulic table, a built-in water-type aspirator, and a state-of-the-art surgery lamp. Blackadar could have the best of two worlds: a new hospital for surgery and the great outdoors for recreation.

With him on the cross-country trip was Shirley, whom he had married four years before. One of her daughters later described her mother as a "real eastern lady." Shirley, however, possessed an adventurous streak of her own. She had served in the Army as a field hospital nutritionist during some of the bloodiest days of the war in the southwest Pacific. In time, she was sent stateside to recover from the debilitating effects of dengue fever which had left her with severe pains in her joints and muscles. During her convalescence, she met the brash, young pre-med student, and their wedding was two years later. Largely overshadowed by her husband's strong personality, she surprised many of her friends and acquaintances who never realized how gritty and determined she was. As her Aunt Evelyn described her, "She was no milk toast."

When they returned to the East after visiting Salmon and other prospects, Blackadar asked Shirley where she would like to live. "If I know you," Shirley replied, "you won't be happy if we don't go back to Salmon." Then, Salmon, Idaho, it would be.

IN September of 1949, Walt and Shirley arrived in Salmon City in a 1948 Chevrolet sedan, top-heavy with luggage tied to the roof, the inside crammed full of their possessions. Packed among blankets, clothing and dishes were their two squirming children, Ruth, nearly 3, and Lois, a few months old.

It was like a dream to Blackadar: all around him—the mountains, the rivers, and the wilderness that lay just beyond the edge of town. He had lived vicariously in wild places when he was a boy in Watchung, New Jersey, reading with relish books by the British doctor Wilfred Thomason Grenfell about his travels by dogsled and missionary adventures in the wilds of Newfoundland. Now here he was, a doctor like Grenfell, on the edge of the Idaho wilderness. He knew precious little about the area, about its wilderness, about its fishing and hunting and the mountain trails. But he was eager to learn.

When Blackadar drove down Salmon's Main Street, the town reflected the prosperity of post-war America. The number of businesses and products available in Salmon in 1949 was probably as diverse as it ever had been or would be. If Blackadar had been in the market for a new car, he had his choice of Fords and Plymouths at Pioneer Garage; Hudsons at Chris' Motor Service; Chevrolets, Cadillacs and Oldsmobiles at Valley Chevrolet Co.; Pontiacs at Benedict's Motor Co.; Jeeps at Lemhi Motors and Studebakers at the Studebaker dealership. Three Studebaker models were displayed in November, and 500 to 600 people came out to look, gobbling 800 doughnuts, 900 sandwiches and 15 to 20 gallons of coffee.

There was a feed store, Army and Navy store, cab service, implement dealer, lumberyard, dairy, dry cleaner, portrait studio, jewelry store, machine shops, furniture stores, insurance agents, real estate firms, cafes, grocery stores, and a mortuary which also provided ambulance service (phone # 71—but never mind about remembering the number; the operator will connect you).

Since the great fluctuations of the boom and bust mining era early in Salmon history, the population of Lemhi County had stabilized and steadily grown to 6,500 in the forties. It remained in the 5,000 to 6,000 range during Blackadar's life there.

Along Main Street stood signs which pointed backward to the town's robust western roots. Two or three log cabins stood along Main Street in 1949, with at least one still roofed with dirt and dating to the 1860s. Other than the log cabins, Salmon in 1949 looked like many growing, rural towns. Neatly painted wood frame houses clustered along side streets. In 1949, if you were in the market for a five-to-six room "completely modern home" with three bedrooms and oil furnace, you would pay anywhere from $7,000 to $11,000.

Social events in the bustling town were equally numerous. In a two-week period at the end of October, the *Recorder Herald* announced a Halloween party at the Elks Hall, a benefit dance at the VFW, a barn dance at the Lemhi Grange Hall, a public card party at the Masonic Hall (refreshments, 50 cents), and another card party at the America Legion Hall (an even better deal than the Masons with both cards and lunch for 50 cents.)

With movies, parties, card games, and dances, the small town offered much for the new arrivals as they settled into a temporary residence. Mulder, an elder at the Presbyterian church, had helped make arrangements for the Blackadars to stay initially at the manse, the church-owned rectory, located two blocks south of Mulder's—and Blackadar's—office on Main. A gravelled road passed by the small brick house in which Shirley had set up her home. In fact, Main Street was the town's only paved road; all the rest of Salmon's side streets were dirt or gravelled. Moreover, once outside the town, considerable lengths of rough, unpaved stretches slowed travel on both US 93 and Idaho 28, the main highways serving Salmon. The conditions of the roads were small reminders that the Blackadars no longer lived in the East.

Another reminder came soon enough. It happened on Friday night, September 22, 1949, the same night that the Salmon High School Savages, playing away from home, racked up their third win that season. A brilliant passing attack led by quarterback Wes Whiting doused Madison High in a 26 to 6 rout. While Whiting was dazzling Savage spectators with his aerial display, three prisoners, Jack Leonard Ashbaugh, Clarence Bauer and Hubert Edwards, quietly worked away with a hacksaw blade. A young friend passed it to them through the window of the Lemhi County jail.

Ashbaugh and Edwards were in on petty crimes and bad check charges, and Bauer was serving out a year's sentence for grand larceny. Bauer's family was particularly well known in the area. Both of his brothers had spent time behind bars; so had his father, Max, who served time on one occasion for dynamiting his father-in-law's house.

The three prisoners sawed through one bar of the pail gate and three small bars across the door. Slipping through the freshly cut bars, they escaped into the night.

For Edwards, freedom was short. A night patrolman spotted him and easily recaptured the escapee. But Bauer and Ashbaugh had better luck, making their getaway in a 1948 Chevrolet sedan belonging to the town's newest doctor.

Blackadar had stored his gun, a .22 Woodsman pistol, and a liberal supply of ammunition in the car, which went with the prisoners. County Sheriff Robert Isley alerted officers throughout east Idaho of the stolen vehicle.

The alert paid off. Ashbaugh was caught in Ogden, Utah, trying to sell Blackadar's pistol, and Bauer surrendered himself to the Blackfoot, Idaho, sheriff. By late September, Blackadar had his Chevy and pistol back.

It had been an extraordinary beginning for Walt and Shirley Blackadar, a reminder that life in Salmon would not be dull. If they hadn't questioned their decision to move to Salmon before, they certainly had ample reason now. In town less than a month, the family car had already been stolen by two prisoners who had hacksawed their way out of the county jail. Yet the vehicle was recovered quickly, and justice was swift. A month later, each of the three escapees was sentenced by Judge Preston Thatcher to a five-year penitentiary term.

For county crime, Blackadar's stolen vehicle and the jail break stand out as news highlights in 1949. Overall, Salmon was a quiet, peaceful town and a good place in which to raise a family. In that year, county records show no homicides, no suicides and only a few petty crimes. The big news in 1949, the year of Dr. Walter Blackadar's arrival, had nothing to do with crime. It had to do with another, more persistent, and far more destructive western antagonist.

THE stories that Blackadar heard of last year's severe winter probably reminded him of scenes from Grenfell's books. It was one of the worst on record for the West. In the plains of eastern Wyoming and Montana, cattle left stranded by the blizzards starved and froze in the white lunar landscape. In Lemhi County, avalanches frequently blocked the highways leading in and out of Salmon, making travel uncertain. If avalanches hadn't blocked roads, then blizzards did. New snow and wind filled in the roads as fast as crews could plow them. In early February, the bus en route from Pocatello, southeast Idaho's largest town, to Salmon in east central Idaho, took an incredible nine days for what was normally a day trip. When it wasn't snowing, it was cold. One of Blackadar's earliest friends in Salmon was pharmacist Roy Durand. Throughout the entire winter, the flowers on Durand's father's newly dug grave remained frozen.

The cold snaps also froze water mains throughout Salmon. Most of the town fended without water as the city workers had no other choice than to wait for warmer weather to repair lines. Even once the ground thawed, some homes continued without water well into the spring. The disastrous winter had left the city's water budget $25,000 in the red. It was obvious that new lines were needed, but the eight-inch steel pipe laid under Main Street in 1910 would not be replaced until years later.*

Blackadar had more than a passing interest in winter conditions. Part of his duties in the partnership included a weekly drive to the Blackbird Mine town site, located deep within the Salmon Mountains, 35 miles south and west of Salmon. The drive took him through country which receives heavy amounts of snow. Once there, Blackadar gave physicals and took care of the health needs of the mine workers and their families. The mine workers lived in a newly constructed company town, which later would be named after the mine's chief commercially marketed product, cobalt.

Once settled into his practice with Mulder, Blackadar wasted no time before he was out fishing. It was fall, and the steelhead were running. Steelhead, a prized catch by any fisherman, is a particular type of rainbow trout that migrates to the ocean where,

---

*Before Blackadar arrived, streets had been dug up everywhere and water mains repaired. Throughout his life in Salmon, the scene of back hoes, piles of dirt, and potholes on Main Street would be as common as colds in the winter. In a never ending search for water breaks, city crews would in the coming years dig up Main Street as many as three times a week.

like salmon, it gorges itself on the ocean riches and grows to an average 10 pounds or more at maturity. Those which spawn in the Salmon River drainage enter the Columbia in the summer, the so-called summer run. Some of that summer run does not arrive in the Salmon City area until February or March of the following year, but a sizeable portion reaches Salmon in the fall.

Blackadar, young, impatient and, increasingly with time, reckless, dove headlong into things. But he also had a calculating, deliberate side. Often when he undertook something new, he sought out those who were known to be the best. It comes as no surprise that his earliest steelhead fishing companion was Roy Durand who was noted around town as an accomplished steelhead fisherman.

He found quickly that steelhead fishing was a different sort of sport, with conditions similar to those of ice fishing. He and Durand would get up on frosty mornings and shiver while working their way along the slippery banks of the Salmon, casting for hours and shaking the ice off their reels and lines. Like most steelhead fishermen they dressed the part: pack boots, bulky canvas trousers, weighty parkas, and caps with wooly ear flaps.

Despite the conditions, it was the excitement of catching steelhead which attracted Blackadar: the flash of the fish, the turbulent, mushroom of water in its wake, the zip and whine of the line running off the reel, the fight that might last 10 minutes or more, and finally, if luck was going his way, a plump 16 pounder.

From steelhead fishing, he went on to big game hunting, and then to duck hunting, and then to trapping and snaring. Soon he was training dogs for pheasant hunting and breaking horses for packing and hunting. The intensity at which he undertook the new sports amazed and even startled some friends. Initially, he felt self-conscious about being a newcomer to the West. He particularly stood out with his New Jersey accent and his eastern sense of etiquette and the manners which his mother had at least been partially successful in instilling.

Jim Caples remembers a breakfast one early morning before a duck hunting trip. The doctor had volunteered to cook, and upon entering the house, the surprised Caples found a carefully arranged New England style table spread "with lots of forks and knives." Caples, enjoying the royal treatment by a hunting pal, thought it all very nice.

It was short-lived. Caples described a later day camping dinner that couldn't have been more different: "He'd seared the duck on each side and then we'd eat it practically raw. There was no silverware. No napkins. No nothing."

"He hated to be from there [the East]," said Nel Bunce, who as a nurse worked with him often. "He was proud of the fact that he was out West. He didn't want anyone to associate him with anywhere but here."

Others agreed. "Walt was trying to be a part of the West," said Jean Tomita, his office manager. Blackadar admired the hero and the rugged individualist of Western mythology. Indeed, if Blackadar's lifestyle in Salmon is compared with the traits of the Western hero which historian Robert Hine has identified, he fits them perfectly. Hine summarized the legendary folk hero as a self-reliant man who is motivated by a competitive spirit, who personifies the individualist and whose strength comes from bouts with the forces of nature. "Alone against the wilderness," wrote Hine, "he [the Western hero] is supreme." There is no better characterization of what Hine describes than Blackadar, years later, running the wild rapids of Turnback Canyon alone.

One additional characteristic defines the Western hero, according to Hine: an individual who knows no moderation. Drinking, hunting, driving—it was all the same. "He always went full speed," said Jim Caples of his friend. He seemed to know no low gear—in his life or Travel-all. On one goose hunting trip, Blackadar drove across a partially frozen marsh covered with three inches of snow. Caples who by now was wise to Blackadar, said, "Doc, you're going to go through the ice." And, of course, that's exactly what happened. Caples spent all that day walking across the ice carrying logs and placing them under the jacked-up Travel-all. By the time they finally got the vehicle out, Caples was completely exhausted. Roy Durand could empathize with Caples. On an elk hunting trip, they managed to get a jeep and one-ton dual-wheel truck carrying two horses stuck after being hit by a three-foot drop of snow. Blackadar, Durand, and their other hunting companions worked with a winch all that night and next morning getting back to town.

*   *

DESPITE Blackadar's penchant for getting his vehicles stuck, both Durand and Caples looked forward to their trips with the doctor. He was fun to be around, full of energy and willing to try just about anything. Interestingly enough, Walt's enthusiasm for the outdoors wasn't something that had been fostered by his father. In many ways, Walt and his father, Lloyd Blackadar, were antipodes to one another. Lloyd was very much a company man, holding a comfortable position as an actuary with Equitable Life, the venerable insurance firm based in New York.

Although Lloyd worked in New York, he had chosen to live and raise his family in Watchung, New Jersey, 40 miles to the southwest. During his years with Equitable, he had made a good salary, and while faced with a long commute in and out of the city, he was satisfied with his ordered, quiet lifestyle in Watchung. The small town, surrounded by hills and forested with maples, oaks and sumacs, was an untroubled haven from the stormy and immoral climate of New York City. A religious man, Lloyd and his wife, Harriett, bundled up their five children and every Sunday attended services at the First Park Baptist Church in nearby Plainfield.

It was Harriett, Walter's mother, who encouraged his childhood interest in the outdoors. Because of work, church and civic responsibilities, Lloyd had little time, nor much of an inclination, for outdoor sports. Harriett, on the other hand, had time and the desire. On one backyard camp-out, Harriett spent the night with Walt and his younger brother, John. They fashioned a candle lantern from a tin can, and she and the boys sat around the glowing lantern telling stories well into the night.

When Walter was older, she joined him, John, and their two cousins on a canoe trip in Canada. At one point, they came to a rapids that Walter was eager to run. It looked dangerous to John, and he refused to accompany his brother. After some discussion, Harriett volunteered to paddle in the bow of Walt's canoe. John protested, but Harriett was determined, and he watched amazed as Walt and his dauntless mother ran the rapids effortlessly.

Harriett couldn't have been more pleased when Walter decided to become a doctor. For her, the daughter of a Baptist minister, it meant that he would be working in a field in which he could truly help others. For Walter, it meant a profession out of the ordinary, one that was stimulating and challenging, and one that would allow him the opportunity to live in a place of his own choosing.

Dr. Walter Blackadar worked away at his job in Salmon, Idaho, treating illnesses, removing fishhooks, setting bones, driving to Cobalt, stitching up lacerations, prescribing medicine for colds and flus, and performing routine surgeries. Like any country doctor, his hours were long, and calls could come at any time of the night. While he immensely enjoyed his work and his place in the community, at the same time he wanted something more than the usual country practice.

Emergencies helped. They galvanized him. Nurses on the hospital staff repeatedly described him as someone who could think clearly and quickly on his feet. He kept a medical bag which was regularly checked and readied for emergency runs. Often on serious cases, he raced ahead and started working on a patient before the ambulance arrived. When Sam Popejoy was shot in the groin in 1951, Blackadar arrived at his cabin 30 miles north of Salmon ahead of even the sheriff. The doctor patched the wound, and once back at the Salmon Hospital, Popejoy recovered.

Blackadar took a more ambitious emergency run in the fall of 1951. A call came for his help when a plane carrying two pilots from Burley, Idaho, crashed in the Chamberlain Basin country of the Idaho Primitive Area. Having no time to change into appropriate clothing, he jumped into a waiting plane, and the pilot flew him to the Root Ranch landing strip. Because of his haste, he still wore a pair of street shoes. It was unwise. He had been transported to the middle of a rugged, mountainous country, covered by a heavy early season snowfall. No horses were available, so he walked six miles through heavy timber and snow to reach the wreckage. He gave plasma and aid to the victims, and then when horses arrived, he helped pack both of them to where they could be flown to the hospital. The newspaper attributed Blackadar, dressed in street shoes and clothing, with saving the men's lives.

IN 1951, Shirley delivered twins, Robert and Nancy. Now that the family numbered six, the Blackadars needed a larger house. (The family would eventually grow to seven with the birth of Sue a year later.) Across the river from the business district on a large bench of land overlooking town—referred to by Salmonites as the "bar"—a house caught Shirley's and Walt's eye. At the southern edge of the bench and at the end of West 4th Avenue stood a large, 4,800-square-foot, two-story house shaded by large cottonwoods and poplars. The property looked out over a curving Salmon River below, a patchwork of irrigated fields south of town, and a collection of gray and brown rooftops which made up Salmon City. It had a big backyard, four acres in all, and, situated at the end of a side street with a hill in back and no neighbors in sight, it was secluded, quiet and idyllic.

Adjacent to their new home, Walt built a corral, and a gentle mare, Lee, became the first of many horses to pasture there. Despite his efforts, however, he never quite mastered the art of handling horses. He fared far better at sports in which he was in control. When a dog or horse entered the picture, things grew more complicated.

Ginger was an example. Ginger, a horse, was traded to Blackadar by one of his patients in lieu of paying a bill. He and his hunting buddy, Joe Nebeker, went to pick up the horse early one morning. They were to meet Ginger's owner at the mouth of Owl Creek, a tributary of the Salmon River north of Salmon City, but when neither his patient nor the horse were there, Blackadar and Nebeker decided to look for them at the patient's cabin, two miles by trail up Owl Creek. It was 3 or 4 in the morning, and Joe described the early morning trip up the steep canyon as uninviting and "so dark that you could almost feel the darkness." They arrived at the cabin. No lights were on.

"Anybody home?" Blackadar yelled in his characteristic dissonant voice that would wake the heaviest of sleepers. Getting no response, he pushed the door open. Everything inside was a mess: the blinds were torn off the windows, a table was upside down, chairs were strewn about, and broken dishes and glass were all over. It looked like a bear had gone on a rampage through the house. "I've never seen such a sight," Joe said, "I believe in the devil, and I believe the devil was in that house." From the darkness, the devil of the house appeared.

"The look on this man's face was like hell itself," Joe Nebeker chillingly recalled. But if the man had any real connection with the underworld, he lost all appearances of it as he stood before them dressed in grey woolen underwear. He explained that his wife had just run off, and overcome by grief and too much drink, he had gotten a little carried away.

By this time, Blackadar had heard and seen enough. He had only one day to go hunting and asked the distraught man to get

Ginger and join them for the hunt. Nodding, the man walked outside and started beating on a tub. To Joe's and Walt's questioning looks, the man explained: "When you want the horse to come, just bang on a tub, and she'll come in for grain." With Ginger and her original owner along, the rest of the day went beautifully. Blackadar had a great day of hunting. He shot an elk, packed it out, and wishing the man well, took Ginger and his elk meat home.

Blackadar and Ginger's relationship, however, was never so ordinary. Ginger had inherited a little of her previous owner's devilish predisposition. On a later hunt, early in the morning before sunrise, Blackadar had sleepily tried to mount Ginger on the wrong side. Suddenly, the tranquility of the morning was broken. Joe Nebeker, who again was with Blackadar, peered through the darkness, saw sparks flying and heard the clattering hooves and Blackadar's excited shouts and curses. Through the early morning dusk, Nebeker caught a glimpse of Blackadar galloping away, trying to throw his other leg over the hapless Ginger. Eventually the clamor quieted, and Blackadar, reeling from the wild ride, trotted back to rejoin his friend.

When the hunt was over, they rode back down to the river. At the river, Blackadar looked for a place to make a crossing to reach the road on the other side. The spot Blackadar chose to ford was above where they had originally crossed.

"Joe, you go first," Blackadar suggested. "You've got a taller horse."

Nebeker agreed, and rode his horse across the river. At one point, his horse teetered a little in the deep water, coming close to swimming. Afraid that the current could push Ginger into a large rock downstream, Nebeker yelled back to Blackadar, warning him not to cross above the rock. Blackadar, not listening, started across where Nebeker had warned him not to be.

Once in the river, the string of packhorses behind Blackadar began to drift in the current, and then chaos broke out as all the horses lost footing, including Ginger. The river washed Ginger into the boulder, toppling the horse and its rider.

Blackadar disappeared. Ginger thrashed in the water, re-gaining her stance. Seconds passed, but no sight of Blackadar. Nebeker's gaze searched the river. Then at last, the doctor popped up like a cork.

"Hell," he sputtered from the river, "that horse was all over me. I couldn't get out from under it."

Nebeker, relieved that the doctor was unhurt, saw some-thing floating downriver which caught his eye: "Doc, your hat's floating away."

"Shoot it!" the aggravated doctor yelled back.

Don Smith, a veteran outfitter and river boat operator on the Salmon, had stopped on the road and watched in amusement as the scene unfolded. Once the embarrassed Blackadar reached the other side of the river with his drenched team of horses, Smith offered to give him a ride back to his vehicle. It was a cold fall day.

"Hell, no, we don't need no ride to our vehicles," Blackadar huffed.

Smith, seeing that his help was unwanted, left them there. Straightening out the horses, Nebeker and Blackadar rode down the road. When they finally reached the vehicles, Nebeker couldn't help but notice the doctor shivering and his teeth chat-tering as he got off Ginger.

Nebeker admired Blackadar's spunk. He didn't have much horse sense; that was obvious. But in Nebeker's eyes, the doctor from the East was turning out to be quite a "rugged character."

II

The Middle and the Main

SOONER OR LATER, Blackadar would run the Salmon River. It was inevitable. A passion for shooting rapids had been in his blood since his boyhood when he ran small rapids in a canoe near his grandfather's cabin in Canada. In the early spring of 1953, he made plans for his first trip down the River of No Return.

The Salmon River originates 30 miles northwest of Sun Valley in Idaho's picturesque Sawtooth Mountains. It runs 170 miles in a general northeasterly direction. The country it passes through changes as the river gains size—first a green, cool broad valley between the Sawtooth and White Cloud Mountain ranges and then through a restricted canyon which twice breaks open at the towns of Challis and Salmon. Twenty miles north of Salmon the river turns sharply, slicing 165 miles west from one side of the state to the other, through the central Idaho mountains, through the largest wilderness in the lower 48 states. It is this rugged stretch of river, known as the River of No Return, which attracted Blackadar.

For 80 miles along this west-seeking stretch no roads run along the river, and even hiking and horse trails only parallel its banks in places. Geologically, here the river has eroded its way into the Idaho Batholith, a large ancient reservoir of molten rock which cooled under the crust. The granite rock which crystallized from the cooling is exposed throughout the area, but no part of it is so dramatically shown along the main stem of the river as in the narrow sculpted granite walls of Black Canyon about midway across the state. The resistant rock has created a falls, known as Black Canyon or Salmon Falls. It is one of the obstacles that Blackadar faced on his journey down the river.

"Deciding there was no time like the present," read the story on the front page of the *Recorder Herald*, "two Salmon residents left Saturday to run the Salmon river in a rubber boat, although neither of them had ever been down the 'River of No Return' before." Leaving March 28, 1953, Blackadar teamed up with Eddie Linck, a stocky and ruddy-faced conservation officer for the Idaho Fish and Game Department. Linck was described by a friend as "one of those guys who'd be the first to try something. He was different." Linck's wife felt that her husband and Blackadar were much the same, both stocky and daring, both a chip off the Old West; both, she felt, would have "fit into the time of the 1800s."

Even though the Salmon River had been run by a fair number of people, the numbers were still small, and by the standards of the town, Blackadar's and Linck's trip was considered adventurous, earning a place in the local newspaper. Having lived in Salmon for a little over three years, Blackadar had heard plenty of stories of the river, and he was anxious to have a go at the rapids. They planned to use a rubber boat with a wooden platform and, in the traditional style of Salmon scows, had mounted sweeps fore and aft.

Blackadar and Linck put their boat in at the Middle Fork confluence, starting on a series of smaller rapids and giving themselves a chance to familiarize themselves with running the sweeps. They "were handling their boat well by the time they reached the end of the river road," the paper reported. Once below the end of the road they were on their own, running each of the Salmon's challenging rapids: Horse Creek, Devils Teeth, Black Canyon Falls, Bailey, Big Mallard, Split Rock, Elk Horn, Growler, Whiplash, Ludwig, Dried Meat, Chittam—each one having its own peculiarities requiring unique routes through the obstacles of holes and rocks.

Away from the cities, away from their jobs, Blackadar and Linck found an undisturbed corner of the old frontier. It was still the same wilderness river that Lewis and Clark had seen and the same powerful rapids run by the original river pilots. When they finally floated out to the road near Riggins at the end of the trip, Blackadar knew that he would return. It was the beginning of a love affair with the river, its rapids, and the few recalcitrant people who lived isolated along its banks, deep in the central Idaho wilderness.

He did return, often, coming back every spring, enjoying the rapids and fishing the early steelhead run. On each trip, he slowly accumulated knowledge of the river, its residents, and their eccentricities. Jim Caples recalled one of his float trips with Blackadar when they stopped at an old cabin opposite Barth Hot Springs, 47 miles downstream from Pine Creek. After a look at the cabin, the group decided that no one had been around for at least a week and made preparations to spend the night there.

Unpacking the boat, the men began carrying their equipment up a steep bank to the cabin. While Blackadar worked on the boat, Caples took up one of the loads. Looking down as he toiled up the steep trail, Caples halted suddenly in front of a pair of feet directly in front of him. He looked up slowly and met the gaze of one of the "biggest set of blue eyes" that he had ever seen. The hands of the figure standing before Caples gripped a rifle.

The blue eyes belonged to Dan Carlson, one of the hermits of the area, who survived by trapping and hunting. He did not own the cabin, but he occupied it, and by backcountry rights that was as good as owning it. Caples, in Carlson's perspective, was trespassing.

Caples, speaking quickly and looking at Carlson's rifle, told Carlson that he was with the Doc Blackadar party. The information put the hermit at ease. He knew Blackadar. After Blackadar arrived and talked with Carlson, they all were invited into the cabin. The hermit, however, made Caples uneasy with his intense stare and the "crazy look" in his eyes. Caples had heard stories about Carlson hiding behind trees and shooting at boats passing by. "You never knew," said Caples, "when the old boy was drawing a bead at your head."

At the first opportunity, Blackadar pulled Caples and his other boating companions aside and suggested that the best way to break the ice with Carlson was to get him into a poker game—and lose to him. Agreeing, everyone chipped in a couple of dollars and did just that. The psychology seemed to work, since the boaters had a restful night's sleep, and in future years, no shots were ever fired at a Blackadar boat.

Blackadar ran the river in a black rubber raft outfitted with a tubular pipe frame molded over the boat's air tubes. A wood floor was bolted into the tubing and ran across the top of the boat. In the front he attached a metal cowling constructed out of sheet metal to break the spray when running rapids. Sometimes, he and his three to five companions would sleep on top of the deck, sheltered by a tarp, covered-wagon style. On an early trip when he was running Black Canyon Falls, now called Salmon Falls, blocks of winter ice still remained on the boulders in the falls. A miscalculation in maneuvering caused the boat to collide against the ice, crushing the metal cowling.

Repairing the cowling and other parts of the boat was always part of the trip. Blackadar's equipment was never in the best of condition. Before leaving on trips, he and his companions would run about town buying hardware and parts to fix the frame or sweeps or raft—or sometimes all three. Once on the river, the boat might bang against ice as it did in Salmon Falls, scrape over a jagged boulder, or bash into a cliff, breaking the sweep. When faced with such problems, Blackadar would rummage around in deserted river cabins for parts, and using wire, rope, rusty hinges, driftwood or whatever else could be found, he patched the damage and continued with the trip.

When Blackadar was in the height of his trapping days, he brought traps on his river trips, setting them at night and checking them in the morning. One night, Caples remembers him trapping three beaver. The next morning, anxious to get on the river, Blackadar and Caples pushed the boat into the river. The doctor started to skin the beaver on the deck, every so often jumping up, and slipping on entrails and sliding across the blood soaked deck, to pull the sweeps to miss a rock. Later the skins were stretched on hoops fashioned from green sticks.

Blackadar also used a small motor to power the boat through some rapids and particularly across the slow lake-like water found on the lower reaches of the river. The small five horse-power Hiawatha motor was in the same kind of condition as his hunting vehicles and the rest of his boating equipment.

"Since the top had fallen off [the motor], you had to wind up the rope manually," said Caples. "The carburetor float valve had to be held open with a stick. In rapids, Walt would use the motor plus the sweeps. We'd go in a rapids, and Walt would yell 'start the motor!' 'Ok!', I'd say and start it, and blue smoke would pour out."

IN addition to stories about the Salmon, Blackadar had heard many tales about the Middle Fork of the Salmon, a tributary of the Main Salmon. A crystal clear mountain stream, it is remote and almost totally ensconced in wilderness. A decade or two after Blackadar began running the river, the Middle Fork would become one of the most popular and well known multi-day wilderness float trips in the United States. On some stretches of the river, one rapid follows another, one on top of another for several miles. It is a smaller river than the Main branch, and maneuvering around its many rocks and through its swift currents with a fully loaded sweep boat challenges the most experienced rafter. With the Main Salmon barely under his belt, Blackadar looked to the Middle Fork.

The Middle Fork begins, from a cartographer's perspective, where Bear Valley and Marsh Creeks come together in a "V" like the tail feathers of an arrow. Ten miles below the tail feather junction is Dagger Falls, formed where the river has met the resistant granite rocks of the Batholith. The river narrows at the falls and drops approximately 30 feet over two jagged ledges of bedrock. The few boaters running the Middle Fork in the early fifties launched their boats from the only road access on upper Bear Valley or Marsh Creeks, ran down to Dagger Falls, portaged their boats around the falls and continued down the river.

At Dagger Falls, Blackadar could watch with regularity one of the most thrilling sights in nature—salmon leaping into the air, slowly climbing the steps of the falls on their instinctual drive which had taken them up the swift rivers of the Pacific Northwest. He wrote of "watching hundreds of huge salmon leave the lower pool and attempt the falls generally to get swept back. Once in a great while a mighty fish would get the correct arc to his leap and land at the brink of the falls and join the quiet water above." Dagger Falls was near the end of the salmon's extraordinary journey from the Pacific Ocean, 800 river miles away.

During Blackadar's early years in Idaho, a person who wished to fish for salmon or to watch the spectacle of chinook surmounting Dagger Falls, walked or rode a boat. Nearly everyone walked, though. It was a wild, demanding raft ride to the falls and then an equally wild and demanding ride beyond. The river quickly separated out the timid and unprepared.*

In the summer of 1953 as the chinook salmon swarmed up the waters of the Middle Fork, Blackadar got a chance to see this challenging stretch of water from the seat of someone else's boat. It was a quick trip with an unusual purpose. The trip started out with Blackadar and a fishing guide by the name of Everett Spaulding, and later, to the confines of their small boat, they added a corpse.

※   ※

IN early July of 1953, Frank Gibson and Wendel Picht were returning to the Bernard Ranger Station, located 68 miles downstream from Dagger Falls. Normally, the men crossed the Middle Fork at a pack bridge, two miles upstream, but Gibson, in order to save a few miles, chose to ford the Middle Fork directly across from the ranger station. Picht decided against it. Gibson rode into the river, trailing a pack mule. His dog followed.

"Gibson suddenly dropped the lead rope and attempted to turn his mount in mid-stream," the *Salmon Herald* reported. "Picht started back to try and assist his partner and when he saw Gibson again he was swimming toward the east bank [from which he had started], about 30 yards out. The struggling forester suddenly went out of sight and Picht was no longer able to see him. The pack animal and the dog succeeded in swimming back to the east bank and the horse was found later on the west bank of the stream."

The search for the body went on for two weeks. Finally,

---

*Things have changed. In the late fifties, the Idaho Fish and Game Department built a road into Dagger Falls to provide access for the construction of a fish ladder alongside the falls in an effort to help salmon reach upper spawning areas. Because the road opened up more of the Middle Fork country, Blackadar and others wanted it closed. But the Fish and Game Department and the Forest Service found it unpopular to stop tourist and fishermen traffic. Float parties were particularly eager to have the road open since they could avoid the shallow and difficult float down Marsh or Bear Valley Creeks and strenuous portage around Dagger Falls.

Everett Spaulding and Woodie Hindman, while guiding a fishing party down the Middle Fork, found Gibson's body. The body drifted into a small eddy near them while they ate lunch. Tying the body to a snag, they floated out and informed the authorities.

The only way to get the corpse out was to float it out. Blackadar, hearing the news, volunteered to accompany Spaulding, who was asked to retrieve the body. Leaving in the morning at Bear Valley, Blackadar and Spaulding floated down to Dagger Falls, portaged the boat around, and continued downstream, running the river's many rapids. Spaulding rowed a plywood, 16-foot-long dorie called a McKenzie, an excellent boat for fly fishing, but one that demands a high degree of skill to maneuver through the rock strewn rapids of the Middle Fork.

Blackadar had his chance to try running the boat, taking the oars in easier sections of the river to relieve the tired Spaulding. Normally, Spaulding took a week floating the river, but the two men rowed steadily, moving quickly downstream. They picked up the body and continued running rapids.

At one particularly tricky rapids, Spaulding stopped. After scouting it, he decided to lighten the load to make the boat more maneuverable. One person was going to have to get out and walk around the rapids. Blackadar, looking at the corpse, said "Looks like he's not going anywhere. I guess I'll walk."

Picking up Blackadar at the bottom of the rapids, Spaulding continued his swift run, floating out to a waiting vehicle at the mouth of the Middle Fork in a record 19 hours. The trip gave Blackadar a chance to watch and learn from one of the best in the business.

With that introduction, Blackadar's next Middle Fork trip came in 1954. Roy Durand and Jerry Butler joined him. They put in at Bear Valley Creek. While running down the shallow, twisting tributary, the front sweep, battered by the river's many rocks, finally broke. Blackadar managed to temporarily patch the sweep, enough so to get them to Dagger Falls. At the falls, they unloaded everything from the raft, carrying first the equipment and then the empty boat to the bottom of the falls.

Just beyond Dagger, Blackadar walked ahead, scouting the next part of the river, almost a continuous stretch of whitewater. Where one rapid ended, another started, and on the river went, tumbling around bends and over boulders. Before getting started, it was obvious that he needed a solid piece of wood for the broken sweep if their boat was to get through the rapids below.

"You know what that little guy did?" Jerry Butler recalled. "He just walked over and took the door off an outhouse and built another sweep!"

With the new sweep fashioned from the outhouse, they worked their way down the river. Beaching the boat every so often, Durand and Blackadar jumped out, scouted rapids ahead, and ran the boat through.

Strong, alert and comfortable in rapids, Blackadar's rafting knowledge and skills were advancing quickly. He was gaining confidence. More and more, Blackadar, who had usually run the sweeps teamed with a partner, asked to run the boat by himself. In mountains with a horse underneath him, he could not always be sure what might happen, but on the river with the sweeps in his hands he was in control. Old home movies show him standing on the deck, his companions hanging tightly to the sides, and the boat bucking in the waves. As he strains against the sweeps, his profile could be that of any of the early western river pilots.

His western conversion was almost complete. One major test loomed.

※　　※

IN the summer of 1955, Blackadar put together a party to run the Middle Fork. He and Salmon Sheriff Bill Baker, Jim Perkins, who was with the State Police, and Don McPherson, a Salmon businessman, launched Blackadar's 10-man raft on Bear Valley Creek. At Dagger Falls, the doctor stopped, planning to portage it over the normal route on the campground side.

Blackadar studied the upper part of the falls. The right side, viewed downstream,* was a sheer drop of what he calculated to be 15 feet. On the left, the water dropped in "stairstep" fashion over four levels. "Below the two water segments lay a sharp rock about 10 feet wide extending to the bottom of the falls," Blackadar wrote. "This dagger-like rock dictated the name of the falls."

They unloaded all their luggage and food and carried it to the pool below the falls. Blackadar, who had been over the portage route four previous times, did not look forward to the steep carry of the boat and frame, a load which, even without their camping equipment, weighed over 250 pounds. He had an idea that might save them the trouble.

He felt sure he could swim out to the dagger rock separating the right and left sides of the top falls. From there he and his companions along the side of the river could ease the loaded boat over the four steps of the falls with a rope, a process called lining. Indeed, this same practice of lining a boat over Dagger Falls had been performed by previous boaters running the river. Everett Spaulding might have talked to him about it.

For protection during his swim, he would hold on to the end of a three-eighths inch rope. If for some reason, he couldn't make the swim all the way across to the center rock, the others would pull him back into the shore. It sounded simple enough.

"I removed my cumbersome life jacket," Blackadar continued in his written version of the events that day. "I needed all the agility I could get—yet knew that rope was protecting me in case of miscalculation. Clutching the rope in my left hand, I dove in well above the falls and swam out hard . . . ." Blackadar's strokes, powered by his strong, bulky shoulders and chest, propelled him so far out in the river that when he looked up to get

---

*Left and right sides of the river are relative, of course, depending how a person views the river. This book follows the accepted river running practice of defining left and right as one looks *downriver*.

his "bearings," he realized to his horror that he had gone too far. The current drew him towards the sheer 15-foot drop on the right side of the river.

His companions on the side misjudged his position and let out more rope, exacerbating Blackadar's predicament. With not enough time to swim back, he was in serious trouble. As he dropped over the edge of the falls, the rope went tight: "There I hung on the rope in the midst of the cascade feeling my arms being pulled out of their sockets." His friends pulled desperately on the rope, but the strength of moving water against an object in rapids—much less against a body in the midst of a falls—exceeds hundreds of pounds of force. Blackadar felt his arms being ripped off like "ancient Christians" whose limbs were pulled off by horses charging in opposite directions. He let go and dropped over, miraculously without hitting a rock.

He was delighted: "I bobbed up almost immediately and paddled around admiring the falls, thinking what a blast it would be to do it again." But euphoria quickly ended as he was jerked under the water by an undertow created by the falls: "I found myself being drawn into a U-shaped indentation in the cliff . . . . I tried to regain the surface but couldn't . . . . I crawled and scratched at the mirror-smooth wall . . . but to no avail. I could easily see the surface and almost reach it with my hand, but it was a world away."

He tried pushing with his legs to get out of the cave, but to no avail. So, "[I] decided to relax and let the current take my body where it would. Immediately the light decreased as I tumbled over and over with the current. Suddenly I saw a huge hole in the rock with the bright evening sun shining through like a searchlight in the night but I was beyond it and could not get back." He thought he might have been able to swim through to safety if he had seen it coming sooner, but as he circled back into the darkness his last hope had been plucked away."

His lungs screamed for air. He started thinking about taking a breath of water, but knew that it would end it all. He felt like he was suspended "at the bottom of a deep well," looking up at the surface, like gazing dreamily up through the tops of "the tallest redwoods in a deep forest." He began sinking into unconsciousness. With his brain deprived of oxygen, he hallucinated, and lightning in brilliant colors flashed through his head. He struggled one last time, trying to swim to the surface. Just as he teetered over the edge of consciousness, he broke the surface and caught several "pants" of air.

The current then swept him toward the lower and last part of the falls. Twisting his body, he attempted to avoid crashing against a rock. His head missed but his pelvis hit the rock, "crunching solidly" as he went over. Baker raced down the rocky shore of the river after the dazed doctor.

Blackadar called out to the sheriff, "If you want me, come and get me."

Baker, who can't swim very well and fortunately still had his life jacket on, dove in and reaching Blackadar, pulled him to shore. Later his friends put him in a sleeping bag and broke out a bottle which, he reported, calmed and revived him after an "hour's shake."

Blackadar seemed to be strangely attracted by the experience. He rarely put pen to paper. It wasn't his form of release. But his close call at Dagger Falls had so moved him that a few years later he wrote about it. Although never published, his explanation of the events of the near drowning was probably prepared for an article. Outside of medical reports and a few letters, it is the only writing that he has left about this period of his life. It was not until 16 years later that he wrote again, and this time it was a far more gripping account of another battle for his life.

While the article needed the help of an editor, the story he told of Dagger Falls is exciting. And through it, he has given us an important look at the forces motivating his life. Danger excites him. When faced with dire consequences, he never gives up, fighting for his life even as unconsciousness overtakes him on his struggle to the surface. Instead of being frightened of water, his ordeal left him confident.

He says at the end of his manuscript that he values "the experience greatly. I proved to myself that I was not afraid to die and that death would be accepted when it came, grudgingly but bravely." Modesty is not his style. He is brave and has no qualms about saying so.

His experience at Dagger Falls was also, on another plane, a rite of passage. Rites of passage are very much a part of Western history and mythology. In one of its forms, the Sun Dance of the Cheyennes, a medicine man slashed the chests of braves and forced sticks beneath the muscles. The sticks were tied to taut ropes hanging from a center pole, and the braves danced facing the sun for hours. "It was," according to one historian, "a rite of initiation, a test of fortitude, and if the supplicant cried out or fainted he would be treated like a squaw for the rest of his life."

Blackadar never cried out. He did not show fear. He passed the test. At 34 years of age, Blackadar had long ago reached manhood, but, in a ceremonious sense at Dagger Falls, he proved to himself that he was worthy of manhood—and a revered place in the West.

III

Esquimautage

"WE WERE BOTH swimming, and horribly unprotected," Blackadar wrote about his earliest whitewater kayaking experience. "No wet suits, water frigid, and almost no flotation in our boats, since I had only a water-ski belt in one end and a beach ball in the other end of my kayak."

The two men had put in on a calm stretch along the Salmon River called Deadwater. Blackadar wore a small 10-pound life jacket and his friend Joe Kinsella wore a water-ski belt. After practicing on the flat water, they felt confident enough to give the rapids below a try, but within a short distance first Kinsella and then Blackadar tipped over. They fell out of their boats and bobbed and swirled out of control down the swollen, muddied waters of the Salmon River.

"Within half a mile," Blackadar continued, "I had both boats by the grab loops and was well upstream, with the kayaks below me. Then, on the first major drop, I was swept into the boats with rib- and jaw-breaking force. I learned fast, and pushed the boats ahead and swam for my life."

For several miles, as the cold water quickly drained their

energy, the two swam frantically, first trying for one bank and then, as the current flushed them around another bend away from the intended shore, struggling for the opposite shore. Blackadar grabbed onto the bow of one of the kayaks while Kinsella held onto the stern. Immediately below a bend, Blackadar "lunged" for an inside eddy. As he dragged the nose of the kayak in with him, the opposite end, held by his friend, "snapped around like a whip."

"My friend, who failed to hold tight," wrote Blackadar, "was flung into the main current. He swam as he never had before, but, being cold and tired and in the middle of the river at flood, he soon faltered." Kinsella, whose small water-ski belt did not provide him with sufficient flotation in the turbulent icy water, struggled to keep his head above water. Exhausted, he looked and saw the life belt which had been jammed into Blackadar's kayak. He reached for the belt, grasped it tightly, and with the few extra pounds of buoyancy, he reached the shore. Cold and tired, they were shaken from the swim but not hurt. Their boats, however, fared worse. Both were destroyed.

THE year was 1967. Blackadar had first developed an interest in kayaking two years earlier when he had met a New Yorker by the name of Nelson Riley. With a flair for doing the unusual, Riley drove into Salmon with a kayak tied to the top of his car and a desire to run some western whitewater. While in the area, Riley ran a stretch on the Main Salmon, including the difficult Pine Creek Rapids. Blackadar, impressed with what Riley had done on the Salmon, ostensibly suggested that Riley try his luck on the more challenging Middle Fork.

Riley took him up on the challenge the next year. While Blackadar ran a supply boat, Riley, his two sons and six other friends ran kayaks and a decked canoe down the Middle Fork. Since he had agreed to run the support raft, Blackadar found himself watching enviously as the slick and agile crafts made easy work of the fast-paced rapids on the Middle Fork. Blackadar did manage to extract compensation for his help. He would run the supply raft and guide them down the river if Riley would give him two kayaks. As agreed, the group presented two boats to Blackadar, who told the Salmon paper that he was "anxious to get a group started here learning the sport."

※   ※

To begin, Blackadar immediately set about learning to roll a kayak. From an upside down position in the water, a kayaker executes the roll by sweeping the paddle in an arc on the surface of the water. A twist of the body, combined with the support given by the sweeping paddle then brings the body back upright. Blackadar knew the importance of the roll. It is the key to kayaking. If one could roll up, nearly any rapids might be runnable—Middle Fork, Main Salmon, and even the big rapids on Hells Canyon or the Colorado River. He had seen the technique demonstrated on Riley's Middle Fork trip. The two boaters in the double canoe could also do a roll. For him, the problem was how to learn.

He started with a book. Using the description and pictures in a small paperback entitled *A White Water Handbook for Canoe and Kayak*, Blackadar, with paddle, splashed and floundered away in a pool. Even though he had been whitewater canoeing and rafting for nearly 30 years, he found that rolling, along with other kayaking skills, was not easily learned. Eventually, he managed to right himself now and then. "I had learned a sloppy roll," Blackadar wrote, "which worked occasionally in a swimming pool but never worked reliably in the river." He learned how unreliable his roll was when he and Joe Kinsella attempted running the Main Salmon below Deadwater in 1967. Their cold exhausting swim proved to Blackadar that he had a long way to go before he could even begin to master the sport.

What he needed, he decided, was a good teacher. But where could he find someone to help him in Idaho? At the time no one else in the state kayaked—at least he knew of no one. He had joined the American Whitewater Affiliation, the only existing national organization of whitewater kayakers and canoers, and he was the organization's sole Idaho member. If he was to get help, expert help, it would have to come from the East where kayaking had taken hold.

Since 1961, one woman from the East was the dominant figure in United States competitive kayaking. A biochemist just getting started on research in the field of cell differentiation, Barbara Wright had tallied an impressive record, and by 1967 she remained undefeated in women's kayaking. Wright's specialty in whitewater competition was the women's one-person kayak category. In competitive lingo, her category is called K-1W. (Other categories include K-2 for two man kayaking, C-1 for one-man canoeing, C-2 for two-man canoeing, C-2M for mixed—man and woman—in a two-person canoe, etc.) In 1967 she placed ninth at the World Championships in K-1W, marking the first time that any American—man or woman—had placed in the top 10. A versatile competitor, she and Bill Bickham also dominated the C-2M category, winning national titles from 1961 to 1965. In her peak year of 1967, she was also the first American to briefly break the dominance of the Europeans, winning at Tacen, Yugoslavia.

Besides her impressive competitive record, she could teach and clearly articulate kayaking technique. In the 1964-65 winter issue of *American White Water*, she wrote an article entitled "Esquimautage Sans Paddle" which described the technique of rolling a kayak (*esquimautage*) without a paddle. Blackadar was trying to learn how to roll a kayak the normal way, with a paddle, and here was a woman so versed in the sport that she was writing about dispensing with a paddle and rolling with two hands and—the ultimate in rolling technique—with one hand. Considering his masculine and competitive nature, Blackadar might have sensed that he would learn better under a woman's tutelage than a man's. Blackadar decided to ask Barb Wright for a lesson.

Wright, living in Boston at the time, received a letter from Blackadar. "He had been a rafter," Wright said, "But he decided that he wanted to try a kayak. He needed a teacher. He liked women and chose me." Blackadar offered her a free trip that summer of 1968 on the Middle Fork of the Salmon in exchange for kayaking and rolling lessons. Since Blackadar had invited other of Wright's competitive friends, the trip looked fun, and Wright eventually took Blackadar up on his offer.

A kind of electricity filled the air surrounding the Blackadars' house overlooking the Salmon River. The early July day buzzed with chatter and cracked with the laughs of old friends meeting and new acquaintances being made. Scattered in piles on the lawn were duffel bags filled with sleeping bags, clothing and tents, fishing poles and tackle, crates of food, bottles of whiskey and more food, and everywhere there lay kayaks, shining and colorful, 15 in all. This was the first of many such scenes, the beginning of the opening of the Blackadar home to the kayaking world, the early spring of a new era of kayaking soon to be re-shaped by the gathering boaters' host.

With Nelson Riley's help, Blackadar had put together a remarkable party. Coming from Canada and the United States, the kayakers were unarguably the *creme de la creme* of North America: former National K-1 Champion Ron Bohlender, former National K-1W Champion Barbara Wright, Canadian Wildwater Champion Herman Kerckhoff, and Eastern K-1W Champion Jan Binger. Herman Kerckhoff and his wife Christa would later develop a Canadian center for kayaking and canoe-ing in Ontario called the Madawaska Kanu Canoe Camp. With the Kerckhoffs were other members of the Ontario Voyagers

Kayak club including Herb May, Steve Knappe, Judge William Sheppard and Klaus Streckman who would later start a whitewater guiding company and pioneer a number of first descents of remote, wild rivers in British Columbia. The indomitable Nelson Riley from the 1966 run of the Middle Fork was back for another go. Others included Jack Nichols, Craig Leonard, Ada Migel, Lynn McAdams, and David Binger, who wrote an article about the trip for *American Whitewater*.

Since Blackadar planned to kayak, his raft which had supported the Nelson Riley kayak party would be left in the garage. In its place, Blackadar had arranged for Bill Guth, an outfitter from Salmon, to run a 24-foot-long sweep boat to carry the gear and seven raft riders.

Binger was immediately impressed with the inexhaustible Blackadar. In his article he described Blackadar as having "more bounce to the ounce than any hoss-wrangler (which he is), or surgeon (which he is), this side of Pecos . . . ." Blackadar scurried about the yard checking food and equipment. He had arranged to have his operating room nurse, Virginia Shumate, join the group as a cook. From the way Blackadar had described the party's cook in his advance letters and phone calls, the male boaters looked forward to having another attractive woman in their midst. "I would love to have recorded the looks on each boater's face when they first met Virginia," Blackadar wrote with relish later. "Virginia was well over 75 at the time, a great gal and great outdoor cook but not quite a honey."

On July 4, the group drove along the Main Salmon, heading upstream through Challis and leaving the river at the town of Stanley, sitting at the base of the Sawtooths. They continued climbing over two passes. The road now led all the way to Dagger Falls. Dropping and winding down the final stretch of narrow dirt road through firs and pines, they caught brief glimpses of the clear, rushing waters of the Middle Fork below.

At Dagger Falls, they unloaded gear and went down to the falls to witness the sight of chinook salmon leaping from the water in their attempt to surmount the cataract. "Watching them," Binger said, "was a magnificent, moving experience." That night Blackadar treated the kayakers to a dinner of wild meat: venison, elk, bear and mountain sheep.

The next morning, the party loaded Guth's raft with all the food and equipment. When the seven raft riders climbed in with the piles of bags and food, it became obvious to Blackadar that the raft was overloaded, but the boat was cast off and the trip began.

The likes of this party had never been seen on the Middle Fork: 15 kayaks, like colorful ducks flapping and darting from eddy to eddy, and in their midst, one giant dark apparition. Within a short distance, the 25-year-old raft established the party's pace for the rest of day. It crashed up against a boulder and stayed. Time after time, the lumbering black boat hung up on rocks and shallows in the river. The kayakers climbed out of their boats and pushed and rocked the raft free, until it ran up against more rocks, requiring once again the tedious process of freeing it.

To lighten the boat's burden, the raft passengers were asked to walk along the bank. The boat continued its ponderous journey, but even without passengers the boat was still too heavy, hanging up and banging and scraping off the boulder-strewn river. "Often when the raft was pushed off from a sharp rock," Binger later described, "a flap of its bottom skin would be torn away, and at one point such a large flap came off that it was decided to beach the raft, unload it, turn it upside down and repair it. This we did, and while Walt and I stitched its dermis, the rest of the party ate, prepared skin grafts for the raft, and did other small chores."

While Blackadar and Binger sewed rips in the floor, a fisherman appeared. His hand was badly infected, and he "was both pleased and surprised to find a doctor doing major surgery on the riverbank." Blackadar cleaned up and bandaged the hand of the fisherman, who had ridden into the area on a trail cycle. The raft was loaded, and once again the party set out, yet "in a few minutes it was hard aground again but this time it had divested itself of its entire bottom, and the pump with which we kept its inflatable wall full of air, fell into the water and started the long trek toward Oregon."

Blackadar examined the damaged raft, and his prognosis wasn't good. The pump was gone, the boat's floor was ripped to shreds, and his group had only made five miles that day. They had five more days and 95 more miles to go. He had organized the trip, inviting some of the best in the nation to accompany him on a run down the famous Middle Fork. Now it wasn't certain if they could even complete the run. His trip, in a nutshell, was in shambles.

Then Blackadar had an idea. Klaus Streckman watched Blackadar walk determinedly toward the bandaged fisherman, who had reappeared on his trail bike. "Hey," Blackadar said, "you've got to give me a ride."

Owing the doctor a favor, the fisherman told him to jump on, and the group watched Blackadar on the back of the smoking bike disappear down the trail.

Blackadar directed the fisherman to take him to the Sulfur Creek Ranch and Landing Strip, seven miles away. When he reached the remote ranch, which is accessible only by trail or plane, he radioed his friend Jim Caples in Salmon and asked him to get the raft ready. Blackadar then called Bill Guth's brother, Norm, who agreed to fly into Sulfur Creek to pick up Blackadar and take him back to Salmon.

Once at Salmon, Blackadar picked up the trailer on which Caples had tied the inflated boat and drove through the night back to Dagger Falls. At first light he slid the boat into the water and, alone, he maneuvered it down the five fast-paced miles of rapids and rocks.

The group, camped at Velvet Falls, awoke that morning. Breakfast preparations had begun while some relaxed in their sleeping bags. Under the circumstances, there didn't seem to be much hurry. They weren't going any place. Sometime around 7:30 and 8:00 a.m., Streckman looked upriver.

"We were having breakfast," Streckman recalled, "when this bloody raft comes down the river." Those watching the approaching raft were astonished. Blackadar, beaming, emerged from the raft, trotted into camp and asked why the group of hearty kayakers was "all lounging around in the sack" when they "should have been up and at 'em and raring to go."

Streckman couldn't believe it. In little more than 12 hours, Blackadar had managed to get out of the remote Middle Fork country, pick up his boat in Salmon, drive four hours back into Dagger Falls and float the upper stretch of the river that had taken the group all of the previous day to negotiate. He arrived bright, happy and ready to go. "It was incredible," said Streckman. "It was just incredible."

Equipment and food were loaded onto Blackadar's raft to lighten the load on Guth's ailing boat. With almost everything sorted out, Blackadar faced one last stumbling block: he did not want to run the raft. After rowing his raft on the last trip for Riley and missing out on kayaking, he was determined this time to paddle a kayak. It was, after all, his reason for putting the trip together in the first place.

The solution, he decided, was to turn his raft over to Craig Leonard. The day before, Leonard, a beginning kayaker, had taken some nasty swims and had badly damaged his kayak. After Velvet Falls, the Middle Fork, at least for a few miles, doesn't require the quick maneuvering demanded of a rafter in the first five miles. It would give Craig a chance to get used to handling the raft.

The athletic Leonard wanted to give it a try. Blackadar gave him some quick instructions on the use of the sweeps, and a short time later Craig found himself running the group's gear down the river. "To sweeten his task," Binger reported, "Kathy Riley, Nelson's pretty young daughter, asked to accompany him on his raft, and with that delectable burden, Craig Leonard began to turn into a first-class raftsman."

Blackadar still had a distance to go before he could be called a first-class kayaker. Barb Wright said that "Walt was mostly upside down on that trip. He was a typical male. He didn't follow instructions."

Barb Wright patiently worked with him, particularly on the roll. "The whole secret," said Wright "is to use the hips." With a proper sweep of the paddle combined with a coordinated hip motion, a kayaker can make effortless rolls, barely requiring any strength. It's all timing and technique. But Blackadar used his arms and shoulders like a wrestler lashing against an opponent and tried to muscle himself up: "He had a macho attitude that if he used the paddle with enough strength he should be able to get up."

With Wright's help his roll became more reliable as the trip progressed. Yet even with expert coaching, Wright felt that he never achieved a highly polished technique. His roll was based more on raw strength than on technique, and as Wright had suspected early on, the lapse haunted him later in his kayaking career.

Whenever a kayaker capsized and swam, which happened regularly to Blackadar on the 1968 Middle Fork trip, other nearby kayakers paddled over to the swimmer and helped haul the boater and his boat to shore. Although it happens even to the best boaters, it is always embarrassing for a kayaker to miss a roll and be forced to swim or be rescued. Blackadar was determined not to have others rescue him, and he kept trying to roll whenever he could.

Despite Wright's difficulties in getting him to roll correctly, Blackadar was an eager pupil. She took advantage of his ingrained competitive nature to add a little amusement to her instructional job. "I'd tell him to go in a hole and he would go in the hole," Wright said. At the same time, Blackadar enjoyed watching the friendly competition between Wright and Kerckhoff, who dared each other to drop into holes. Joining in the games, Blackadar dropped into a hole which Wright had edged by safely. Thrown upside down, he ended swimming. But he climbed back in his boat and was ready for more. After Blackadar had been knocked over in another hole, Wright dropped into the same hole, and this time it was Blackadar who got the laugh as the top U.S. woman's kayaker took a swim.

✳   ✳

BLACKADAR kept the trip lively. His kayaking companions quickly understood why Blackadar's hunting buddies all could count on a fun trip if Walt was along. Streckman described the trip as "always happy hour." There was plenty of booze and good fun. At one time Streckman watched some members of the party fishing from a cliff. Fish were jumping but no one was having any luck. Then, suddenly, Streckman heard a gun blasting. It was Blackadar; with a .44 magnum pistol he had shot a salmon for dinner.*

His laugh rang out from around the campfires at night. He drank and shouted and animated stories to the Easterners who watched disbelieving. The wild Westerner dominated the group. One evening the discussion centered around gun control measures which were under consideration by Congress. Barely a month earlier, Robert Kennedy, while campaigning for the Democratic nomination for president, had been shot and killed by a Palestinian fanatic. The assassination was still fresh in the minds of everyone, and the Easterners favored limiting availability of handguns.

"Blackadar was drinking," remembered Lynn McAdams, a friend of Blackadar's from Montana, "and disagreeing with them. He pulled out his .44 magnum, got some girl's cap, threw it, and tried to hit it." Unable to hit it, Blackadar stomped back and re-entered the argument.

*Shooting any kind of fish with a firearm was and is illegal in Idaho.

47

"We need our guns out in the West," Blackadar boomed at the group. "We need to protect our wives and kids from the animals!"

Lynn McAdams couldn't believe it: "I suppose they [the Easterners] thought 'this guy is a real animal.'" Most of the group did disagree with him about gun control, but his fun-loving, wild antics were hard to rebuff. "Blackadar was never cranky, never down," McAdams said, "He acted as though this may be the last week you'll live, so you might as well enjoy it."

Amidst all the revelry, Barb Wright discerned something else beyond the playful exterior of Walt Blackadar. There was more than met the eye.

"He had charisma. He could grab you," she observed. "There was a black image that he created. Everyone turned and looked at him. It was not the noise. He had a personality that was very black—very strong. I don't mean black in a negative way."

For many, Blackadar's presence, his "black image," made him exciting to be around. But for some men, his personality was too strong, too domineering, too competitive, too arrogant.

For the other gender, it was different. "Women," Barb Wright perceptively observed, "were either frightened by him or intrigued." Blackadar enjoyed the companionship of women. He flirted outwardly with them, often unabashedly, in front of husbands or boyfriends.

"He scared a lot of women by playing games," said Wright. But even if startled by his direct advances, some women were attracted by the brash style and the excitement which surrounded him. At least superficially, his appeal wasn't motivated by a physical attraction—he lacked a movie star face or an athlete's well proportioned build. In reality, he was, as Barb Wright described him, "a little man . . . not a very attractive man." But an aura surrounded him. "Whatever it was, he had it."

AS the trip approached the end, Blackadar and Guth began to play an old river runner's game to heighten the suspense for the climactic last day of rapids. "After three pleasant days, Dr. Blackadar put the psychological squeeze on the party," Binger told the *Herald*. "He kept telling of the horrible rapids ahead with the first below the Flying B Ranch. We were so worried we could hardly eat our lunch and when we got to the first 'rapids,' there was nothing there. But the doctor's prediction came true. The river narrowed as it ran through the gorge with the water likes of which the Easterners had never seen."

When paddling into one of the "gorge" cataracts called Rubber Rapid, Binger was flipped upside down: "My helmet was sucked right off my head, chin strap and all, and I had a long and invigorating swim in suds that were so thick they looked as if there had been an explosion at the old corner brewery. Barb Wright went over, but rolled up, and then several other bodies and boats came floating through." The huge standing waves of the next rapid, Hancock, left them breathless. After maneuvering through a few more rapids, the excited kayakers reached their vehicles at the confluence of the Middle Fork and the Main Salmon. Despite all the troubles the party experienced on the upper river, they arrived at 1 p.m. July 10, 15 minutes after Blackadar's original estimated time of arrival.

DURING the decade of the sixties when Blackadar took up kayaking, many changes were occurring in Salmon and the rest of the country. One issue that challenged Blackadar's conservative political philosophy more than any other related to the environment. The decade had opened with a portent signaling trouble for Salmon River fisheries. On March 16, 1960, the Washington Public Power Supply System applied to the Federal Power Commission for a license to build what was called the

Nez Perce Dam. Previous dam applications for hydro projects on the Snake above the Salmon confluence had been made, but this dam located at river mile 186.2, one mile below the confluence of the Salmon and Snake Rivers, would have an effect on anadromous fish runs like no other. In one grand sweep, the 715-foot-high concrete dam would create two reservoirs: 61 miles of the Snake *and* 53 miles of the Salmon River. The dam, there was no doubt in Blackadar's mind, would put a complete end to the salmon and steelhead runs in Idaho.

Already, three dams on the Columbia River—Bonneville, McNary and The Dalles—were causing reductions in Idaho salmon runs, and an alarming flurry of dam construction on the Snake-Columbia system was under way: Ice Harbor, John Day, Lower Monumental, Little Goose, and Lower Granite. The dams were outfitted with fish ladders, but still salmon were dying. The problem was not a simple one. Research biologists were finding that fish mortality came—and still comes—from a variety of causes, including poisoning by super saturations of nitrogen below spillways, battering against the blades of turbines, increased predation by "trash fish," which reservoir environments promote, and confusion of salmon directional instincts by the slack water in reservoirs.

But the dams on the Columbia and the Snake River were only part of a great plan to harness the rivers of the Northwest. Dam sites also had been located all throughout the Salmon River drainage—on both the Main and Middle Forks of the Salmon. The eight dams planned for the Middle Fork would have made the beautiful whitewater river into one long lake. The Salmon River drainage possessed, according to a US Geological report, more than one third of the gross theoretical power of the state of Idaho. It had, in short, the potential of providing great wealth to imaginative investors.

Not only was dam construction a threat to fisheries, but the effects of logging were also being felt. The problems were never so evident as in what was occurring on the South Fork of the Salmon, the large tributary of the Main Salmon that Blackadar passed on his annual spring float trips. Logging roads and clear cuts continued to proliferate throughout the early sixties. Then it happened. In 1964 and 1965, rapidly melting snow combined with periodic heavy rains sent torrents of water washing across the bare soils of roads and trails. Tons of silt, mud and sand carried by side streams dumped into the river, muddying the turgid waters. When the waters receded, settling silt and sand clogged the river's deep pools.

The silt load from the eroding network of logging roads was so great that the river's current could no longer cleanse the gravel river bed in which salmon deposit their eggs. The gravel of one famous hole popular with salmon fishermen was covered by as much as 18 feet of silt. The salmon fry hatched from the eggs laid in the silt suffocated and died.

The result was one of Idaho's greatest ecological disasters. The salmon declined dramatically until the run of wild chinook on the South Fork, the single most important spawning stream in Idaho and the Columbia River drainage, teetered precipitously close to extinction. For salmon fishermen, the decline was numbing. On opening day of the 1960 salmon fishing season, South Fork campgrounds were filled with tents and campers. Cars and trucks lined up along South Fork roads. Eager salmon fishermen spent more than 10,000 angler days that year casting and catching 3,927 of the big fish. Five years later, the French proverb—if the salmon die, man is imperiled—seemed hauntingly true. On opening day in 1965, the campgrounds were empty and the roads deserted. The Idaho Fish and Game Department had no other choice. To protect the few remaining fish from extinction, the South Fork of the Salmon was closed to salmon fishing.*

*The salmon fishing closure precipitated by severe erosion of logging roads still remains in effect at the time of this writing, 29 years later.

There were more warnings. At the Blackbird Mine which Blackadar had served in his early days in Salmon, toxic chemicals leached from the mine tailings into Panther Creek. Before Blackadar, arrived Panther Creek was used by chinook salmon, rainbow trout, eastern brook trout, Dolly Varden and cutthroat trout. The first records of large fish kills occurred in March, April and July of 1954. Among the fish reported killed were 200 adult chinook salmon. Thereafter, numbers of fish steadily declined and even after the mine was closed, toxic seepage from the tailings continued to pollute Panther Creek.

The signs were too clear to be ignored. Increased, unregulated development was destroying the very thing that had attracted Blackadar to Salmon. He was a conservative, but he found no solace in Idaho Republicans who were either reluctantly embracing conservation legislation or were outright antagonistic to it. On the other hand, the liberal Democrat, Frank Church, had pushed through the Wilderness Bill in 1964. He also worked on a Wild Rivers Bill with the expressed purpose of keeping dams off the Salmon River to protect anadromous fish runs. Blackadar's political allegiances began to shift.

By the mid-sixties, Blackadar was writing letters. On April 2, 1965, Blackadar wrote to Stewart Udall, Secretary of Interior, supporting the idea of designating the Salmon River as a wild river. Concerned about dams, he asked for the "entire" river to be protected, particularly mentioning the stretch from Riggins to its mouth at the Snake ("the wildest water and the most scenic run of the entire river"), in an obvious attempt to prevent the destructive Nez Perce Dam which would flood this area of the river. He also opposed a house bill which reopened mining activities and location of claims along the Salmon River. Blackadar, though he had good friends from the Blackbird mining days, didn't like what mining was doing to fish and wildlife and felt that the boom-bust mining industry held little economic promise. Rather, he told Udahl, "our main future is wildlife and wild rivers."

Blackadar was not alone in his efforts to protect rivers, wildlife habitat, and wilderness. Although the economy of Salmon and the rest of Idaho was tied closely to resource extraction, a small but growing group of environmental activists in Idaho was beginning to question giving free rein to resource exploiters. They advocated limiting development in wild areas of Idaho, better laws to protect wildlife, and legislative protection of rivers and pristine wilderness.

Many of the early environmentalists were, like Blackadar, hunters and fishermen who were fed up with dwindling salmon runs, polluted streams and logging roads in prime big game habitat. They included people like the quiet and unassuming Ted Trueblood, a hunter and fisherman and an editor with *Field and Stream* magazine living in Nampa, Idaho.

Trueblood, Blackadar and most of the others in Idaho's fledgling environmental movement were reluctant activists. They had no interest in attending hearings and getting into the fray of political fights, but they soon found themselves deep in the quagmire of Idaho politics. What was happening in Idaho would have repercussions elsewhere in the country. An Idaho environmental issue would demonstrate how important such issues had become to the electorate and would in a few short years determine the outcome of the Idaho gubernatorial race.

IV
Emergency Call from North Fork

A T THE END of 1968, Blackadar was the only whitewater kayaker in Idaho. But things were changing. The following spring, Dick Roberts, Bill Kendall, a dentist and a doctor from Twin Falls, and Al Beam, a perennial Sun Valley ski bum, joined Blackadar for a day of kayaking on the Salmon. They were hooked, and the new converts to the sport sat around with Blackadar afterwards eagerly discussing other rivers to run. At last, Blackadar had some company in Idaho that shared his passion for kayaking. Kendall suggested that they take a stab at the Bruneau River, a remote, desert river in southwest Idaho, west of Twin Falls.

A couple of weeks later, they were on the river and on their way to making a descent of the wild Bruneau. With only the previous summer of kayaking, Walt Blackadar was already starting to lead rapids. Psychologically, leading rapids, showing the way, is considerably more difficult than following. The leader deals with unknowns and must find a pathway in the rapid through the maze of rocks and holes.

Yet not only was Blackadar leading, he was also beginning to run whitewater others passed around. At one point on the river, Joe Trotta, an experienced eastern kayaker who joined the party for the trip, looked at a rapids and felt it was impossible to run. Trotta carried his kayak around, but Blackadar looked carefully at it, felt it could be run, and ran it. "He may be the only man to have run the entire route without carrying his boat around any of the rapids," Roberts told the Twin Falls newspaper which reported their journey. Within a year, Blackadar had begun to develop a reputation in the sport.

He had another sort of reputation, of course, for his medical practice in Salmon, but now kayaking was giving him broader recognition. Dave Binger's article on the Middle Fork trip had been recently published in *American White Water*, bringing his name to light among river runners. The Twin Falls newspaper, a daily with a much larger circulation than the small weekly Salmon newspaper, called him "one of the most experienced authorities on kayak river running in the West . . . ."

That title stretches the truth. He had only learned how to roll reliably less than a year prior to the article, and by any measure, he would need at least one or two more years before deserving the "experienced" label. Nonetheless, his confident mannerisms and his already total commitment to the sport had left his newly gained admirers and friends in Twin Falls with the impression that he was an "authority" and perhaps something more. Dick Roberts summed up his own feelings about Blackadar: "On the Bruneau. That's when he became my idol."

❋ ❋

In Salmon, it was a different story. Throughout the late sixties and into the seventies as he was gaining a reputation in kayaking, the doctor's relationship with the community was becoming increasingly strained. His bold stands on river preservation, mining restrictions, and wilderness designation pitted him against those in the town who depended on resource extraction for their livelihoods. The tempo had been building for some time, and the town of Salmon, caught in the middle, felt the jarring impacts of that clash, like felled trees crashing on the forest floor.

The initial reverberations came from plans to cut trees in an unroaded area 25 miles west of Salmon called the Clear Creek-Garden Creek area. Blackadar often passed through the area on his way to hunt in the Big Horn Crags. The 80,000-acre roadless area is important habitat for deer, bear, bighorn sheep, mountain goat, and cougar, and it is prime elk country with open south-facing slopes which provide winter range, and nearby stands of timber, which provide needed cover and protection. It was the timber, of course, in the Clear Creek area that drew the attention of Salmon's logging industry.

When Blackadar first moved to Salmon, the timber business was small, self-reliant, and mostly served the needs of the community. But during the heady days of the fifties and sixties housing booms, it expanded and evolved into an industry nearly overnight. The five family-owned mills operating in 1951 went out of business or were bought out by larger companies, and by the sixties, surrounding timber was cut almost exclusively for three firms. The largest of the three was Intermountain Lumber, owned by Montana investors. The company grew exponentially from 3 million board feet of lumber in 1953 to 19 million board feet in 1965.

In a way, logging in Salmon was similar to mining in that it too depended upon government subsidies to survive. For the timber industry, the subsidy came and still comes in the form of roads provided by the U.S. Forest Service. In a central Idaho forest, timber is marginal. The lush stands of pines and firs in northern Idaho, Oregon, California, and Washington are easier to get to and more profitable. In the large roadless Salmon National Forest, new road networks needed to be constructed to reach the timber. Roads are expensive, particularly when constructed carefully to avoid environmental damage—damage which could be extremely costly as was demonstrated when the poor roads and logging practices decimated the salmon runs in the South Fork of the Salmon.

The Forest Service allowed only a certain amount of timber to be cut each year, but the growing timber industry pushed for larger cuts. Under pressure from the industry, the Forest Service pushed up its allowable cut ceilings.

By the late sixties, Gordon Crupper, manager of Salmon's Intermountain Lumber mill, often served as the industry spokesman. Blackadar knew Crupper well. They were fellow Chamber members, and Crupper had served as Chamber president. But like two similarly positively charged particles, they moved steadily apart. During the fifties, Blackadar, like his father and most of Salmon, was conservative and Republican. But because of his interest in protecting rivers, he gradually began supporting Idaho Democrats like Frank Church who sponsored the Wilderness and Wild River Bills.

Crupper steadfastly supported Republicans, even heading the Lemhi County's Republican Central Committee. Crupper, understandably protective of his mill and its workers, looked suspiciously at any kind of government legislation which might interfere with logging. And Blackadar, more and more a preservationist, pushed for federal protection of his beloved rivers and hunting areas. On the Clear Creek issue, the two locked horns.

For some time, the Forest Service had been eyeing the timber in Clear Creek, estimated to be 72 million board feet at the time. Under increased pressure from the Salmon logging industry, the Forest Service finally moved to obtain a right of way for logging access across a small ranch at the mouth of Clear Creek. They were held up when Keith Hansen, the original owner, and Dr. Gil Bacon, an orthopedist and a friend of Blackadar's from Pocatello, refused to grant the right of way.

The delay slowed up the planned timber sales just enough

for those opposed to the development of the area to organize. Mounting opposition rallied by Blackadar and other conservationists in the state resulted in the Forest Service holding a key hearing early in 1970. Blackadar called and wrote his new kayak friends, Dick and Muff Roberts, Al Beam and others, asking them to write or come to the hearings.

The Clear Creek hearing was held in March of 1970 in the Salmon Elks Hall on a Saturday afternoon. Crupper, collected and logical, argued the importance of logging for the county, citing employment figures. Blackadar was more pointed. He wanted no logging in Clear Creek and proposed that the area be merged with the Idaho Primitive Area. "Man and his machines," he said, "are altering nature and her animals with ever increasing impact on our area. Historians may well decide that these 20 years have been the dark ages of our area. I am not sure that we haven't already strangled the goose that lays this golden egg by means of our timber oriented land practices dictated largely by the propaganda paid for by the timber industry."

Other timber officials sided with Crupper, repeating the industry's favorite phrase: protecting the area was "a lock up." "Lemhi County already contributes enough of their tax base for rich boys' playgrounds," said John Jacobson of the Intermountain Company. "Now we have the preservationist interests using this one more wedge to attempt to lock up more land for single purpose rather than accepting the principles of the multiple use act . . . . ," said Dave Ainsworth of Salmon.

Among the timber representatives, others spoke in favor of logging Clear Creek, including an official from Idaho Power, chairman of the Lemhi County Commissioners, and the district superintendent of schools. Those for preserving the area included Peter Henault of the Idaho Alpine Club, Franklin Jones of the Idaho Wildlife Federation, Gerald Jayne of the Idaho Environmental Council, John Merriam of the Greater Sawtooth Preservation Council, Ernest Day of the Idaho Wilderness Committee, Doris Miler of the Montana Wilderness Association, Ken

Collins, a Salmon school teacher, Bill Guth, a Salmon outfitter, Al Beam, and Dick and Muff Roberts.

What happened over the next few weeks astonished nearly everyone. After the hearing, letters favoring protection of the area poured into the Forest Service office. Over a thousand letters in all were sent in by people throughout the country. The vast majority opposed development of the area. Swelling the total were those from university students and school children, including 50 members of a ninth grade environment class in Michigan, urging that the area be preserved as wilderness.

A month after the hearing, in late April, high school students staged Earth Day in Salmon. The idea of students marching in Salmon raised eyebrows. "Students had hoped to march up and down Main Street carrying placards as a protest to man's destruction of his own environment," reported the *Herald*, "but the plan met with little favor from officials." Ken Collins, the high school teacher who had spoken against logging in Clear Creek and served as the students' spokesman, persisted. Finally, the parade was allowed but to discourage participation, the Salmon police chief required all students to have signed parental permission slips. The inoffensive parade finally came off. Some 20 students who had managed to produce permission slips marched up and down Main Street carrying a banner, "Are you a litterbug?" A garbage truck followed the marchers.

All in all it was harmless. The students were well-behaved, and demonstrating against littering could hardly upset anyone. But it did serve in another sense to call attention to a growing polarization of the community. Two archetypes which best personified the opposite ends of the polarity were Blackadar and Crupper. Both were invited to speak at the high school as part of Earth Day events.

Although a few other friends in town supported Blackadar's attempts to protect Clear Creek, only two or three were as vocal as he. The issue no longer could be argued rationally. It had become emotional. Logging families felt that their jobs were threatened, and many people who might have supported Blackadar remained quiet. One of Blackadar's friends in Salmon who was unafraid and unrestrained in his public expression of preserving Clear Creek was Richard Smith. A dentist from California, he had met Blackadar while on a hunting trip. Smith, later invited by Blackadar to set up a dental office in his medical building, accepted and moved to Salmon in the summer of 1969.

Smith had testified at the Clear Creek hearing and strongly supported preservation of the area. He was one of only five from Salmon reported by the *Herald* to take that position. All other conservation supporters came from out of town. In an urban area, one can take unpopular stands and still enjoy the support from a number of similarly inclined friends, but in a small town, unpopular stands are lonely. Nonetheless, Smith was undaunted. He was a hunter and had seen too much evidence of logging operations adversely affecting big game populations. Clear Creek was an important big game area and ought to remain so, he said in a guest editorial in the *Recorder Herald*. Hissing could be heard all over town.

In a virulent opposing guest article authored by Mrs. Glenn Biggs, the wife of a logger, Smith was called "a co-hort of Dr. Blackadar." His article was "propaganda." She called Smith and Blackadar a part of the "favored few" and said that he might be able to meander through the "pine covered hills of Clear Creek" but not loggers who must work for their living. Her article contained a veiled threat that both Smith and Blackadar had better wise up and realize where their livelihood was coming from. "I wonder how many of your patients are loggers or connected with the timber industry?" she asked. "Has Dr. Blackadar ever rented a home to the Forest Service, mill workers, loggers?"

"How do you manage these pleasurable leisure hours of 'meandering?'" she asked, and answered it: "Dollars and enough of them! And where do you get these dollars? It would be interesting if you would check your clientele. So I say, you

61

should talk!"

Smith and Blackadar found themselves in a small-town hornet's nest. It was almost as if they were heretics, the two of them against the rest of the town. The name calling began— "bird-watching squirrel chasers" was one of the polite names— and rumors and innuendos circulated.

*   *

IN the spring of 1970 while Clear Creek was on the minds of Salmon residents, Tullio Celano and Roger Hazelwood, both with the Air Force at the Mountain Home Base near Boise, wanted to do some kayaking. Celano, who owned a kayak, walked into a Boise sporting goods store: "I talked to some kid," said Celano. "I asked him 'Is there anyone who kayaks around here?' And the kid said, 'There's some doctor up in Salmon. I think his name is Dr. Mustard.'"

Celano called Salmon information and asked for the phone number of a Dr. Mustard. The operator told him that there was none. Celano persisted, "Do you know a doctor who kayaks?" And she said, "Oh, you must mean Dr. Blackadar." Celano reached the doctor's house, and after a chat, Blackadar invited Celano to join him for a roll session at the Challis Hot Springs pool.

Like Beam and Roberts the year before, Hazelwood and Celano, who attended the rolling session, grew ever more excited about the sport and became the latest members of the state's small coterie of kayakers. After the roll session, Blackadar gave Celano a call and asked him if he wanted to try running the North Fork of the Payette. Celano indicated interest and Blackadar said he'd be up on May 6.

The North Fork is one of Idaho's premier stretches of Class V whitewater. Rapids are rated on a scale where Class I is easy, flat water and Class VI is the ultimate in difficulty and life threatening. Blackadar had not run anything harder than Class

IV except, perhaps, a short drop on the Bruneau. The North Fork was different and much harder, with continuous, fast paced whitewater. At the time, it was one of the most difficult and challenging stretches of whitewater in the nation—and still is considered a celebrated test of advanced kayaking skill. Located north of Boise, the river is bounded by a road on one side and a railroad on the other. Because of the confining canyon, debris from road and rail construction has been pushed into the river, making its bed unnaturally obstructed. The river visibly slants downward, tumbling over a maze of boulders, one nearly uninterrupted sheet of bubbling whitewater. One or two kayak attempts had been made on short portions of the river, but most of the river had not been run.

Celano, not having much experience in rivers, drove up to have a look at the North Fork six days before Blackadar came up. Deciding to make a short trial run, he stopped his car above a railroad bridge, unfastened his boat from the top of the car, and, alone, paddled down the stream.

Immediately the current swept him away, and he was in for the ride of his life. He rolled a couple of times, but soon came out of his boat. The kayak swirled out of control, and further down it smashed against rocks, totally destroying it.

Celano had managed to struggle to the shore. "I was on the wrong side of the river," explained Celano. "So I swam across." It was a dangerous swim in a dangerous river. Celano was lucky; he reached the other side. If he had been swept down the river, he could have drowned. "I'd walk 10 miles before I'd do that again," he said.

Blackadar received a call from Celano who told him that he just lost his boat and the North Fork looked pretty bad.

"Don't worry," Blackadar replied, "I'll bring you another one."

Blackadar arrived with a boat and his friend, Al Beam, who had decided to run the North Fork also. "Al Beam looked at the river," remembered Celano, "and his face turned white." Celano knew from prior experience that the river was one wild stretch of water, but "I figured that as long as Walt was there, he'd take care of me."

They put in just beyond a rapid called Hound's Tooth. Blackadar pulled out of the current into an eddy about a half mile down. Celano tried to stop to stay behind the more experienced kayaker but he was swept downstream. When he managed to look back upstream, he saw to his horror that Blackadar, who had been caught in a hole, was now spinning wildly about in the current, out of his boat. With Blackadar out of his boat, Celano lost all of his confidence, tipped over and was swept away from his boat on a second careening ride down the river.

Beam, who had managed to stay up, helped Blackadar off to the side of the river. Blackadar slowly pulled himself out of the swift river. In his swim, he had banged against rocks, and his leg was bruised and bleeding. That was plenty for Beam. "I decided," he said, "that I had enough of that goddamned river." They walked downstream, with Blackadar limping, looking for Celano. Finally they found him, collapsed and exhausted alongside the river.

"I was lying on a beach panting," said Celano, "when Blackadar yelled at me to come on." Celano dragged himself up to the road, and they drove downriver looking for the boats. Unfortunately, the boats were on the opposite side of the river. Celano couldn't be coaxed into crossing the river: "After the week before, there was no way I was going to swim after a boat." Blackadar resigned himself to the job, and stroking across, he retrieved the boats.

Blackadar arrived home early the next morning and jotted a note off to Beam: "Home safe . . . . OK to paddle, not walk. Boat repairs start soon 7:30 PM. All go on Bruneau & no swims!" A bruising swim like Blackadar's on the North Fork of the Payette can do much to lessen one's enthusiasm for kayaking. But the same night of his return, Blackadar was already repairing his kayaks and telling Beam that he was all set for an early June trip on one of the upper branches of the Bruneau called the Jarbidge.

✳   ✳

THE plans for the summer of 1970 were even more ambitious than the summer before. Enabling him to take more time was the addition of a partner in his practice, the first since he split with Mulder years before. Blackadar had interested Boyd Simmons, a doctor from Seattle, in a partnership by offering him an arrangement where Simmons would start earning income from the onset and work into a 50-50 split. Simmons agreed and moved into a new office wing which Blackadar had just recently added to his building.

Blackadar later explained his thinking: "I spent 10 years in a partnership with an elderly M.D. and 10 years solo before inviting Boyd, a Mormon with eight children, to join me—a perfect choice since he doesn't kayak." Kayaking is exactly what Blackadar did. While Blackadar was out on kayaking trips, Simmons "worked hard." "Walt took off a lot of time," Simmons said, "but from his standpoint he thought it was fair since he contributed a lot of surgery."

A few days after the Jarbidge River, Blackadar was out of the office again, teaming up for another trip with Al Beam. Blackadar may have not realized it at the time, but he was just beginning to close in on a new type of kayaking. He had gotten an early taste of it when he and Red Edwards had rafted Buck Creek Rapids in 1955. Buck Creek was the largest rapid in Hells Canyon, but it was destroyed when the Hells Canyon Dam was built. Later, in a kayak, he had run Wolf Creek on the Selway, and Granite and Wild Sheep, the two large rapids still not inundated by dams, in lower Hells Canyon. In 1970, he drew closer. By then he knew it had something to do with big water.

In Idaho, the biggest water conditions come in May or June

when snow melt is at its peak. Early in June 1970, the rivers throughout central Idaho were rising impressively, fueled by plentiful snow pack. As the water on the Middle Fork rose to a peak, Blackadar and Al Beam drove to Dagger Falls to make a high water attempt.

Once at the Falls, they found company. Bob Smith was there also, loading an unusual piece of baggage, a Volkswagen bus, on his 34-foot-long sweep boat. The Flying-B Ranch downriver had contracted Smith to float the vehicle to the ranch where, among other purposes, they planned to use the bus to transport guests between the ranch and airstrip. Smith had chosen high water for the trip in order to avoid having to maneuver his heavy load through the maze of rocks exposed in lower river flows.

The ranch was located in the middle of the greatest expanse of roadless country in the lower 48, and floating the bus was the only economical way of getting it there. Smith built a platform on top of the sweep boat on which the bus, minus the tires, was chained. An impressed Blackadar and Beam talked with Smith and volunteered to go ahead and point out the best route as the raft progressed down the river. The turgid waters of the river below the Dagger Falls campground rushed by. It would be a challenging run for Smith, and having the kayaks along might be helpful in an emergency.

The night before they left, Beam and Blackadar talked with Dan Sullivan, a packer out of Challis. They invited Sullivan to go on the trip, but Sullivan didn't want to have anything to do with the flooding river. "No, boys," he told them. "That river's going faster than a Mormon going on a mission."

The next day, the odd-looking raft and the two kayaks rifled down the Middle Fork. Blackadar loved it. It was big forceful water. Beam described one rapids as a "big artesian well in the middle of the river." In another rapids, Beam was thrown upside down and tried rolling three or four times on his right side, and finally switching to his left, he popped up. Washing down to the bottom of the rapids, the exhausted Beam was met by a grinning Blackadar, obviously delighting in his friend's struggle. "I was waiting for you, Beam," he said dryly.

With only a few close calls, the small armada pulled into Flying-B, a distance of 66 miles covered in only eight hours. Smith unloaded the bus, which had been undamaged in the extraordinary trip. Blackadar and Beam spent the night at the ranch and then paddled out the next day in a few hours.

✳   ✳

BLACKADAR was elated about the high water run down the Middle Fork. He loved the feeling of flirting with the powerful waves and was anxious later that summer to try his hand on bigger rapids. In all levels of water, the Middle Fork was a beautiful, special place to him, but he had been disturbed about a state-sponsored project which had destroyed some of the river's virginal loveliness. It had been gnawing on him, and after he and Beam returned from the Middle Fork, he did something about it.

In the late fifties, the Idaho Fish and Game Department had built a road into Dagger Falls and constructed a fish ladder to help salmon reach their spawning grounds. In itself, the fish ladder was not a bad idea, but Blackadar had not been happy with the methods employed by Idaho Fish and Game in constructing and maintaining the ladder. After the trip, he wrote a fiery letter to John Woodworth, director of the Fish and Game Department.

He complained in his letter that the road which had been built to service the fish ladder remained open to public travel, opening up a previously large roadless section of the Middle Fork country. On top of that, the department had constructed a chain-link fence above the project, which added still more scars to the area's beauty and made it difficult for people to view the beautiful falls. If that weren't enough, an incongruous metal shed was built in which maintenance tools were kept.

In Blackadar's mind, the worst of the department's indiscretions was what had been done to the Falls. He described the debacle as "the rape of Dagger Falls." "[L]arge portions of the beautiful falls and surrounding rock were blown free and a monstrosity of cement was placed instead surrounded by a jungle of wire," he wrote. "Just because a beautiful virgin is raped by one of your friends does not mean that it is right. This is the worst mess your department . . . has ever done."

He told Woodworth to remove the tin shack, take down the fence "and your nasty [no trespassing] signs, which are out of place and totally illegal since man has a right to tread on this federal ground in spite of what the Fish and Game has done."

Woodworth politely replied to Blackadar later in August, explaining that the department had tried to minimize the aesthetic impacts while building the Falls. The fence was necessary because of concern for the public's safety. He could do nothing about the signs. They were federal signs. Woodworth agreed that the metal shack was not in keeping with the area. A wooden building would be more appropriate, but wooden buildings, he explained, were often destroyed for fuel for campfires.

Blackadar might have remembered that he had removed the door of a wooden outhouse at Dagger Falls years before to repair the sweep on his boat. But, nevertheless, he had made a good point. The construction and metal fence at the Falls was and remains atrocious, starkly out of place with the beauty of the upper Middle Fork. Blackadar didn't push the issue much further, but thereafter he continued to refer to the mess as the "rape of Dagger Falls."

＊　　＊

THE big trip for the summer of 1970 was a kayak foray down the Grand Canyon of the Colorado. It is known the world over for its big, challenging whitewater, and Blackadar, coming ever closer to finding his niche in the whitewater world, had been working on the trip since the previous fall. He had sent out letters to "everyone" on his kayaking list, more than 40 people. The job of organizing the trip was a mammoth undertaking which involved arranging for raft support, corresponding with kayakers and even buying life jackets for everyone. Loren Smith of the American Guides Association agreed to run rafts and carry the group's supplies. Smith insisted that in addition to the raft oarsmen, he did not want to support more than eight additional raft passengers and 26 kayakers. In the end, 27 kayaks, consisting of seven Canadians and 20 Americans, were scheduled to go on the trip.

In his correspondence with prospective kayakers, Blackadar told them that the Grand Canyon Park Service required all rafters and kayakers to wear a large Type I life preserver. Blackadar realized that many of the kayakers might not like the idea since the jackets were bulky, consisting of two plump kidney shaped flotation chambers in the front and another square chamber behind the neck. It is "harder to paddle in," he admitted to his friends. "We tried it this weekend, however, and it is possible to paddle and roll successfully with the jacket on. I have found a wholesale source of supply, and have ordered 25 jackets for the paddlers, at $7.50 each. They will not let us start without each person having one of these jackets on. Later on, when we are on our own, you can shift to your own pet jacket if you so desire. However, many of the previous boaters [on the Colorado River] tell me that these jackets are much more comfortable to swim in, especially in some of the nasty holes and whirlpools which we can expect."

On August 3, 1970, the group assembled at Lee's Ferry, where all Grand Canyon trips originate. Joining Blackadar were old friends of the 1968 Middle Fork trip, including Herman and Christa Kerckhoff, Herb May, Steve Knappe, Barb Wright, Klaus Streckman, Lynn McAdams, as well as more recent friends and new acquaintances, Al Beam, Bill Koch, Al Chase, Linda

69

Hibbard, Gunter Hemmersbach, Sumner Bennett, Roger Parsons, Jan Showacre, Kay Swanson, Jack Wright, and others. The kayakers, divided into three contingents, and Loren Smith with his four 22-foot pontoon rafts and one smaller 10-man raft, all carrying the food and equipment, floated away from the launch site. It was the kind of trip, large and logistically difficult (Blackadar had called it "a massive excursion"), that he delighted in and had become proficient at putting together.

The group camped beside House Rock Rapid, known for its two house-sized holes on the left side of the river. Many of the kayakers had walked around the rapid. "Next morning we arose early," wrote Roger Parsons who kept notes on the trip. "The water had dropped 2½ feet overnight and the rapids had taken on a whole new appearance. William Koch, a U.S. paddler and a purported millionaire, had brought his own cameraman along to make a film of the trip and was looking for volunteers to re-run House Rock at its new level." Al Chase from Oregon, who was the only one among the kayakers to paddle a closed canoe, volunteered to make the run. The current swept Chase into the first hole, capsizing him, and after washing out, he rolled back up, then spilled twice more before reaching the bottom.

After Chase's dramatic ride, Jack Wright volunteered to run it. Wright had already begun to grate on the nerves of some members of the party. "He was a good boater but a show-off," said McAdams. Beam agreed, saying that Wright and Blackadar "didn't mix at all." Blackadar, obviously, was a show-off too, but his histrionics seemed more acceptable to the group, and it was, after all, Blackadar's work which had made the trip possible. In any case, Jack Wright, as Parsons explained, "decided he would show us how it should be done. As he slid into the first hole, the kayak was stopped dead by the haystack below. It slid back, pearled, and did two consecutive somersaults before turning upside down, still in the hole. Finally after a couple more flips it came out but there was no sign of Jack. The boat, now we could see, was badly damaged, then Jack's head appeared about

100 feet downstream and two kayakers sped out to rescue him."

Tied to a raft, Wright's boat, missing four feet of its stern, was damaged beyond repair. That left Wright without a boat. Not to be undone, Wright hitched a ride on a big motorized raft which was going much faster than Blackadar's group. He was planning to get out at Phantom Ranch, in the Middle of the Grand Canyon, where he could hike out the trail and pick up another kayak, hike back into the canyon, and rejoin the party. Blackadar figured that Wright's plan was impossible, and that night he announced that carrying Wright's kayak was an embarrassment to the group. "It looks like we're incompetent," he said.

At Blackadar's urging on the fourth morning, Wright's kayak "was stood on its broken end on top of the fire and as it was gleefully consumed we all sang praises to the river gods and danced around it like Indians. Following this we drank what was left of Jack's beer saying 'good old Jack.' After all, park rules stated that anything that can't be burned must be carried out."

"Good old Jack," however, had managed to get another kayak and carry it down the steep, switch-backing trails of the canyon. He caught up to the party sometime after his boat had been burned and all his beer drunk. He wasn't happy about his boat. He had thought that he might have been able to repair it once out of the canyon. And "he was bummed that we had drank his beer," said McAdams. But any ill feeling past, he seemed to get along well with everyone afterwards.

Blackadar was starting to pick out some of the larger holes in the river to run. One well-respected patch of whitewater on the Colorado is a series of violent holes making up the left side of Crystal Rapid. Blackadar ran them. Barb Wright, after watching Blackadar's run, looked over at the members of the party watching the stunt and said, "That's the gutsiest thing I ever have seen." "Walt was running stuff that we thought would drown him," said Kay Swanson. "He would go into the damnedest things and make them look easy."

Lava Falls is the largest, most revered of the Colorado's famous rapids. Although Lava is now run routinely in kayaks, in 1970 it was still new to do so. The falls had only been attempted by kayakers one or two times before, and most river runners felt it was an extremely risky undertaking in small craft. When the party reached the falls, many of the kayakers took one look and portaged their boats around. Blackadar scouted the rapid from one side of the river and then paddled over to the other and scouted it again. "It's a son of a bitch," he pronounced.

Blackadar started his run on the left center, and a large wave slapped him upside down. He rolled up, paddled to the side of the river and decided to try it again. Three more times, Blackadar ran Lava Falls, each time getting thrown over in the rapid, but always rolling and paddling out to the end of the rapids. By the end of the trip, Blackadar, according to McAdams, "was a top quality big river boater. There's no doubt about it. He had a roll that was absolutely non-failing."

Although Blackadar lacked the technical finesse of many of the other kayakers on the Colorado trip, he had developed an alternative, his own brash western style of boating. It was a style of boating that could open the door to a new and fascinating realm of river exploration. And if he went after the right opportunities, it could send him to the breathless heights of the sport. By the end of the 1970 season, he was almost there.

❋   ❋

WHEN Blackadar returned from the Colorado River, the Idaho gubernatorial campaign was under way. The incumbent, Don Samuelson, was a likable Republican who was running against Cecil Andrus, a 39-year-old insurance executive who had been the unsuccessful Democratic candidate in the 1966 election. The race began heating up in October over three issues—taxes, education, and the environment. Concern over Idaho's environment had reached an all-time high, and nothing symbolized public sentiment more than plans to mine the White Cloud Mountains.

The White Clouds are located 80 miles to the southwest of Salmon near the source of the Salmon River and across the valley from the Sawtooths. The name comes from a light beige hue of some of its peaks which appear as low-lying clouds from a distance. The highest point of the range is a regally prominent mountain, poised above pine forests and a multitude of small lakes, called Castle Peak.

On May 15 of 1968, the American Smelting and Refining Company (ASARCO) set up a camp at the base of Castle Peak and began diamond drilling for molybdenite, a mineral used in steel hardening applications. No roads were built. All transportation to and from the site was done by helicopter. Upon completion of the initial work, enough of the mineral had been located from the exploratory drilling to warrant development of a large-scale mining operation. In 1969, the company proposed to the Challis National Forest to build a road into the area.

At the hearings called by the Forest Service in response to the road application, it quickly became obvious how controversial the White Clouds mine had become. Testimony at hearings held in Boise and Idaho Falls was overwhelmingly against the mine. But at a hearing in Challis, upriver from Salmon, sentiment from Custer County, where the mine would be located, and nearby Lemhi County was overwhelmingly in favor of developing the White Clouds. Those in favor of the mine included Lemhi County legislators, county commissioners, various mining companies, and the timber companies. Gordon Crupper, Blackadar's nemesis, supported the mine: "The natural resources of Custer County and any other county in the United States are the only true sources of wealth. The wise use of these natural resources is essential to our continued strength as a state and as a nation."

The White Clouds became one of the major issues of the

1970 election. Samuelson supported the mine. "The Good Lord never intended us to lock up our resources," he said. Andrus opposed the mine. "We can't afford to destroy this high altitude, alpine area to mine a low-grade, export ore for the temporary economic gain of a few," said Andrus.

Andrus also took a strong position on protecting Salmon runs. He vigorously opposed dams in Hells Canyon, "a natural resource which is beautiful beyond description." Samuelson favored dams in Hells Canyon, as long as "Idaho shares in the benefits." There's no doubt who Blackadar supported in the election. But Blackadar's opinion was a minority view in Salmon. When Lemhi election returns came in, Samuelson had garnered nearly three times as many votes as Andrus, soundly defeating him in Blackadar's county. Statewide, however, Andrus beat Samuelson in a close race. It was a significant win, both from a state and national perspective. Andrus broke a 26-year Republican hold on the governor's office.

The election had been won on "lifestyle" and environmental issues, said the *Post Register*. Industry and economic development, of course, were important, but "Andrus would apply a criteria [sic] for the new industry he would promote to preserve Idaho's liveability." *Time* magazine agreed, saying the Andrus win was in part due to his opposition to a Samuelson-backed mining development in the White Clouds.

THREE days after the election, on the morning of November 6, Roy Wells of Torrance, California, and Thomas Sterling of Santa Monica traveled south on U.S. 93, north of Salmon. They were road hunting, searching the open fields and hillsides for signs of deer. Wells, driving, steered his pickup truck with a white camper off to the side of the road for a closer look at the area.

At 7:15 that morning, 6-year-old Karyn Prestwich, dressed

in a red dress, put on her brown furry jacket, told her mother good-bye and walked from their white and red-trimmed trailer house across the open fields towards the school bus stop. Her father, Don Prestwich, had left earlier for his job with the Forest Service. That morning he would be marking timber for a logging sale near Ebenezer Creek.

In hunting, there is a period of intense arousal, a time when deep primordial instincts stir within. When it goes awry, it is called buck fever. Good hunters learn to keep it in check. Others, however, when sighting down the barrel of their rifle, may begin trembling or shaking. Some become so anxious that they shoot off to the side or above their prey. Some hunters lose touch with all reality, shooting at anything—bushes, trees, mailboxes, thinking that the objects are animals.

Wells had buck fever.

Sitting and sighting his 30-06 rifle through the open window of his truck, he turned until the girl in the brown jacket came in his sights 250 yards away. Karyn turned towards the truck, her jacket open, the red dress in view.

From inside the trailer, Marsha Prestwich heard the hollow muffled thud of the bullet. Instinctively, she knew what had happened. The highway, nearly a city block away, was too far for her to reach. She watched horrified as Wells, who had suddenly shaken from his stupor, ran, picked up her wounded daughter and drove madly towards North Fork.

When the call came, Blackadar was scrubbing up for a surgery. He immediately cancelled his surgery and waited for the arrival. At 8:30 a.m., one hour and 10 minutes after the shooting, Prestwich was carried into the hospital. Wells turned himself in to Sheriff Baker. A complaint issued shortly after charged Wells with assault with a deadly weapon.

At the hospital, Blackadar looked at the first grader. The bullet had entered through the front of her abdomen and exited through the right hip. The femoral artery, the major blood source to the legs, hung by a thread. He wasn't sure why she hadn't bled to death on the way there. Marsha Prestwich arrived, and Blackadar was waiting for her. "It's real bad," he began and described what he knew.

"Walt told me like it was," said Marsha Prestwich. "I appreciated it. I wouldn't have been prepared otherwise. I appreciated his bluntness."

Blackadar went into surgery at 9:00 a.m. and didn't finish until 3:00 that afternoon. Among the damage, the urethra was torn and the sciatic nerve severed. He had difficulty locating the wounded kidney. Twice during the surgery, Blackadar thought he might be losing her, but the little girl battled back. He took out bullet fragments, removed a two-foot section of the small intestine and repaired the artery. It was a trying, difficult surgery, and it took all his skill as a surgeon.

After the surgery, Karyn woke, but as Blackadar had expected, her kidneys were not properly removing wastes. He wanted to get Karyn to a Salt Lake City hospital to the needed sophisticated equipment and the care of specialists, but he couldn't move her until she showed some kind of improvement.

Whenever Blackadar asked the first grader how she was doing, her answer was always a weak "fine." In her arms, she grasped a talking Barbie doll and occasionally pulled the string to make the doll talk. On one visit, he asked what she had there, but she was too weak to pull the string. It was a disheartening sign. He couldn't control his emotions and left the room. His eyes moist, he told Marsha Prestwich, "I just think she's going to make it."

Exactly one week later, Karyn Prestwich was flown to the intensive care unit at the University of Utah Medical Center in Salt Lake City. The kidney continued to malfunction, but at Salt Lake she was able to be connected to a dialysis machine.

Meanwhile, word of the shooting made national news. A fund which was set up to help pay her bills received donations from throughout the country. Primarily, the money would be needed for the long stay and expensive medical bills that would be necessary in Utah. In the Salmon hospital, however, the bill for Karyn's one-week stay was, according to her parents, only $550.

The spunky Karyn Prestwich would have a long, slow recovery but she would recover. It was one of Blackadar's greatest challenges and certainly the most rewarding success of his career in medicine.

V

A Look in the Mirror

AMONG THE TWISTS and turns of his life, it was matter of chance that Blackadar learned of Turnback Canyon on the Alsek River. The news came at an opportune time. By the end of 1970, he had built up just enough confidence in kayaking to imagine such a river might be runnable. And, most importantly, events in his life led him to believe that he could be the one to do it.

It was an audacious belief, for the river is not an ordinary river, nor does it lie in an ordinary place.

A palpable air of potency hangs above the Alsek river valley. It can be felt in the bite of the valley's interminable winds, and it can be seen. Deep in the interior of the St. Elias Range, what is now called Mt. Blackadar rises above an incomparable tableau. Below, the Alsek River, wide and shimmering leadenly, curves gracefully one direction, then slips gracefully back again. Streaks of gray and green reach up out of the valley and merge in the compelling white of the snow-covered and glaciated peaks of the St. Elias Range.

There is so much white that the gently curving river is an anomaly in this world of tortured starkness. Much of the Alsek lies within the Kluane National Park of extreme northwestern British Columbia and southern Yukon Territory and more than half of the park is covered with snow and ice year round.

Snow and ice. And more snow. Snow, sometimes accumulating to depths of 3,000 feet, forms the glaciers of the St. Elias, which are among the most massive and geologically active on the North American continent. Within its icy boundaries is Mt. Logan, at 19,850 feet the highest peak in Canada—and Mt. St. Elias which, 30 miles from the Gulf of Alaska, rises an astonishing 18,008 feet. This is a wild, capricious land of blowing snow, wind-sculpted summits, of groaning ice and crevasses, and, where there is not snow, of steep hillsides, tangled with impenetrable growths of alders and thorny devils club: a vast uninhabited wilderness battered endlessly by violent winds and storms off the Gulf of Alaska. It is no wonder that the area was only recently mapped, and to this day it remains one of the least known regions on the continent.

Between the toe of the immense Tweedsmuir Glacier and the southern extension of the Blackadar massif, the river nearly disappears. There the river is pinched into the dark narrow gorge of Turnback Canyon. It is between the pinched walls of Turnback Canyon, unobtrusive amongst the massive scale surrounding it, where lies a dangerous five-mile stretch of turbulent, boiling whitewater. In 1970 it had repelled any attempts by river runners, and it was thought to be impossible to run.

THE canyon's name probably originated from the gold rush of 1898, since it formed a barrier, turning away a few adventuring miners—usually reported to be starving, near death, and scared by marauding bears—in unsuccessful attempts to find new riches or a new river route to the Klondike. In 1970 the canyon was largely unknown to river runners. The disheartening ill-fated journeys of a few unwitting '98'ers and any memories of what they saw at the canyon had been forgotten. There were tales, of course, of a miner's lost gold mine and of a native legend of the river disappearing into the ground—a legend, it appears, that is very likely more truth than fiction. Glaciers in the St. Elias Range are so active that they can and have surged across the river, blocking it. In at least one case witnessed by explorers, the displaced river flowed over the top of an advancing glacier and in a great, spiraling torrent, disappeared from their view down a hole in the ice.

The first known descent of the river draining this most unpredictable land was made in 1961 by Clem Rawert and John Dawson. Following Rawert, two more small parties struggled down the Alsek, and then again in 1970 Rawert, along with five others, ran the river in Klepper kayaks. What they found was an inhospitable place of cold, wind and, big rapids.

By far the biggest obstacle on the river was Turnback Canyon. Upon nearing the mouth of the ominous canyon, they climbed out of their boats and made their way across a glacier, until they could peer over the edge of the canyon. The river, squeezed between dark walls, turned into a fury of treacherous cataracts. The only way to continue was to carry their boats and equipment beyond the canyon over an arduous portage route across ice and the slippery moraine of the Tweedsmuir Glacier. To run Turnback Canyon, it was clear to those early river explorers, would be certain death.

SHORTLY after Karyn Prestwich was moved to Salt Lake, winter settled heavily into the Salmon valley. By late December of 1970, Lost Trail Pass, north of Salmon, had collected five feet of snow. Temperatures in town dropped to -24 degrees, and upriver in the Sawtooth Valley, Stanley recorded a bitter -52 degrees. The Salmon River, normally clear near town, flowed sluggishly under the Salmon bridge, carrying slush and chunks of ice.

Blackadar was taking advantage of the snow, enjoying a number of good skiing weekends and spending much of his free time with Shirley at their Sun Valley Wildwood condominium. Family life had quieted considerably. His father's illness and death was now two years behind the family. During Lloyd's lingering bout with Parkinson's disease, Blackadar remarked to his office manager, Jean Tomita, that he didn't know why his father would not take hold and try to do something for himself. Then again, he and his father were two very different people, and Blackadar must have understood that. Clearly, he never had much regard for his father's eastern lifestyle. His own move to Salmon and his vigorous, outdoor lifestyle almost seemed to be an expression of defiance, a way of severing the paternal tie and removing himself as far as possible from that life. When Lloyd finally died, the suffering was over, and Blackadar was relieved.

All was quiet elsewhere in the family. By the winter of 1970-71, his children lived away from Salmon: three of his daughters had married, and the fourth, Sue, was a freshman at the University of Idaho. His son Bob was also enrolled in school at the College of Idaho.

On his visits to Sun Valley, he often skied with Al Beam. The year before, Beam had given him a few skiing lessons, and Blackadar was impressed. He wrote him after one of their ski outings, chortling: "Hi 'Wild Al.' What a skier! [Y]ou are more suicidal than I!" Two months later, he wrote to Barb Wright telling her that he hadn't "mastered the French style of skiing," though he was working on it. "Al has finally gotten me to keep my shoulders straight and knees wiggling," he wrote, "but what a crash when I tried to pass him while he was packing the mail!"

Blackadar was also pleased with the progress that Beam had made in his new river guiding business. Familiar with Idaho guiding and outfitting law, the doctor had helped him get started and had loaned Beam his sweep boat to use to take passengers.

The prospects for the whitewater business looked rosy, and Beam was busy planning more trips for the coming summer season.

In mid-February, Blackadar joined Kay Swanson for three days of skiing at Bridger Bowl in Bozeman. While together, he talked with Swanson about making copies of Klaus Streckman's films of the previous summer's kayaking trip on the Colorado. Blackadar, already having a collection of home movies of many of his early rafting trips, particularly wanted the shots showing his four kayak runs of Lava Falls. He enjoyed showing his films to friends and visiting kayakers, and he was just beginning to get a few requests to talk for clubs and organizations outside of Salmon.

As the winter progressed, Karyn Prestwich went through a series of operations in Salt Lake. Hundreds of letters addressed to Karyn arrived in Salt Lake and Salmon, many containing money. Thirty-five cents was enclosed in one letter from a man from Washington who said that it was all the money he had. Another $499 was received from American Airlines employees, $800 from Forest Service employees, and $500 from Roy Wells, the hunter who mistook her for a deer. By the end of the winter, $16,000 had been received, enough to cover her medical expenses to that point. In addition to donations, some people wrote letters of encouragement. A 9-year-old girl wrote to cheer Karyn up, telling her that she had been shot four years earlier but now only a few scars remained to remind her of the accident.

News of Karyn Prestwich's improvements pleased Blackadar. He was also pleased when the supervisor of the Salmon National Forest announced that as a result of the Clear Creek hearings, area would be studied for possible inclusion along with the Idaho Primitive Area when it was reviewed for wilderness classification. Intermountain Lumber, under Gordon Crupper's management, and Salmon's two other logging firms filed an appeal with the regional forester, but late in 1971, the appeal was denied. Blackadar had won this round with Crupper, but he knew that Clear Creek, like the White Clouds, was still not free of development. Nonetheless, at least the area had been granted a reprieve. Roads most certainly would have been built and Blackadar's hunting grounds partly logged by now had not he and his fellow conservationists acted when they did.

✻   ✻

In February, the March 1970 issue of *Alaska* magazine appeared, and Blackadar upon paging through it came upon an article on page 36 entitled "Running the Alsek." The three-sentence teaser superimposed on a picture of the river was the kind of introduction that would undoubtedly pique his interest: "The Alsek River is a major stream that pours into the Gulf of Alaska. Its waters are swift, dangerous, and virtually unknown. Six of us challenge this remote river with kayaks." The accompanying full-page picture shows the river in the foreground and one large glaciated mountain dominating the background.*

The article, written by Richard D. Tero and illustrated with 10 color photographs taken by Dee Crouch, recounted their June 1970 trip down the Alsek. One of the members of the party was Clem Rawert, who had made the first known complete descent of the Alsek nine years earlier. In Blackadar's copy of the magazine which has survived, he marked one of the article's paragraphs in blue pen. The paragraph describes their exploratory walk on the Tweedsmuir Glacier and scout of Turnback Canyon: "Exploring was handicapped by the rugged terminal moraine, topped by young willows—and clouds of mosquitoes. The canyon rim is 500 feet above the water and a serious rock climb to the water's edge. We could hear the roar as the water crashed against the walls. In places the solid granite was undercut by the river. It might be navigable in a balloon. Bill and Dee, who have run the Grand Canyon in big navy assault rafts,

---

*Ironically, the mountain pictured prominently in *Alaska* magazine, unnamed at that time, is Mt. Blackadar.

thought it would be more difficult than anything in the Grand, because one rapids leads to another without pullout possibilities, and rescue from the 500-foot-high sheer walls would be impossible."

Blackadar, still effervescing from last summer's Colorado trip, was now interested in any water that might have Grand Canyon-type rapids. Turnback Canyon, with "the roar of water crashing against the walls," literally sounded right up his alley. The description left plenty of room for Blackadar to believe that an attempt on Turnback might be possible. It was no doubt difficult and dangerous, with the sheer walls and no stopping possibilities, but nothing in the article ever mentions that the canyon is utterly impossible. Particularly, no mention is made of high falls which would indisputably block any run of the canyon.

The Alsek article came at a time when Blackadar was ripe to try something new in kayaking. He had tried rafting, but kayaking, from the standpoint of big water, promised even greater possibilities. It was, however, contrary to what whitewater boaters believed possible. In the early seventies, the idea that a kayak was superior to rafts in big water was ridiculous. Conventional wisdom dictated that large rafts, or even three rafts tied together known as triple rigs, were the safest craft to use for big stuff. Blackadar was convinced, however, that despite the fact that rivers like the Colorado were being run primarily in large rafts, a maneuverable kayak—with the ability to roll up if knocked over—could run and survive in far harder rapids than large rafts.

His curiosity aroused, he started testing the waters. On February 26, he wrote Klaus Streckman and told him to read the March issue of *Alaska*. On the same day, he also wrote to Barb Wright, describing a "new" river: "Sounds like a fun trip. We should consider it in '72 or perhaps even this year." Continuing in his letter, he tells Wright that the 10-mile portage of Turnback Canyon doesn't "appeal" to him. "We'll plan to run that part unless it's a no-no. This is beautiful country and should be seen before Niagara!" The reference to Niagara Falls concerns a fanciful plan between Wright and Blackadar to attempt one final kayak run over Niagara Falls. Blackadar's boasting that he could survive the run would always be good for a round of laughter in the evening after a day on the river.

A month later, he sent another letter to Streckman. Although he was still gathering information, Blackadar invited Streckman to go on the Alsek, proposing July 6 to 20 as the dates. Streckman and Wright doubted that they could go on the trip, but Blackadar's interest in the Alsek continued to snowball, and in early April, he had decided to bring a navy 10-man landing boat to carry supplies.

He made his first contact with Richard Tero, the author of the Alsek article: "I have been very intrigued by your excellent adventure on the Alsek River and am planning to bring a group of expert kayakers up to run this river either in July or August of 1971 or 1972." He told Tero that he would be taking a raft which was of the appropriate design to run the big rapids of the Colorado. Because of the size and weight of the raft, he realized that he would not be able to portage Turnback Canyon and asked for more specific information from Tero: "Our present plan is to scout the canyon somewhat and have two expert kayakers paddle through the gorge and walk back before the rest of the group proceeds on. We then will either carry our gear by and turn the raft loose to be picked up at the lower end or ride the raft through, etc. I would surely appreciate a brief comment from you as to the feasibility of this undertaking."

Tero immediately replied, telling him the "feasibility" was nil. Blackadar also tried to call Clem Rawert for his opinion but was unable to reach him. He did, however, reach Dee Crouch by mail, and Crouch gave him more discouraging news: Turnback was impossible. "I repeated it again in a subsequent phone conversation," said Crouch. "I thought it couldn't be scouted, and the water was too turbulent anyway."

Crouch, who had experience in running the Grand Canyon, knew what he was talking about, but Blackadar remained skeptical. From his own experiences in big water, he had formed a new concept of what was possible and impossible, and if he could have a look at the canyon, he might see its rapids in an entirely different light. Moreover, he wasn't committing his party to a run of the canyon. His group could portage the canyon and otherwise have an enjoyable trip down an Alaskan river. Yet, when he had suggested the trip with a planned portage of the canyon, he was still unable to enlist support from dispassionate kayaking friends. He had even asked Crouch to accompany him, but Crouch decided against it.

Unable to attract others to the trip, he must have at this point begun to consider the idea of kayaking the Alsek alone. It was an intimidating and unnerving proposition, and it appears that he hesitated and put the trip on the back burner. Other than writing some friends in Alaska about transporting boats and equipment, his enthusiasm cooled. From April until well into the summer, he left no further correspondence or notes about the project.

❄   ❄

AN April domestic disaster was partially responsible for diverting his attention away from Alaskan rivers. It occurred while his wife was away visiting their daughter and son-in-law in California. The winter of 1971, which had kept the valley well in its grasp, flung one last storm and 14 inches of wet snow at the town. The heavy snow knocked out service to some 300 telephones, television went off the air, branches fell across the highways, a large awning over the entrance of the hospital emergency room collapsed, and a rock slide, triggered by wet soil, slid down the hillside behind Blackadar's house and demolished his garage. Blackadar and his other son-in-law, Butch Howick, went to work, moving tons of rock, and rebuilt the garage in a less hazardous site.

Late in April he went on a Hells Canyon river trip and gave a few kayak lessons to Oregon Senator Packwood who had been working on protective legislation to prevent further hydroelectric development on the river. With a good snowpack in the mountains, the rivers ran full as the summer came on, and whitewater boating fell into full swing. During the 1971 season, more and more boaters converged and staged their river trips from the Blackadar house, now well established as the kayaking center in Idaho. The scattered boats, paddles, damp wet suits, plastic float bags, and tents on the lawn must not have been a welcome sight to Shirley. With her children now gone, she had looked forward to unhindered time with her husband. Instead she found her home surrounded by sunburned boaters from all over the country. Yet she never displayed any displeasure, making all welcome, unenviably finding plenty to do keeping "washer and dishwasher busy."

Her husband made use of every spare weekend and vacation day to run rivers. Blackadar's river list reads like Teddy Roosevelt's notes after a day of hunting in Dakota. Besides Hells Canyon he knocked off the Owyhee, Jarbidge, Bruneau, and the Middle Fork of the Flathead over the Fourth of July. In mid-July he ran the Selway, and he pioneered two previously unrun sections of the technical upper South Fork of the Salmon in Idaho.

Meanwhile that summer, the Alsek country was making news in Alaska. On June 24, Kenneth Wayne Anderson and his 23-year-old son, Gary, had been flying from Anchorage to Juneau. Caught in bad weather, Anderson had been forced to attempt a dangerous emergency landing in their Stinson pontoon plane. The large river which Anderson found to land on was the Alsek. Immediately upon touching down, the powerful current capsized the plane and spilled both its occupants into the river. Both wore life jackets. The gray water swept the father ahead, and in the struggle for his own life, Gary Anderson lost track of him.

Gary managed to swim to shore in the cold water and spent three days walking along the river in search of his father, finding only the wreckage of their plane. Authorities started a search as soon as their plane turned up missing, but a week later, when no sign was found of them, the Andersons were given up for lost, and the search was officially called off.

Gary Anderson, however, was very much alive, but he was alone with no food in the midst of a great wilderness. Finding an abandoned hunter's camp near the confluence of the Tatshenshini and Alsek Rivers, downstream from Turnback Canyon, he built a rudimentary shelter and kept himself alive by eating roots. In what was an extraordinary test of human endurance and the will to live, he survived a total of 38 days.

His SOS stamped on the soft silt of the river bank was located by a plane passing overhead, and Anderson, gaunt, having lost 50 pounds, was finally rescued. His father was never found.

When Gary Anderson was located on August 2, Blackadar was still uncertain about whether his Alsek trip would go. Although the Anderson story was extensively reported by Alaskan newspapers, it's not certain that, while in Idaho, Blackadar knew about the 23-year-old's ordeal. The doctor did know by now that the Alsek country was a harsh place, and it was more remote and more threatening than any of the wildernesses to which he was accustomed in Idaho.

His friends certainly saw red flags. Despite his efforts, no enthusiastic responses were received from boating companions to whom he had proposed the trip. Al Beam regarded the trip as "ill-prepared." "It was too much of a hairball thing to do at the time," said Beam, who was busy with his river company.

By now Blackadar had given up any idea of bringing a support raft. He wrote Tero, telling him that "I cancelled plans to take a group of 10 after learning of the canyon in detail." By this time, it was clear: if he wanted to run the Alsek, he would have to do it alone.

On August 13, 1971, he turned 49. He made the first entry in his Alsek diary: "My birthday! Looked in the mirror and realized I wasn't getting any younger. After spending a sleepless night, I decided to paddle the Alsek and to do it this year solo if I can't get a competent boater to go with me. Take-off date—next Wednesday evening."

The decision was made. He would run the river.

*   *

BLACKADAR wasn't by nature a solitary person, and he desired companionship for the trip. At the same time, he also realized the seriousness of the undertaking, and his last-minute search for boating partners seemed only half-heartedly attempted. In his original diary, he wrote that he had asked boating friends to accompany him, but he "did not want to urge [them]." Barb Wright believes that, at least as far as she was concerned, Blackadar knew her answer before asking. Given more time, he might have been able to interest at least one other person to go with him, but he had set a deadline for himself, and as time drew closer to his departure, he knew fully that he would be running the river solo.

He also knew that he was dealing with a great unknown. It wasn't the Alsek River itself that drew him to Alaska; rather it was the possibility of running Turnback Canyon. The only thing that he knew about Turnback Canyon was what Crouch and Tero had told him, and the crucial question of whether it was even runnable must have caused doubts. Making plans for the trip, he decided to reserve judgment until he had a chance to fly the canyon before he ran the river. If the aerial scout proved the canyon impossible, he would pass on Turnback. However, if Turnback looked remotely feasible, there seems to be little question about what he would do.

"I'm not suicidal," he wrote in his diary, "but I get depressed watching so many patients with incurable diseases."

Death and suffering surrounded him. He explained to a writer preparing a profile on him: "I lost a good patient, a man my age, to a coronary that day [August 13, his birthday]. I was depressed about it. I was painfully aware of how fragile life is and I figured 'what the hell, we're all going to die eventually anyway.'"

In fact, it had been a particularly bad year. Besides the coronary death, another friend, Lucile Herndon, had cancer and died two days before he left for the Alsek. Lucile was the wife of Charles Herndon, a good friend of Blackadar's and a Democratic candidate for governor. He had been killed in a tragic plane crash in the Sawtooth Mountains while campaigning four years before. Even more depressing, cancer had struck several children in the small community: Linda Howell, 18 years old; his trapping friend Jack Nancolas' daughter, Shelli, who was only 14 years old; and even his partner's son.

He had, after all, become a doctor because, like Grenfell, he wanted to save lives. Yet, for every Karyn Prestwich, there were 10 or 20 patients who could not be saved. No matter how impartial he might try to be, he was intimately involved with the suffering of others. He had lost other patients in the past, but now nearly 50 years old, the reality of age seemed ever more closer. While still able, and before unexpectedly being snatched away by an "incurable disease," he must live his life to its fullest—and kayaking the big "hair" whitewater of the Colorado or Turnback Canyon or any other big river, more than anything he had ever done, allowed him the means to do it.

There was probably more involved. Ever since his childhood, it had been his nature to seek out new sensations and novel experiences in the outdoors. Among individuals possessing the propensity for sensation seeking, Blackadar would have easily fallen into a particular personality type which has been identified by psychologists as Type T. The "T" is for thrill seeking. Type T's are driven psychologically and perhaps biologically to take risks and to pursue, according to one researcher, "the unknown, the uncertain." As he familiarized himself with one level of uncertainty in kayaking, he pushed on to another level, and on to another, and still another, until Turnback Canyon loomed in his sights.

His partner in the Salmon Medical Clinic offered another reason behind his decision. "He had a super big ego," Boyd Simmons said, "and once becoming committed, he couldn't back down." Blackadar had begun planning the Alsek trip in early March and had talked to many of his boating friends about the possibility of running the canyon. By 1971, he had developed a reputation among respected kayakers from Canada and the U.S., both in and out of the competitive world. He enjoyed the attention and even cultivated his own unique image by referring to himself to one non-kayaking friend as "a screw-ball whitewater kayaker." Events leading up to the Alsek might have taken on a life of their own, parlaying on top of each other until his going on the river was a foregone conclusion.

Compelled by *fait accompli* or not, he fully understood the dangers. Before leaving, he took out a $50,000 two-week accident insurance policy which he calculated would pay off his debts and leave a reserve for his wife. He also left a note with his daughter, Sue, who was working as a receptionist in his office that summer. The note, to be opened in the event that he turned up missing on the Alsek, instructed Shirley to spend $2,000 to $5,000 to prove him "alive or dead": "If my boat is found swamped and no sign of me for 10 to 14 days, I am dead. I will stay with the river!"

He called Barb Wright to let her know he was going. Wright knew that she could do little to stop him, but incensed at his plans to go alone, she told him that he was "stupid." Her tone probably delighted the playful Blackadar. On Thursday, August 19, he tied his fiberglass Vector kayak atop his car, and after finishing all of what he called his "honey-dos," he left Salmon at noon and drove north to Missoula.

❋   ❋

LYNN McAdams was in the middle of painting his house when Blackadar pulled into the driveway. Putting down his brush, McAdams, who had kayaked with Blackadar on the Middle Fork and Selway, listened as the doctor explained his plans. Lynn had never heard of the Alsek, but Blackadar painted a vivid picture, describing the big water in Turnback Canyon in a way that sounded "pretty damn scary."

Blackadar's stop in Missoula was more than social; he needed McAdam's fiberglassing expertise in concealing a .44 Magnum pistol under the seat of his boat. The veteran Idaho and Alaskan hunter had great respect for grizzly bears and wanted a weapon along. He could not carry a rifle in his boat— it was too heavy and wouldn't fit properly anyway, so he had decided to take a pistol. There was one problem. It was illegal to take a pistol across the Canadian border.

Wrapping the gun and ammunition in plastic, McAdams fashioned a housing around the weapon out of fiberglass cloth and resin. He placed the housing under the seat of the kayak and finished off his work with a black gel coating to match the seat's color. Blackadar was satisfied. The new addition looked like a natural extension of the boat's seat and should easily pass through customs.

Blackadar then left McAdams' house, driving all night to Seattle where he caught a commercial flight to Juneau and talked the agent into shipping his boat on the same flight as air freight. When he arrived in Juneau, he contacted Layton Bennett, a well-known charter pilot in Southeast Alaska, to do a flyover of the river. He was anxious to do the aerial reconnaissance to determine whether he had a chance to run the canyon.

Rain and poor flying conditions held up the flight until 5:20 p.m. Finally, Bennett was able to take off, and Blackadar looked down for his first view of the river which he had first heard of only six months before. Bennett, a large man with a wry sense of humor, gave Blackadar an exciting ride. "He wanted to see every rapids, so I made sure he got a good look," said Bennett, who did not gain a reputation by boring his passengers. For Blackadar the flight was far from dull: he vomited. "After he threw up," said Bennett, "I wondered if the guy was going to make it."*

The white-faced Blackadar, buckled into the small plane, scanned the river below while the cheerful pilot sitting to his side banked the plane sharply for a closer look. After at least three trips through the canyon and with "wingtips nearly touching the Canyon walls," he had had enough. "I called a halt to the low flying. A kayak would be safer," Blackadar wrote.

Despite the nauseating flight, he had managed to make a careful study of the canyon. Turnback looked runnable. He was surprised to learn that the worst of the whitewater was only five miles long as opposed to previous estimates of 12 miles. The eddies looked difficult to catch, but if he could stop himself, it appeared that he could climb out of his boat and scout some of the rapids from the ground level. If necessary, it also appeared that he could carry his kayak around some of the hardest rapids. He observed that the walls of the canyon on the glacier side did not look as severe as he imagined, and if he ran into trouble, he might be able to climb out in a place or two.

The most intimidating water was in the first half of the canyon. "Several very impressive boiling pots with boils ten to twenty feet high," he wrote. "Very active. I think I can avoid these. One roller all the way across which will be a sure flip but I don't believe it will hold. In fact I saw several sure flips but no holding holes and no danger to me unless I swim."

That was the one problem. There was little margin for error; he must not come out of his boat. But there was another

*On a Bennett piloted reconnaissance flight of the canyon in 1983 in preparation for the Alsek-Mt. Blackadar Memorial Expedition, one passenger vomited before reaching the destination and the other upon landing.

problem. He was looking at the river from several hundred feet in the air and the size of what he saw below could be tricking him: "I'm not sure of the magnitude but they look big." One rumor of a possible big falls was put to rest. None was found. He wrote, "I saw a couple of drops but nothing that I didn't feel was [un]runnable. There is nothing in the Grand Canyon however with as much violence or power or water hydraulics."

He was glad to be alone on this trip now that he had scouted the canyon from the air. If he had been with others, he was certain that he would have abandoned plans to run the river and returned to Idaho. Though it appeared extremely difficult, he believed that he could paddle the canyon. At least he felt that he had a fighting chance and it was worth paddling down to the entrance of the canyon.

After returning to Juneau, he firmed up arrangements with Bennett. Blackadar allowed himself 10 days to run the river, and if he had not made it to Dry Bay by September 2, he authorized the pilot to spend $1,000 in flying expenses to look for him. The kayaker planned to carry a small battery-powered citizens band channel nine radio with which he would be able to communicate with Bennett in case of emergency. To conserve batteries, he planned only to use the radio when he could see or hear Bennett's plane.

The wilderness-wise Bennett had pointed out a number of sandbars which would serve as possible landing sites in case Blackadar ran into trouble or was stranded. Of course, the doctor would be on his own in the canyon, but if he could manage to get to a sandbar above or below Turnback, the pilot could help. Bennett gave him instructions on how to mark off 1,000 feet of runway on a sandbar.

In case he was found dead, Blackadar instructed Bennett to bury him there and send positive identification to Shirley. This was a noble wish, but Bennett probably realized that it wouldn't wash with the authorities. A coroner would be required and an examination and determination of cause of death probably requested, none of which would have been done on a sandbar along the Alsek.

The next day, Saturday, August 21, a friend, Harvey King, took him from Juneau to Haines on his 50-foot launch. At Haines he hitched a ride with a schoolteacher in a pickup who took him and his kayak to the small town of Haines Junction located on the Alaska Highway. Arriving early evening Sunday, he checked in with the "Mounties" at Kluane National Park. The Park Service wardens told him that on the 24th they would be taking a helicopter to count game and would check on him if possible.

He made his final preparations for the journey, readying his boat and finishing up the first part of his diary. His launching place was at a bridge where the Alaska Highway crosses over the Dezadeash River at the edge of Haines Junction. From there the small river flows south through a gap in a treeless, scree-covered band of mountains and then, out of Blackadar's sight, flows deep into the icy bleakness of the St. Elias Range. No more roads cross the river. From there to the ocean, the Alsek is surrounded by hundreds of miles of wilderness.

VI

"In the Gorge and Stranded"

DAY THREE, AUGUST 24. Forty-seven miles into the trip. The fast-paced current pushed him around a broad bend. To his right, the ice of Lowell Glacier was barely visible under a lamination of grey dust and broken morainal debris. Then as the current slowed and dissipated in the calm waters of a small lake, his surroundings dramatically changed. He was in a foreign world, a world of stillness and of ice forms which, like existential souls, floated strangely around him.

Here the ice, recently sheered from the active toe of the glacier, had lost its grey coating. The "Lowell Glacier, off to the right, is tremendous," he wrote excitedly. "It is a mile of bright blue ice wall over 100 feet high and extending out into the Alsek, which undercuts the cliff."

From the ice wall at the river, the Lowell Glacier arcs upward to the perpetual snowfields of some of the St. Elias' highest peaks, including Mt. Alverstone at 14,501 and Mt. Kennedy at 13,907. The vertical relief from the summit of Mt. Alverstone to the river is an incredible 13,000 feet. As Blackadar paddled through Lowell Lake, far below the snowy summits, a great calve of the ice, "two-thirds the size of a football field," crashed into the river, shattering the cool silence and sending out shock waves which tossed his kayak about. The glacier had dislodged so much ice that Lowell Lake was a maze of icebergs, and Blackadar wrote that he "became lost in the floating ice but continued on to the end and found the runout OK."

The large amount of ice encountered by Blackadar indicates that Lowell Glacier was in the process of what glacialists call a surge. During a surge, glacier movement is accelerated many-fold. An advancing glacier might move at a normal annual pace of a few feet, but in a surge the same glacier may move hundreds of feet in a year. One glacier in the St. Elias Range, the Steele, usually advances less than 30 feet a year, yet during one remark-able surge it moved seven miles over a four-month period.

After Lowell Glacier, Blackadar made good time, carried along by the fast current of the river. He came to the first major rapid on the Alsek five miles below the Lowell; in another five miles he came to the second. Blackadar didn't scout either rapid, staying in the center, but the size of the water impressed him. It was probably the second rapid which gave him a small taste of the power of the river. Several very large holes guard the en-trance of the rapid. As the river cuts left and widens slightly, it fills with large waves and more menacing holes and eventually slams up against a cliff on the right bank. Blackadar managed to keep upright, but his heart was pounding as he was thrown by "cliffs with boils and huge hydraulics."

He observed in his notes that the water was cold, so cold that he can't force himself to try a practice roll. (In fact, the Alsek's water is about as frigid as river water can be. River temperature readings taken by research biologist James Brock put the summer water temperatures of the river below Lowell Glacier at one to two degrees above the freezing point.) He mentioned that a practice roll in the glacial water would help him prepare psychologically for the canyon, but he forewent it: "It's ice and brown—about like halfway through the Grand [Canyon of the Colorado]. One can still read the water . . . but it's thick."

After the second rapid, the Alsek cuts into bedrock, and for several miles the scenery resembles that of a river canyon one might expect in the lower western U.S. Here, the expansive glacial vistas of the upper river are restricted by chalky colored walls and grassy hillsides which are grazed by Dall sheep. Every so often, through a break in the canyon or a bend in the river, the scene brightens like a slide flashing on a screen, with the brilliant, bleached-white mountains of the St. Elias. The dazzling scenery, though familiar to mountaineers, is foreign to river runners who spend much of their time deep in the earth's recesses.

Blackadar doesn't mention the beauty of this part of the canyon. Perhaps it was shrouded in clouds. Or perhaps he was more interested in what lay below. One wonders if he paused to admire a broad mountain that resembles an inverted porcelain bowl with a broken and fragmented top and side. Hanging glaciers cling to its precipitous north face which starts within a short distance of the river and ascends 5,000 feet. If the clouds were not too low, there was no way that Blackadar could have missed it. This lovely spacious mountain, which dominates the downriver view for miles, would later be named after Blackadar.

※　※

BLACKADAR had a healthy respect for grizzlies. On his journey down the Alsek, he couldn't help seeing signs of bear. The signs are everywhere: tracks on beaches, piles of black scat, and heavily worn trails along the river. In 1961, Clem Rawert and John Dawson were camped on the Alsek near Bates River, 30 miles above Turnback Canyon. During the cool of the evening the river dropped, exposing a layer of damp silt near their campsite. They awoke the next morning to find in the silt fresh tracks of at least 12 different bears that had passed within a hundred feet—and some within five to six feet—of their tent during the night. They had never heard a thing.

Before leaving for the Alsek, Blackadar had called Dee Crouch, who had traveled often in Alaska's bear country, and asked how he felt about the effectiveness of a pistol against bears. Crouch told him that a person shooting at a charging bear couldn't survive at anything less than rifle range. But a rifle wouldn't fit in his kayak, and he told Crouch that from his own hunting experiences he felt a .44 magnum pistol might do the job, if done right. To other friends he once explained that the only way to stop a bear is to aim for the head. Wait until the bear is five feet away. Then shoot. Then jump.

At the start of the Alsek trip, he had taken his knife and cut away the fiberglass compartment that Lynn McAdams had fashioned for him and removed the gun, placing it in his watertight float bag. Nonetheless, he knew that his gun would be practically worthless while inside a tent. That night, settled in at his camp, he wrote in his diary that he was worried about the positioning of his tent. The tent opening was facing upstream. Since an up-canyon wind was blowing, a wandering bear approaching the rear of his tent might not be warned away by his scent and "surprise us both." Though protected by an overhanging bank, he figured that it would take only two jumps by a determined bear to reach him.

"The amazing thing was that Walt was in there alone," said Dick Tero, who has run the river twice and has written about the history of the area. "That is an awesome wilderness. There was nobody to talk with. Bear prints are all over the place on the beaches down there. That's spooky when you're camping out alone."

The camp where he was concerned about a rear surprise attack from a bear was only a few miles above Tweedsmuir Glacier. He was close now. He planned to sleep late in the morning, and if he reached the entrance of Turnback Canyon before 2 p.m., he would start into the gorge. "Otherwise," he writes, "I will wait until the next day at noon." His notes indicate that he made a quick review of his equipment: He was wearing a complete wet suit with gloves, but he hoped that he might be able to take his gloves off to grip his paddle firmly for running the canyon. He had matches and emergency supplies sewn into his large buoyancy life jacket, the same type of life jacket that he used on the Grand Canyon. He was three days ahead of schedule, and he was relieved to see that his 25 ounces of vodka was still holding strong, enough, he wrote, to "see me home with spare."

He realized the danger of the solo undertaking, but he reassured himself that having a companion along would not have helped his chances of survival. "Rescue by another boater in water which could drown me would be nearly impossible," he wrote. Turning to a lighter subject, he concluded the day's diary entry with the wildlife count: "two golden eagles and a friendly shore bird . . . ."

The next morning, the fourth day, he rose, packed, and started down the river, reaching the Tweedsmuir Glacier a short time later. The 40-mile-long glacier, to his right, was named in the winter of 1935 by explorer and cartographer Bradford Washburn for his personal friend, Lord Tweedsmuir, the governor general of Canada. It is one of the largest glaciers in the Alsek Valley. For most of its length it is nearly three miles wide, but the glacier fans out to a width of 10 miles where it butts up against the river. When viewed from a distance, the Tweedsmuir is a great faint blue sheet with broad, parallel stripes of dark rock debris that curve broadly down from surrounding peaks.

When Blackadar arrived on August 25, 1971, the Tweedsmuir was beginning to surge. Ice calves weighing tons fractured off the exposed toe of the glacier and swirled towards the canyon. The ante was upped, the dangers of running Turnback Canyon multiplied.

✳   ✳

THE Alsek River just before Turnback is a half mile wide, and upon entering the canyon, the river narrows to perhaps 100 feet. Once inside, the gray ice walls of the glacier are replaced by the black, polished rock walls of the gorge. The right side rises up 200 to 400 feet to the toe of Tweedsmuir Glacier, and the left side climbs steeply, finally culminating in glaciated summits, a mile vertical above the river. At some locations within the canyon, the Alsek River is radically constricted by solid rock banks only 35 to 40 feet wide.

Although no accurate geodetic surveying has been done, there's probably not a significant drop of river level through Turnback Canyon—at least not the dramatic drop that would be expected of such a notorious stretch of whitewater. Water dropping steeply over boulders and riverbed obstructions is normally what causes rapids. But in Turnback Canyon, the savage turbulence of the rapids appears to be the result of a great volume of water squeezed through a confined area.

As the glaciers melt in the summer warmth and river volume increases, so does the severity of the turbulence in Turnback. Peak flows for the Alsek River come when melting reaches its greatest intensity at the end of July and first part of August. During this time river flows exceed 50,000 cubic feet per second (cfs) in Turnback Canyon. Such a volume passing through the canyon is twice that of the normal summer flows of the Grand Canyon, and nothing on the Colorado approaches the tortured constrictions of Turnback. While the level of the Alsek River had probably dropped some since early August, Blackadar, nevertheless, was attempting the canyon during a period of dangerously high water.

He paddled past the last portage of the canyon on his right. The river began to narrow. The current increased. His boat bounced through a few building swells. Ahead, the river narrowed even further.

For 49 years, his life seemed to build up to this one grand challenge, one *tour de force*, one man facing overwhelming forces alone: we picture him in the moments before starting in the whitewater as one small, insignificant white and orange dot floating on a vast grey river, the sound of glacial silt scraping against naked rock, the groaning bulk of the nearby glacier, the white glaciated peaks above, the boat disappearing into the portal of the gorge.

SHORTLY after the canyon narrows, the river begins twisting and the current accelerates.

"I suddenly felt trapped and committed," he wrote. The water seemed to take him by surprise, and he appeared not to be boating in the careful calculating manner that, despite all the braggadocio connected with him, his many companions insist that he had. Approaching the first major set of rapids, he searched for a place to stop. He seemed anxious and picked a poor location to try to get out of his boat. That he finally realized he must scout had almost come too late for he was nearly in the midst of the whitewater.

The normal method of getting out of a kayak along the side of a river is to slip the paddle behind the body, against the cockpit rim. The kayaker reaches back, gripping the paddle and cockpit rim together, and balancing on the length of the paddle on the shore, the boater can ease up out of the kayak. Without a firm place on which to rest the paddle, climbing out of the boat can be exceedingly difficult or impossible.

Blackadar, forced to pick a takeout against a cliff, was unable to get a proper purchase for his paddle. Trying a different tack, he threw his paddle up on a small ledge above him, but the paddle bounced off the rocks and fell back down towards the water. After several tries, he finally "tossed it some distance above where it lodged. Then in trying to get out on the precipitous cliff I nearly turned over 2 or 3 times."

He was indecisive. Throwing his paddle above him, he realized now, was a foolish error. He could not afford foolish errors. "I tried & tried to regain my paddle so I could go on without scouting but couldn't reach it." He was nearly swamped several times in his desperate attempts, but eventually he managed to delicately lift himself and his boat out of the water by pulling himself up on the rock. Had he slipped, he "would have had to swim the entire gorge!" "[U]nlike my teacher," he said, referring to Barb Wright who could do an esquimautage sans paddle, "I can't roll up without a paddle."

He climbed out of his boat and scouted the first rapid. The rapid, now called the S-turns, consists of several twisting bends of the river and nearly continuous whitewater. He climbed back in his boat and started his run, in the company of icebergs which had calved off the surging Tweedsmuir. He hit two of the unyielding blocks of ice hard, but his boat survived.* The water knocked him over twice, but he rolled upright easily. At one point the current pinned him up against a cliff. Holding the paddle in one hand to free his other hand, he pushed himself forward and freed himself from the trap.

After the S-turns, the river widens and the rapids ease up some. Blackadar stopped again on the left. This time he picked a good place to get out of his boat. He seemed now to be under better control; he was anticipating and planning. Yet what he saw ahead during his scout was sobering: "A huge 45-degree drop of 30 feet or more into a boiling hell."

At Blackadar's Boiling Hell, the river is pinched through a 35-foot-wide opening in the polished walls of canyon. During August flow levels, the top wave curls, crashing back on itself, followed by a steep drop of 10 feet. The full force of the drop-

---

*In his notes, Blackadar is a little vague on the exact location of his first two collisions with icebergs. It appears from where the passage is located in the diary that the incidents occurred in the S-turns.

ping river piles 15 feet high against the right wall. Recoiling and surging up and down, the river rushes back to the left into an undercut wall and finally drops into an erratic and boiling cauldron of water. For 200 feet the river broadens and flows unbroken by rapids, and then it disappears between the closing narrow walls ahead.*

After scouting, Blackadar decided to carry around the Boiling Hell. The river in this area hourglasses in and out. His planned portage route led from the left side of an eddy in an enlarged alcove to a wider, less turbulent bulge in the river below Boiling Hell.

He never made the intended portage. Just before he reached the stopping point, his boat was jerked away and caught by a whirlpool: "The boat was sucked by the stern into a perfectly vertical position, then whirled 1½ times around and plopped in upside down. I rolled up immediately and easily caught the eddy as planned, but in the wrong place."

He struggled to get into the necessary position but he judged that the lower end of the eddy where he needed to take out was 10 feet higher than his location on the upstream side of the eddy. While he was attempting to reach his intended stopping point, the current caught him again and flung him toward the Boiling Hell. He could not stop now. He had to run it.

"Now I knew I had a paddle ahead!" he wrote. "Just then an iceberg the size of my bedroom appeared alongside, charging for the drop. I hurriedly turned my boat around and paddled upstream with all my strength while sliding backward into the 'falls.' Missed the iceberg which went ahead, flipped and hung upside down while the boat was tossed out of the most violent boils before rolling up." Somehow, in the confusion, he had avoided a collision with the iceberg, successfully run the Boiling Hell and rolled.

---

*Both Klaus Streckman and Rob Lesser, who have studied Turnback's rapids, feel that this rapid is what Lesser later named "Dyna-Flow." Blackadar's more descriptive "Boiling Hell" is used in this account.

He was "euphoric." He had come through unscathed, and his roll was confident and strong. Paddling to the side, he stopped for a brief rest among ice chunks which had washed into his stopping eddy. He thought that he would be out soon. A cliff blocked his view of the next section of the canyon, so he continued on, blind to what awaited him:

> Suddenly, I was in a frothy mess that was far worse than anything I've seen. I don't know how far the hair lasted and would not go back to check if I could, but I am sure it was 20 degrees down with the most gigantic waves and foam and holes on all sides of me. Very narrow—like trying to run down a coiled rattler's back, the rattler striking me from all sides. I was shoved to the left bank about an inch from the cliff where a foot-wide eddy existed. For perhaps a mile I skidded and swirled and turned down this narrow line. I kept telling myself, "You can roll in this," but all the time I knew I couldn't. I expected to get jammed into the cliff but never touched it. Eventually, I squirted out into a pool right side up and safe, only to flip in another whirlpool before reaching shore.

He got out of his boat and scouted ahead—this time on the right bank. He was drained and hoping that he was near the end of the gorge, but what was coming was his biggest test yet.

He hiked down and found "an immense cresting wave blocking the way, the one I had seen seven days before from the air." Referring to the wave as the "roller," he scouted it from a 500-foot cliff and also was able to work his way down to the river bank close to the wave.

Blackadar described the roller as a smooth wave, 20 feet deep, curling back at the top. The immense size of the roller wasn't the problem; it was the foaming, curling-back part that alarmed him. The wave's symmetrical shape created a strong flow of surface water which rushed upstream just beyond the trough of the wave. Called a reversal, such waves are anathemas to boaters. Because of the upstream forces created by

reversals, a kayaker or boater may not be able to develop sufficient forward momentum to pass through. A boat can fall back
into the reversal, and particularly if the boat turns sideways, it
can become entrapped. A prime example of a reversal is the
wave found at the bottom of small dams. Even a dam three or
four feet high can create a deadly reversal. Unwary boaters
drifting into such reversals have been trapped for hours. If not
released by the reversal or pulled out by rescuers, they eventually die. Death may come relatively swiftly by being held under
by violent currents and being unable to reach the surface of the
water. Or it may come slowly as the victim's strength ebbs away
while he fights for air and struggles to escape.

He studied the roller and thought he might be able to force
his way through on the right side. On the right, though, just
downstream from the roller was a large, violent hole. He wrote,
"I was sure the roller would hold a boat if it turned sideways &
didn't think the hole would." But the addition of the hole complicated the situation. He was concerned about the power of the
roller, and if forced to swim, the prospects were frightening,
washing through the hole and into more bad rapids below.

Awed by the power of the great roller, he tried out the various scenarios in his mind and speculated on his chances of surviving it: "After scouting I thought there was a good chance I
could get flipped upstream before I could get my body & paddle
thru the crest & if so I would join the roller forever unless I did
a deep exit in which I [would have] had a hell of a swim ahead."
Exiting from his boat, however, would have left him "in the
middle of the river heading for some rapids below with little
chance of reaching shore. If I did, I would be afoot with no
supplies since my empty boat would stay sideways in the wave."

He vacillated. For an hour, he surveyed the roller and
weighed the options. Finally, he scrambled back up-canyon to
where he had left his boat. No more hesitation. He was going
to run it.

Blackadar paddled "furiously" to a point on the right side of the roller where he felt he had a chance to break through. It was a chancy run since he risked "plummeting" into the troubling hole below.

His boat climbed up the huge wave. He reached out with his paddle, trying to propel himself through the wall of water caused by the reversal. Crashing into the wall, he was stopped dead and violently thrown upside down. The turbulent water pummeled his boat, and it felt to him that his boat was tearing apart. His boat was caught: "[I] could feel the tug of war. The boat bouncing in the roller sideways." He tried reaching with his paddle and pulling. Then as he strained against the incredible force of the water, the fiberglass on the left side of the deck of his kayak ripped. Water poured into the boat, making it heavy and unwieldy. Yet it was the added weight of water in his boat which finally released him, pushing him far enough under the water to reach downstream current which flushed him out of the reversal.

He tried a roll and missed. While upside down he realized that his body had partially slipped out of the boat. "I forced myself not to swim for the surface," he explained later. "I knew it'd be all over if I did. So I climbed back into that kayak even though all my nerves were screaming to head for the surface. Before I could roll up I found myself being beaten and shook and mauled for all I was worth in that feared hole."

Now he found himself caught again, this time in the hole below the roller. He tried four more rolls: "I got scrubbed, tumbled and shaken; rolled and missed—rolled and missed. Finally I caught a breath, calmed my nerves, jammed my knees solidly into the sides of the boat and on my sixth try made a perfect roll and popped up. I found the boat swamped and uncontrollable in the middle of the river. Only the air bladders were keeping it afloat. My body was in water to the armpits, and I was heading for a rapids far worse than Lava Falls . . . . I made a tremendous effort to force the swamped boat to the shore, using all my reserve. Finally I reached the bank holding onto the kayak by a strap, and as I rolled out on the bank I said, 'thanks.'"

Exhausted but safely on the shore, he inspected his boat and found the left deck of the boat split and left thigh hook sheared off.

As it often does on the Alsek, it was drizzling. He erected his air mattress over the kayak to try to dry it and planned to patch the torn deck with the small fiberglass repair kit he had brought with him. Sitting down in the rain, he began to write in his diary, the terror and shock of the last few hours fresh, alive and burning like a fever. He was obviously aroused and rattled. His words are full of emotion.

"In the gorge and stranded!" he began, and after describing his location, he continued: "This has been a day! I want any other kayaker or would-be expert to read my words well! The Alsek Gorge is unpaddleable!"

He described "one huge horrendous mile of hair (the worst foamy rapids a kayaker can imagine), 30 feet wide, 50,000 cubic feet per second and a 20-degree downgrade going like hell. Incredible! I didn't flip in that mile or I wouldn't be writing." And then he ends his short proem and goes back to detail about entering the canyon, the S-turns, the iceberg and the Boiling Hell, the Canyon of the Coiled Rattler, and Blackadar's Roller. Then the same feelings with which he had opened flood back: "I'm not coming back. Not for $50,000, not for all the tea in China. Read my words well and don't be a fool. It's unpaddleable."

The sequence of his story changed little from his original diary. It wasn't planned. It flowed naturally, cascading across the notebook paper while rain fell on his tent, and the gray river rushed below him.

Dick Tero, besides being a Catholic priest and Alsek explorer, is an aesthete of adventure literature. He feels that Blackadar's piece on the Alsek is the best that he has ever read on a kayaking adventure. The reason it is so good, according to

Tero, is that it was written in the heat of the moment.

Blackadar finished all his vodka and completed putting the first fiberglass patch on his boat, which he kept covered with his air mattress to keep it dry. He was on the left bank of the river, across from an "impressive waterfall." His tent, a hundred yards upstream from the damaged boat, was "cozy," and he had found wood for his supper fire.

*   *

THE next day, August 26, he placed another fiberglass patch on his boat. By 2 p.m. the fiberglass had set and dried sufficiently for him to continue. He was close to the end, but a few more rapids remained. Careening down the last turbulent rapids of the Alsek, he barely missed a large hole caused by a two-story sized rock. "I slipped by the edge but spun around and gushed down the chute backward, crashed into the cliff with my stern but didn't flip. I scouted then for two miles and found nothing else. It's a good thing because I'd had enough."

The Alsek, however, hadn't had enough of him, for he was pulled backwards into a hole, flipping him vertically up and over, forcing him to make what counted as his seventh roll. He described the last part of the canyon as "tough," mentioning a narrowing of the river to 40 feet, which is probably the last major constriction of the gorge, but it "was nothing like the previous."

Once out of the dark canyon, the river flattens and the valley opens up to grand, spacious vistas of the Icefield Range to the west and the Noisy Range to the east. Blackadar paddled only a few miles from the canyon to the base of the Vern Ritche Glacier. His recorded observations of the wildlife—even grizzlies seemed a fitting respite to the trepidations of the canyon: "Now relaxing and glad I am out . . . . Bald eagle and one other larger arctic gull-like bird—friendly, came to visit and stood around. Saw two big grizzlies today and another just now out my back door. I hope he goes by."

The next day he paddled past the Alsek confluence with the Tatshenshini. Beyond here, the river size swells over fourfold, joined by the Tatshenshini and dozens of major glacial tributaries, creating a great wide river which in places stretches several miles from bank to bank. From the air it appears as a vast moving gray ribbon, curling beneath ever larger glaciers descending from unnamed valleys and from unnamed peaks. It is enormous, awesomely wild country.

He did not describe the country. With Turnback behind him, he was intent on getting out. He paddled 70 miles the next day, eventually reaching Dry Bay. Not able to find the airfield and exhausted, he made camp and did not even build a fire, his first night without one.

On a map, Dry Bay resembles the head of a tadpole, and the wide river flowing into the bay forms the tadpole's wriggling tail. The river slows and empties into channels that shift with years. Stunted willows and brush cover the low-lying delta and tidal flat created by the river's heavy load of glacial silt. A cabin or two and fish drying racks appear in breaks in the brush. The most conspicuous sign of habitation is the small Dry Bay Fish Company packing plant. The small plant and its 4,000-foot air strip at one time were on the main river channel but are now along a sluggish slough, victims of the river's capricious ways.

The next day Blackadar located the fish camp. Among those who greeted him was Arnie Israelson. Israelson remembered Blackadar as "woozy, shaken and talking about how he didn't know how he had gotten through and how he would have portaged if he had been able."

Layton Bennett was called from a radio at the fish camp and agreed to fly him out. Alex Brogle from the Alaskan Fish and Game Department stopped in to talk to him about his run. Brogle told him that the powerful current in Turnback Canyon prevents salmon, even the powerful king salmon, from migrating up its waters. Salmon are normally stopped by waterfalls and dams, but Turnback Canyon, Blackadar learned, is "the only spot known where the speed of the water stops fish."

It was one more interesting piece of information that Blackadar learned about a place that could only be described by superlatives. For the time being, however, he had seen enough and experienced enough. He was happy to be alive, happy to be returning to home in his beloved Salmon River country. He had survived an incredible test and wasn't anxious to repeat it.

"I know the area well," Blackadar wrote. "Too well. I won't be coming back. Ever."

VII

The Big Su

WHEN BLACKADAR RETURNED to Idaho, he knew that he had accomplished something extraordinary in river running. But just how important was his run compared with what others were doing? Certainly in North America, Blackadar's achievement on the Alsek in the early 1970s was on the cutting edge of kayaking. No one person—nor any boating team—had ever attempted more intimidating or powerful whitewater. But how does his descent of Turnback Canyon compare on an international basis? Was he a Bannister or a Hillary of river exploration?

In one sense, it depends on the type of river being compared. Blackadar was not a technical boater, and he did not possess the skills of kayakers trained in the European tradition of slalom competition—catching minute eddies, ferrying accurately from river seam to river seam, and paddling forward or backward between two narrow vertical poles hanging from wires. On lower-volume, technical rivers, there were many kayakers better than Blackadar.

But when the comparison is made with big water and big rivers, then Blackadar stands out. For mountaineering, it is the big mountains, the Himalayas, Mt. Everest, K-2, which are symbols of the supreme tests of the sport. In whitewater river running, it is the same. The advance of river running is influenced by big, high volume rivers with large waves and powerful hydraulics. It is on such rivers that psychological barriers are broken, where human limits are explored. Such rivers are the kind that stir the imagination and require something more than just technical skill to be able to run.

Overseas, the comparative kayak scene was dominated by the British. Although the Europeans on the continent were gradually descending one Alpine river after another, the British were the major players in expeditionary river running. During the 1970s the outstanding British big water kayaker was Mike Jones. At half the age of Blackadar and topped with a mop of floppy blond hair—in some river photos Jones resembles a disheveled rock star after a concert—he couldn't have been more opposite from the short-cropped doctor from Salmon. But in other ways, almost bordering on the occult, the two were strangely similar. Both fearlessly attacked whitewater, both were practicing medical doctors, and both died while kayaking in the same year.

Jones' first accomplishment which moved him into the limelight occurred in 1969 when, as a member of a British team, he successfully conquered the rapids of Switzerland's Inn River. The descent of the Inn was an extremely technical undertaking, and it was described by climber and writer Chris Bonnington as the equivalent of climbing the North Face of the Eiger.

Jones' major achievement in river running, however, was his descent of the Dudh Kosi, the river draining off Mt. Everest. The expedition, taking place in 1976, ran many difficult sections of the river. Parts of the river which Jones' team found not runnable were portaged with the help of porters.

It is difficult to make a comparison between the rivers since the Alsek and the Dudh Kosi are altogether two different types of runs. The Alsek is a larger river than the Dudh Kosi and located deep within a wilderness area. The Dudh Kosi is decidedly more technical than the Alsek—Turnback has no rocks to maneuver around. Turnback's strength over the Dudh Kosi is the size of the water, its extreme turbulence, and its remoteness.

Rob Lesser, who has built an impressive record of big water kayak descents, including a number of first descents overseas, feels that the Dudh Kosi doesn't compare with the big water of the Alsek, or to other big water rivers such as the Susitna or Stikine. According to Lesser, the Dudh Kosi is "technically difficult but not big stuff." Lesser has boated with Mick Hopkinson, Jones' kayaking partner, in the U.S. and New Zealand, and found Hopkinson suitably impressed with the size of North American water and special techniques used by Lesser and others in big water. Hopkinson's impressions led Lesser to believe, that at least for big water, Blackadar's descent on the Alsek was internationally far ahead of its time.

The most significant difference between the two runs is that the Alsek was run solo with no support, and it was run in 1971, five years before the Dudh Kosi descent. Blackadar's run in no way minimizes Jones' achievement, but symbolically, the Alsek assumes an historical place, a beginning of a new age of the sport built around the powerful story about one 49-year-old individual with a bold dream. It is river running's Everest. The psychological barrier had been broken, and a new array of opportunities was possible.

Although Blackadar's run on the Alsek, like the successful ascent of Everest, did not precipitate the events to follow, it was on the leading edge of a flood tide which brought swelling numbers of new individuals into river running. In the early seventies, the marketplace began its steady expansion in the river business with new rafts, frames, inflatables and kayaks appearing and becoming more readily available. Like eager climbers looking for unclimbed mountains, river pioneers made new river descents. Rivers became so crowded that by the mid-seventies many of the popular multi-day rivers in the West required potential river runners to submit applications which would be drawn out of a hat.

A new age of river sport had begun. Among the thousands taking up the sport, a handful of individuals was out in front, pushing the limits and setting the tone for the sport. With his accomplishment on the Alsek, Blackadar was now unquestionably the leader.

❋   ❋

SHORTLY after Blackadar returned from the Alsek, he sent Barb Wright a copy of his diary with several pages of additional notes and drawings. He asked Wright to help him tidy it up some and get it ready to send to potential magazines. In his note to Wright, he is intoxicated with the journey. "I'll agree it was a crazy trip," he wrote, "but I would do it again on another river."

After Barb Wright had commented on his diary article, he sent it off to *Reader's Digest* in early September. "If they don't give encouragement," Blackadar wrote to Wright, "perhaps we should just send it to the AWA or the round file." By AWA, he meant American Whitewater Affiliation. He had been a member for some time, regularly receiving and reading its quarterly journal. Recently, he had written a piece for the AWA Journal on big water techniques, which appeared that winter. It was Blackadar's first published kayaking article.

By late 1971, he had sent a copy of his diary to *Alaska* magazine and *Sports Illustrated*. There is no record of the *Reader's Digest* response, but *Alaska* magazine was enthusiastic: "Thanks for letting us see your Alsek River diary. Going through Hair was hairy indeed. Very well done. Gripping, exciting and tight," wrote Ed Fortnier, the editor. Fortnier wanted to use it, but he knew that *Alaska* couldn't compete with the rates paid by *Reader's Digest* and *Sports Illustrated*. If they turned Blackadar down, "*Alaska* would be happy to have it."

Alaska wasn't to have it. *Sports Illustrated* was biting. An editor had asked for more information on the Alsek, which Blackadar provided. He heard nothing for more than a month. Then bingo! On January 31 of 1972, Pat Ryan of *Sports Illustrated* wrote to inform Blackadar that he wanted the article.

"Before, I had just a hint of your accomplishment," Ryan wrote. "Now I am filled with awe." Ryan offered Blackadar $1,000 for it. Not hesitating, Blackadar accepted.

Although Ryan's editing helped polish the article, she otherwise left in place Blackadar's descriptive language, his metaphors, and his overall structure. The article to appear in the summer of 1972 was entitled "Caught Up in a Hell of White Water." Boiled down to its basics, the solitary figure fighting the hellish rapids of Turnback Canyon is the same lone, rugged individualist who had so attracted Blackadar since moving to the West. He had never come closer to becoming a part of this elusive, legendary character than in two frightening days on the Alsek River. For Blackadar, it had been a dizzy ride down the back of the coiled rattlesnake—and an equally dizzy ride to the summit of his sport.

He was ready for more. With the *Sports Illustrated* article soon to throw him in the national limelight, Blackadar knew that if he was to remain on the top, he would need to continue to pioneer new runs. Indeed, within a few months of returning from Alaska, he told Barb Wright that he wouldn't mind repeating the experience on another river. It wasn't all for recognition. Kayaking also gave him something else. "I think life is for living," he once said. "Part of living, for me, is facing a challenge and overcoming it. The feeling that comes over you, once you've conquered the impossible, is one of absolute exhilaration." Now that the Alsek was out of the way, he began looking for the next "impossible."

While he considered options, more problems were brewing over undeveloped forest lands in the Salmon area, and once again Blackadar sided against the local logging interests. If the logging companies were temporarily stopped from cutting in the Clear Creek area, they wanted into other roadless areas like Clear Creek. Logging in itself he accepted, but he scorned the roads that necessarily accompanied timber harvesting. More roads into the backcountry, the dismantling of old frontier, was one of the obvious signs of change in the River of No Return country.

He said that much at a Forest Service hearing in the spring of 1972, called to determine the future of undeveloped lands on the Salmon forest.

"We cannot desecrate the land," Blackadar admonished at the hearing. Gordon Crupper, however, did not see it that way. He countered: "Our use of land must be managed so as to produce the material needs of our people on every acre capable of producing those material needs." To Crupper and the logging industry "every acre" meant Clear Creek, the central Idaho wilderness lands, and any other acreage with timber.

It made little sense to Blackadar: why develop "every acre" now? Why not wisely use presently developed areas on the forest to provide for the needs of people? He was a true conservative in that regard, agreeing with the philosophy of his environmental friends that setting aside roadless lands was nothing more than careful investing, like placing money in savings, and if some day, a desperate nation needed the marginal timber or minerals in wilderness areas on the Salmon National Forest, they would still be there. At the same time, and more important to him, by placing areas in reserve, fish, wildlife and recreation values would be protected. "We should not make all the decisions in our lifetime, but wait until other generations come along to see if we are right," he said.

As in the past, Blackadar and Richard Smith were nearly alone in their sentiments. *Recorder Herald* reports on the crowded March 1972 meeting attribute only their statements in support of protecting roadless areas. All other comments at the Salmon meeting agreed with Crupper's point of view. The Clear

Creek controversy and proposals to protect more lands had done little to heal the division. A few months earlier, the *Herald* had foretold the dominant community position in a sharp anti-wilderness editorial, describing wilderness programs as "a continuing threat to the proper management of federal land" and "a major concern to those who abhor waste."

But as anti-preservation stances solidified in Salmon, Blackadar and Smith were able to rejoice over important progress made in protecting the Sawtooths and White Clouds. Compromise legislation in Congress finally passed in 1972, creating the Sawtooth Recreation Area. Although the bill was not as good as Idaho conservationists had hoped, it helped postpone* the destructive White Clouds mine and stopped the ragtag developments which were marring the beauty of the agrarian Sawtooth Valley. Money appropriated through the bill would buy scenic easements and clean up some of the valley's worst eyesores. Years later travelers driving north of Sun Valley and through the Sawtooth National Recreation Area would be treated to one of the most beautiful panoramas in all of Idaho, thanks to the fight put up by Blackadar and his conservation friends.

＊   ＊

ALTHOUGH kayaking now overshadowed his sports interests, throughout the seventies, Blackadar still managed to continue his regular hunting trips. Little had changed. On one hunting trip, he and his son-in-law, Cary Cook, took his Travelall to Leesburg. They had killed two elk, but while Blackadar was moving the Travel-all, he ran it over a sharp rock. "I could hear wind blowing out of the tire." remembered Cook. Looking, they found not one tire flattening but two others deflating, two

---

*At this writing, the future of the White Clouds still remains uncertain. Idaho conservationists have proposed that the area be designated as a wilderness. The designation will not stop the mine, but it would make the White Clouds less appealing for development.

on the truck and one on the horse trailer. Blackadar looked for his spares and found both of them flat. That made a total of five flat tires. "We were trying to get out of there before snow came," said Cook. "So Walt packed out the tires on the horses."

Cook, who had no food, made a shish kebab out of some of the elk meat and went to sleep by the fire. Meanwhile, Blackadar reached the main road and hid the horses. Not about to stand around, trying to thumb a ride back to town, Blackadar laid the tires down in the middle of the road. He stopped the first car, climbed in, and some time around 4 the next morning, he returned to Cook.

"He was always trying to get the maximum amount out of his tires," said Cook, "He was an expert at getting rides. One time along the Payette River [near Boise] he blew a tire—and the spare was flat. He just ran out in the road. The pickup coming had to stop or run over him. He grabbed the tire, threw it in the back and told the driver that he needed to get to a service station. He never even asked!"

That was Blackadar's style. He never ceased to astonish those around him. In the spring of 1972, he traveled to Salt Lake and met Dick Tero and Dee Crouch, whose article and pictures in *Alaska* magazine had first attracted him to the Alsek. After running a small river in the Wasatch Mountains, they all met at Crouch's house for drinks. Tero and Crouch, two of the very few who had actually looked down into Turnback Canyon, greatly admired the doctor for his kayaking accomplishment. But now that Blackadar, all 175 pounds of him, sat in their presence pouring down vodka, it was hard to believe.

"He stunned us," said Tero. "Dee and I were both in our late 20s and to see this guy with a paunch and 50 years old—he was 20 years older than us. We couldn't imagine a guy in Walt's shape doing what he was doing."

He planned to keep on doing what he was doing. That evening, Blackadar talked about running another river in Alaska, called the Susitna. While the Alsek was the major drainage of

CANADA
U.S.

WASHINGTON

Lake Pend Oreille

N

○ Coeur d' Alene

Clearwater

Lochsa

○ Lewiston

Selway Falls

Selway

Selway-Bitteroot Wilderness

OREGON

Salmon River

Riggins ○

River of No Return Wilderness

North Fork

South Fork

Middle Fork

Salmon ○

MONTANA

Salmon River

North Fork

Big Falls

Dagger Falls

Garden Valley ○

South Fork Payette River

Stanley ○

White Cloud Mountains

IDAHO

Payette

Sawtooth Wilderness

Hells Canyon

Snake River

Boise ○

Sun Valley ○

Craters of The Moon Nat. Monument

The Great Rift

○ Idaho Falls

WYOMING

○ Pocatello

Owyhee River

Bruneau

Jarbidge

Indian Hot Sprgs.

Snake River

Twin Falls ○

West Fork

Julie Wilson Falls

NEVADA

UTAH

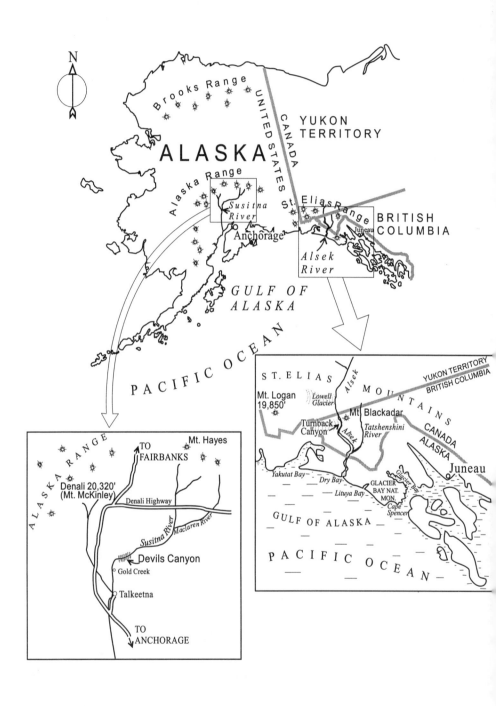

N

Brooks Range

UNITED STATES
CANADA

YUKON
TERRITORY

ALASKA

Alaska Range

Susitna
River

St. Elias Range

BRITISH
COLUMBIA

Juneau

Anchorage

Alsek
River

GULF OF
ALASKA

PACIFIC OCEAN

ALASKA RANGE

TO
FAIRBANKS

Mt. Hayes

Denali 20,320'
(Mt. McKinley)

Denali Highway

Susitna River

Maclaren River

Devils Canyon

Gold Creek

Talkeetna

TO
ANCHORAGE

ST. ELIAS

Mt. Logan
19,850'

Lowell
Glacier

Alsek

MOUNTAINS

YUKON TERRITORY
BRITISH COLUMBIA

Mt. Blackadar

Turnback
Canyon

Alsek

Tatshenshini
River

CANADA
ALASKA

Juneau

Yakutat Bay

Dry Bay

Glacier Bay

GLACIER
BAY NAT.
MON.

Lituya Bay

Cape
Spencer

GULF OF ALASKA

PACIFIC OCEAN

Harriett and Lloyd Blackadar. Harriett, Walter's mother, was the daughter of a Baptist minister, and Lloyd, his father, was an actuary with the Equitable Life Company in New York. It was Harriett who encouraged Walt's childhood interest in the outdoors.

Walter Lloyd Blackadar (middle) at about 10 years old. Two of his three brothers are pictured with him: John (left) and Gordon (right).

A dapper Walt Blackadar during his college days. In 1940, Walt Blackadar started his pre-medical studies at Dartmouth and eventually finished his medical training at Columbia in New York in 1946.

Shirley Clement. Shirley served as a field hospital nutritionist in the southwest Pacific during some of the bloodiest days of World War II. While on overseas duty, she contracted dengue fever and in 1943, was sent stateside to recover. During her convalescence, she met Walt. They were married in June of 1945.

The Blackadar home in Salmon City. In the early fifties, Walt and Shirley moved into this 4,800-square-foot home on a large bench overlooking the Salmon River.

Walt and his 4-year-old daughter, Ruth. It didn't take long before Walt Blackadar dove headlong into outdoor sports. In this photo taken in 1950, a year after he moved to Salmon, he shows off a prized steelhead nearly as long as Ruth is tall.

On one of his annual spring steelhead fishing trips down the Salmon River Walt stands in the middle of the sweep boat with his sister Joy and her husband John Dean.

Holding the sweeps of his raft, Walt Blackadar strikes a pose reminiscent of the early Salmon River pilots. Blackadar greatly admired the rugged individualists of Western mythology and managed to achieve his own place in Western lore after his famous solo run down the rapids of Turnback Canyon.

Very much the versatile country doctor, Blackadar built a busy practice in Salmon. Adventurous in his practice as he was in outdoor sports, he was trained in and regularly performed a number of different surgical procedures.

Doc Blackadar was well known among the sparse residents living in the wilderness along the Salmon River. Here, in Don Smith's outfitting cabin, he performs minor surgery (with a pair of pliers and a nail) on a hunter whose toe had been smashed by a horse.

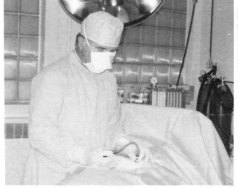

Barbara Wright and Walt. In the late sixties, Wright was the dominant figure in United States competitive kayaking. Blackadar, who at that time was just beginning to learn the sport, offered her a free trip down the Middle Fork of the Salmon in exchange for kayaking lessons. She took him up on the offer, and in 1968 on a memorable Middle Fork trip, Barb taught him the Eskimo roll and other kayaking techniques. The trip marked the beginning of a close and supportive friendship that lasted until his death. This photo was taken on the Main Salmon in July of 1973.

Dick Tero was an important influence in Walt's life. It was Tero's article on the Alsek River that appeared in the March 1971 issue of *Alaska Magazine* that first interested Blackadar in running the river—and Turnback Canyon.

Opposite: The Alsek River cuts a path through the wild and capricious St. Elias Range, a land of blowing snow, wind-sculpted summits, and groaning ice and crevasses.

JAMES T. BROCK

An aerial view of Turnback Canyon. Since Blackadar's solo run, it has become one of the world's most famous whitewater canyons.

BOB BLACKADAR COLLECTION

This recently discovered photograph was apparently taken by Blackadar during his aerial reconnaissance of Turnback Canyon with his pilot, Layton Bennett. The river is flowing from the bottom to the top of the photograph. He had intended to portage the rapids in the lower right-hand corner, but was washed through it, out of control. After that rapids, he pulled into an eddy and tried to get off the river to see what lay ahead, but the surging water, icebergs and slippery rock walls blocked his attempt to scout. On the back of the photograph, he has written: "A. is the intended carry eddy.   B. The pause in that iceberg eddy with no way out.   C. The narrow eddy line I slipped down on the left.   D. Note iceberg just above C." The photo shows that the water level in the canyon was high and dangerous.

The next party attempting to run the Alsek River after Blackadar's famous 1971 descent was made up of Dee Crouch, Dick Tero and Klaus Streckman. But their 1974 attempt was halted by the surging Tweedsmuir Glacier shown in this photo, moving across the river from the right. Massive icebergs calving off the glacier were blocking and pushing the Alsek River up against the far bank, creating terrifying rapids of foaming gray water and shredded ice. Unable to continue downriver, the three men left their boats behind and began a 65-mile epic walk out.

Walt, Roger Hazelwood and Kay Swanson at the beginning of their intrepid 1972 journey down the Susitna River. A few days after this photo was taken, they were battling the powerful, silt-laden rapids of Devils Canyon.

Aerial photograph of the beginning of the Pearly Gates in Devils Canyon. During the confusion of the last half mile of the Pearly Gates, Blackadar became separated from both of his companions. He was flushed out, but Roger and Kay were missing, trapped somewhere back in the gorge.

Julie Wilson and Walt Blackadar on his ranch north of Salmon. Although it is difficult to pinpoint the date of this photo, it is likely that it was taken in the spring of 1974, only a few days before Julie died in a kayaking accident on the West Fork of the Bruneau. Her death haunted him until his own death four years later.

The camera crew for ABC's *American Sportsman* prepares to film Blackadar on the Colorado River. The filming took place in 1974, and the program aired on national television in 1975.

John Dondero outfitted with a camera on his helmet. Enlisted to help with the filming, John took on-the-river shots of Walt and the other kayakers featured in the *American Sportsman* program.

Always the life of the party, Blackadar arrives at John Dondero's Sun Valley wedding in his kayak. The kayak was made by John's company, Natural Progression.

Roger Brown, one of the outdoor world's most innovative cinematographers, created several films in which Blackadar was featured.

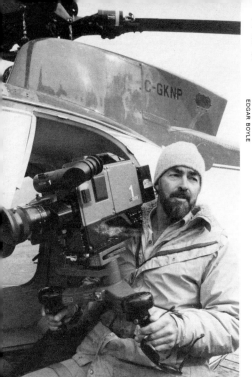

A "wild track" recording session is conducted with boaters during the 1976 descent of the Susitna River. From left: Walt, John Dondero, and Walt's son Bob. In the foreground with his back to the picture, an unidentified sound technician monitors the conversation.

Aerial view of Devil Creek Rapids on the Susitna River. The river flows toward the front of the photo. Just slightly above center in the photograph is the most difficult part of the rapids. The Nozzle, where Blackadar and some of the other members of the 1976 party had trouble, is located where the river dramatically widens just slightly below center.

Blackadar descends a deep trough before the maelstrom of Devil Creek Rapids. Photo taken during the 1976 Susitna trip. (Summit Films Collection.)

Walt struggles to stay up in Devil Creek Rapids. "Rollups and rollups, flips on flips, blurred my mind into a drunken stupor ...." Photo taken during the 1976 Susitna trip.

A towel-clad Blackadar enjoys an early season dip in a hot springs.

The 1977 Susitna River party: Al Lowande, Ron Frye, Walt, and a playful Rob Lesser.

High on the Susitna River near the starting point: Walt with the Alaska Range in the background. The photo was taken on the 1977 trip. (Rob Lesser Photo.)

Walt maneuvers one of the drops in Cross Mountain Canyon. It was obvious to his boating companions on the Cross Mountain trip that Blackadar's shoulder problems and physical condition were seriously impairing his kayaking technique.

Pictured above is Cross Mountain Canyon in Colorado, Walt's last film project. Roger Brown was planning to feature Blackadar in a 1978 *American Sportsman* program along with Eric Evans, Linda Hibbard, and other kayakers.

The South Fork of the Payette River. This rapids, now known as Blackadar Rapids, was the site of Blackadar's drowning in 1978.

A river level view of Blackadar Rapids. In this photograph taken by Rob Lesser, the log on which Walt Blackadar was pinned and drowned is visible immediately below and to the left of the kayaker. The photo was taken about a month before Walt's death. Since it is covered by a wave, the left half of the log is not visible in the photo, but the log does extend all the way to the left bank. The photo clearly shows that there is very little space between the end of the log and the right shore. When Blackadar ran the river, the water level was higher and the log mostly obscured.

Walter Lloyd Blackadar's grave in Pioneer Cemetery, Garden Valley, Idaho.

Walt Blackadar along the Salmon River, The River of No Return.

After the accident on the South Fork of the Payette, Klaus Streckman, Walt's good friend and boating companion, worked with the Canadian government and was successful in having the mountain at the mouth of Turnback Canyon named in Blackadar's honor.

Next page: Mt. Blackadar. The mountain dominates the Alsek River valley for several miles before the river pinches between the walls of Turnback Canyon. (James T. Brock Photo.)

the St. Elias Range, which included the highest peaks of Canada, the Susitna was the major drainage of the Alaska Range, which included Mt. McKinley and the highest peaks of North America. Crouch had mentioned the Susitna in a prior phone conversation. Initially flying over the canyon in a jet fighter in 1969, Crouch later had a closer look at the gorge's impressive rapids from a helicopter.

Crouch related to Blackadar what he knew. In 1970, two friends of Crouch's, Jack Hession and Dave Christie, attempted a run of the river. Just above the entrance of the canyon, Christie flipped and came out of his boat. As they swung around a corner in midstream, Hession heard the deafening roar of a rapid just below them. To shed weight, Christie let go of his boat, and Hession paddled frantically, towing his companion and reaching the shore at the last possible point before the current would have swept them into a rapids which they believed to be "certain death." The other rapids in the canyon looked just as terrifying, and abandoning Hession's boat, the only one still in one piece, they spent four long days walking back to an outpost of civilization.

Blackadar, closing in on another impossible, told Crouch and Tero that he might travel up to Alaska to have a look at the Susitna for himself.

✳   ✳

BEFORE taking any more trips to Alaska, he had lined up an attempt on a new river descent in Idaho. The location was the Bruneau desert again. He had run the main part of the Bruneau and one of its upper tributaries called the Jarbidge. That left one last major upper tributary, the West Fork of the Bruneau.

By now the number of kayakers in Idaho was on the rise, and he had no trouble putting together a group. For his West Fork trip he was joined by Al Beam, John Dondero, and Bruce Malone of Sun Valley; Tullio Celano, Roger Hazelwood and

Keith Taylor of Boise, and others. Before starting the run, Blackadar wanted to check the water level on a gauge near the town of Bruneau. His previous run on the Jarbidge and Bruneau was at a level of seven feet on the gauge, and impressed at the river at that level, he didn't want to do it much higher. Blackadar stayed in the truck and told the others to go down and check the water level. They walked down to the gauge, and, according to Hazelwood, "We made a pact that no matter what the level was we should tell Walt that the level was eight feet on the gauge. When we told him, Walt was nervous as hell."

With the nervous Blackadar, the group of kayakers put in at a bridge over the West Fork, north of the Idaho-Nevada border. At first the river was narrow and meandering but it began to pick up 10 miles after the put-in with a major rapid. Five miles later they found a suitable camp spot and stopped for the night. Blackadar, still concerned about the water level, drank his vodka and Wyler's lemonade mix and paced around the tent that night, occasionally walking down to the river, watching for signs that the water level might be going higher. His companions kept up the charade, and it wasn't until they reached the main Bruneau that Blackadar realized that all his worrying was unwarranted and that the water wasn't any higher than the previous year.

On the second day of the trip, the group encountered several difficult rocky drops. "Walt was in the lead," said John Dondero. "It is the kind of river where it's small with quite a bit of brush on the sides. We did a lot of eddy hopping all the way down. No one wanted to get in a position where he might wash over a falls."

On one steep rocky rapids, Blackadar ran a slot on the right, hitting several rocks. Taylor followed, but his kayak washed up and broached against one rock, and he quickly ejected from the boat and swam to safety. "Then I ran it," Tullio Celano later wrote of the trip, "but broached on the same rock that Keith [Taylor] had. My boat was pinned. I scrambled out as my boat buckled and broke." Celano used duct tape to repair the boat, and the group continued down to the next major obstacle.

This rapids started with an eight-foot falls, followed by smaller drops straining through a maze of rocks. The falls and the rocky mess behind didn't look good to Blackadar so he paddled to an eddy on the left. John Dondero pulled in behind and signaled to the approaching boaters to pull off.

Beam was the last in the group to see the warning. "Malone was sitting on the right bank," noted Beam. "He motioned me to pull off, but it wasn't an urgent wave. If it had been me, I'd have been waving, really trying to get the message across."

Unaware of the severity of the rapid below, Beam floated closer to a log which was sitting about 18 inches above the surface of the river. To avoid hitting the log with his body, he rolled upside down and waited until he had floated under the log.

John Dondero watched anxiously from the side: "Beam waited and waited, while edging closer to the edge of the falls. Finally he rolled up just as he was dropping over. He had these goofy glasses with white duct tape which were off to an angle. He came up paddling, head back and disappeared over the next drop." Blackadar and Dondero moved quickly down the river, looking for any sign of Beam.

Beam remembers dropping over the waterfall backwards: "I got up, got knocked over and rolled up. In the next set of falls I was still backwards. I hit a rock with my head while upside down. By this time I said 'screw this' and bailed out and had a nasty swim." When Blackadar and Dondero reached Beam, he sat, dazed, at the bottom of the rapids, still holding onto his bent paddle. "Where's my boat?" he asked vacantly. Fortunately, the boat was found lodged against a cliff, saving Beam a difficult evacuation from the rugged canyon.

It had been a frightening swim. Hazelwood remembers it as the only time he had seen anyone physically hurt on the river. Al Beam, to the relief of the party, recovered and was able to paddle out. But at the same rapids on a future Blackadar trip, another boating companion would not be so lucky.

❋   ❋

DEVILS CANYON. Devils Gorge. Even knowing little about
the river, the name itself would attract Blackadar. In some ways,
Blackadar might be predestined to grapple with Devils Canyon.
His own name is a derivative of the Scottish word, blackadder,
meaning black water. Devils Canyon, black water: both names
conjure images of dim and dark places, of danger and foreboding. Blackadar played upon the name. "Before you go to hell
. . . Paddle the devil," he titled an article about the river.

Indeed, the devil of the Susitna held a powerful grip on
Blackadar. After his first try at the canyon in the summer of
1972, he returned twice more to struggle with its hellish water.
Yet, of all his trips on the Susitna, none was more adventurous
than the first one, when he and two others explored and attempted to run the powerful and unknown rapids rumbling within
the walls of the canyon.

Fifty miles north, towering above the depths of Devils Canyon, the Alaska Range, the roof of North America, arcs across
the horizon. On maps the great arc roughly approximates the
top curve of the Gulf of Alaska. Anchorage lies on the inside of
the arc to the south, and Fairbanks lies on the outside to the
north. Like the blood vessels gathering into the retinal vein in
the back of the eye, the glaciated tributaries of the southern
Alaska range gather into the Susitna River and flow into the
Cook Inlet, 30 miles west of Anchorage. The river begins from
the outflows of the glaciers of Mt. Deborah (12,339 feet) and
Mt. Hayes (13,832 feet). It flows south, then turns sharply west
between green canyon walls of black spruce, sedge grass, mat
and cushion tundra and birch shrub. The last part of the canyon,
a 10-mile stretch called Devils Canyon, is the most dramatic on
its course.

Most of the distance the Susitna flows sluggishly, but at

Devils Canyon, several impressive rapids are formed as the river drops. To the Upper Inlet Athapaskans, Devils Canyon was "Nutughil'ut," meaning the current flows down, descends. The most precipitous part of Devils Canyon is the final two miles, where the river has cut a narrow "V" shaped slot, 500 to 700 feet high, through gray, metamorphic bedrock. This part of the canyon is called the Pearly Gates.

After Devils Canyon, the walls fall away to a broad lowlands of cottonwood, birch, spruce, alder and willow. The river flows by Talkeetna, the small town from which most mountaineering expeditions are launched into the Alaska Range. Water draining off Mt. McKinley joins the Susitna, near here, and the great river, filled with its enormous load of glacial silt, empties into the ocean. The grey silt is what gave the river its name. Susitnu, or syitnu, the sand river, is what the Upper Inlet Athapaskans called the river. Locals often call it "the Big Su."

FROM the start Blackadar wasn't sure that he would run Devils Canyon. The plan was to go up and kayak a few rivers around Anchorage and then fly over the Susitna to see how difficult Devils Canyon looked from the air. On this trip to Alaska, he wasn't going alone. Kay Swanson and Roger Hazelwood, both good kayakers whose abilities Blackadar respected, joined him for the trip. In early August of 1972, Blackadar and Hazelwood flew to Alaska and were met by Swanson, who had driven up with his wife Gloria and their children, and who had brought all the kayaks tied to the top of his camper.

They boated with Jack Hession, who two years before had attempted to run the Susitna and was forced to walk out; Hession's wife Mary Kaye; Richard Tero, who had finished seminary training and was now a Catholic priest; John Spencer, a beginning but athletic boater who would later make some impressive river descents, and other local boaters. The number of Alaska whitewater kayakers at that time was about the same as Idaho boaters, and everyone knew each other.

In the early seventies Alaskan whitewater kayaking was in its infancy—enthusiasts were just beginning to roll and look about for suitable whitewater rivers. Blackadar's trips to Alaska helped stimulate exploration of more challenging stretches of whitewater. Starting on the Kenai Peninsula, the group ran the East Fork Gorge, then onto the lively Six Mile, and finally two days on the Eagle and Nenana, both fairly easy runs.

In Talkeetna, they asked about running Devils Gorge, but received "furtive glances" from skeptical locals. It hasn't been boated and it won't be, they were told. "[A]fter hearing these fearsome stories of the Devil and his river gorge, we decided to look it over for ourselves," Blackadar wrote. Upon flying the canyon with Cliff Hudson, a well-known pilot to mountaineers, Blackadar wasn't hopeful. "I felt we . . . should find another easier river, but I was alone in my fears." Both Hazelwood and Swanson wanted to give it a try. "I could come along or stay with Gloria," Blackadar mused; of course, he would go along.

After the flyover, they stopped in the Fairview Inn, a regular watering hole for mountaineers in Talkeetna. Over beers, the kayakers, still hyped up from their flight, tried to describe to their Alaskan kayaking friends what they had seen. Then Dick Tero noticed the appearance of Ray Genet, a mountaineering guide in the Alaska Range and most known for his role in the first winter ascent of McKinley. Blackadar had read about Genet in a riveting account of the climb portrayed in *Minus -148*. Tero introduced the two. "Hey," Blackadar said. "You're the one in the book." Hitting it off well, they sat down and talked—Genet telling climbing stories and Blackadar telling kayaking stories. Both were pioneers, possessing an adventurous nature that motivated them to risk beyond normal boundaries. To Tero, very much an adventurer himself, it was a treat: It was the meeting of "two super wilderness people."

The next day, the three kayakers from the lower 48 drove up the Denali Highway which crosses the Susitna near its source. From there the river flows into pure Alaskan wilderness and for 150 miles doesn't again come close to any outposts of civilization until Gold Creek, the Alaska Railroad crossing downstream from Devils Canyon, where they planned to catch a train ride into Talkeetna. While preparing their boats for the trip, Blackadar still had doubts. If his companions weren't fully aware of what they were getting themselves into, he was. He had experience with viewing rapids from the air, and he knew that the rapids he had seen from Hudson's plane were huge.

"I looked for signs of indecision by my partners and saw none," he wrote. "I had already made up my mind to go if they went and said nothing, but I was fearful!"

They calculated that the trip down the river and through Devils Canyon would take five days. If they hadn't shown up by the sixth day, Gloria was to notify Cliff Hudson, who would start a search for them. Getting under way, the first day they paddled about 15 miles, setting up a camp in a wet, mossy area near a small creek. Although progress the next day remained slow, they had seen a fair amount of wildlife, including grizzly bear, caribou and moose. On the third day they passed a small bush landing strip where they met three geologists who were likely doing exploratory work on the proposed dams for the Susitna River. The small group was the only people they saw the entire trip.

The closer they came to Devils Canyon, the more serious the mood that filled their night's camp. "We began to feel tense, and we talked about the strategy of running Devil Creek [rapid] and the gorge below it," Swanson wrote. "We quit early [the third] day because we knew we would need a good night's sleep, and we didn't want to camp right above the roar of the rapids."

Finally, late the afternoon of the fourth day, while rounding a bend, they saw the clear water of Devil Creek joining the grey river on the right (north) bank of the river. There was no doubt they were at the top of Devils Canyon. Below, said Swanson, "we could see the boiling white water and hear the roar."

They got out of their boats on the left bank and climbed along the steep banks to scout the Devil Creek Rapids, the first and the most difficult of the rapids in the Canyon. "[We] found it unbelievably tougher than it looked from the air," said Blackadar in his notes, referring to a "nightmare" wave which blocked the near side, and a series of huge cresting waves 30 feet high, which followed. The far side didn't look any better. It consisted of a series of waterfalls with symmetrical holes which could "stop a kayak forever."

"I don't see how we can run this," Blackadar told his friends. Hazelwood suggested one possible route, but it was difficult to see the entire rapids from their position on the cliff above. Blackadar didn't like its looks. Perhaps the memory of the Alsek was still fresh in his mind. Perhaps he was being more cautious now that others were with him.

Whatever his reason, he made his decision: "If you guys want to run that, you can run it by yourselves."

Hazelwood and Swanson weren't about to do that, and they joined Blackadar in looking for a portage route. The rapids continued for a mile but after the initial major blow at the top, the size of the waves and difficulty of maneuvering decreased. If they could carry their boats around on the slippery cliffs, they might be able to kayak the rest of the canyon. It was either attempt the portage or begin walking out. They returned to their camp, spent the night, and began the portage at 4 the next morning.

THE portage was arduous. They hoisted their boats up steep outcroppings and over mounds of slippery moss. A side ravine slicing down to the river blocked a direct path and forced them to detour up, climbing nearly 750 feet, before dropping back to the river. It was a grueling seven-hour portage, which would have taken not more than a half hour could they have walked along the river.

"Walt was having a hard time," said Swanson. "He was getting chest pains." The sharp pains in the chest bothered Swanson, a doctor, and he talked with Blackadar about the possibility that they might be angina. (On future trips with Blackadar, Swanson as a precaution would carry coronary first aid supplies such as lidocaine, morphine, and nitroglycerin.) Hazelwood stayed with Blackadar as Swanson moved ahead, losing contact with his two companions.

Around his neck, Blackadar carried a pair of binoculars which were the type that required him to screw each of the individual eyepieces to focus. Tired and frustrated with trying to adjust the knobs, he threw the binoculars to the ground. "Somebody else can have it," he told Hazelwood. As Blackadar walked on, Hazelwood picked up the binoculars and packed them out of the river.

Swanson reached the river below and out of sight of the others. The put-in was difficult: "When I finally got down to the river, I had to use a rope to get my boat down into a big eddy." Then Swanson, having no other choice, jumped off the cliff into the river. Standing in thigh deep water, he managed to stabilize the boat enough to climb in.

At the same time, Blackadar and Hazelwood had climbed down to the river's bank to a lower section of first rapids, now known as the Nozzle. It is a squirrely place. The Nozzle is a major constriction in the river where the water gushes through, causing whirlpools and strong swirling currents. Blackadar slipped into his boat and paddled out toward the current: "Three times I charged the gusher only to end up back where I started, driven into a violent series of whirlpools."

Hazelwood figured that it took them 10 to 15 minutes of paddling before they could get near the downstream jet of current. Hazelwood finally broke through the turbulent wall of water, and like a free falling object, he accelerated down the river. Catching a quick look back, he saw Blackadar still trying to get out of the eddy. Hazelwood had no desire to go ahead, but he had no choice. The overpowering current flung him rapidly away from Blackadar. He was alone and anxious.

The next major drop below the Nozzle is a rapid which now is known to kayakers as "Hotel Rock." A hotel-sized rock sits in the middle of a narrow gap in the river, with most of the river pouring to either side of the rock. (In high water conditions, water goes over the top of the rock.) "All of sudden I came around a corner and it's there," said Hazelwood. "We hadn't scouted it, and I didn't have any idea of what it was like. I got spun around backwards and dropped through and surfed out in the eddy below."

Hazelwood made it. The river pushed him safely past the rock, but he was "emotionally drained, exhausted and scared." He looked back upriver to see Blackadar spinning down out of control and going backward over rock.

Both Hazelwood and Blackadar paddled to the side and gave themselves a few minutes to recover from the ride. They had both been humbled by the river's power. "After gathering our wits," Blackadar wrote, "we continued on together and soon met Dr. Kay who had carried a quarter mile further and rappelled off the back side of the mountain to avoid that feared hotel-rock we had just passed."

Now regrouped, the three kayakers continued paddling down the river. The current eased some, giving them a chance to adjust to the big waves in the rapids midway through the canyon. They stopped and "scouted a time or two" but found no major difficulties. Just before a twisting turn, first right and then sharp left, they stopped. Looking downriver, they quickly realized that the rapids, since named "Screaming Left Hand Turn," would require skillful kayaking. Blackadar led off, stopping behind a large rock on the right. The others followed, and from his position, Blackadar waved them to the inside of the sharp left bend. He was forced to run some holes on the outside but paddled them handily and joined his friends below.

"Roger scouted the next big turn for a mile," Blackadar wrote, "and reported all OK, but soon after leading us thru the first wave his spray skirt failed and he frantically waved . . . ." With Hazelwood's spray skirt off, water poured in and sloshed from side to side in his boat, leaving him with little control. In the swells and rolling waves, Hazelwood had all he could do to keep his boat upright. Blackadar, looking for a safe eddy, paddled next to him and talked him towards the shore. Finally, he saw a good stopping place, and Hazelwood charged and reached the bank. Swanson and Blackadar repaired Hazelwood's loose spray skirt and drained his boat.

They were now past the halfway point. Continuing on, they reached a cable bridge over the river. The bridge had been built for studies of the Devils Canyon dam, which if constructed would flood the stretch of river they had just run. Under the conditions they didn't have much time to reflect on the consequences of the dam. This was their fifth day, and if they failed to reach Gold Creek that night, Cliff Hudson would begin a search for them. The last set of major rapids loomed ahead, dropping through the narrowest part of the canyon, the Pearly Gates.

They climbed out of their boats and walked up to an overgrown airstrip near the cable, immediately above the Gates. Blackadar felt he could run at least the first part. He went back down the bank to his boat while Swanson and Hazelwood climbed higher to get a look at the rapids deeper in the gorge. Blackadar waited for 30 minutes. When they didn't return, "I climbed the hill to recheck, finding them lying solidly entrenched—looking at the unknown turn beyond which we had no way to scout or carry," Blackadar wrote.

Swanson said later: "We couldn't see into it very well because the sun was low, shining into our eyes and making the shadows in the gorge even deeper. The walls were nearly sheer cliffs 1000 feet high, making it impossible to walk along the bank or even to see the entire rapids. But what we could see was ominous. This river was larger than the Colorado River in the Grand Canyon. In the gorge there are spots where it is squeezed down to about 20 yards wide. The waves that we could see looked over 20 feet high. I felt weak."

Hazelwood described it as "solid whitewater with big waves exploding in the air." They saw no reasonable portage route around the gorge. With time they might have been able to find a way to walk out, but it would be difficult, particularly for Blackadar. Their problem—and they knew it—was that they had only seen the rapids within the gorge from the air. That view from a thousand feet up gave them no idea of what was really there. Now that they were on the ground, they could see even less. The steep cliffs of the gorge prevented them from getting any closer. If they started kayaking into the gorge, they would be running completely unknown water. It was a big risk. They might not come out alive.

One of their options was to sit tight and wait for Hudson to fly in and rescue them. But Blackadar dreaded the humbling experience of having to be rescued. "You guys can stay here," he said. "They're not coming in for me."

Swanson reminded him of their aerial reconnaissance: "Walt, look, we saw a couple more real bad rapids below this when we flew over the other day."

"Hell, it's getting late," Blackadar blurted out. "I'm going to run it."

"It's bad, Walt, I don't think we can make it," said Swanson.

Impulsive and decisive, Blackadar had made up his mind and started off down the hill. He intended to run the river. Hazelwood and Swanson had to make a quick decision: "Roger and I decided that if he was going, we were, too."

Blackadar looked over at his friends as they braced themselves in their kayaks. "Spread out so we don't bump into each other," he barked.

Then shoving away from the bank, he shouted, "Boys, follow me!"

* *

"WALT started first, followed by Roger and then me," wrote Swanson. "We were separated by 75 yards and we entered the gorge in the center as it made a bend. We struck some very big waves, then paddled like mad to get over to the left side and away from a large hole that would have crushed us. Soon we were forced into the middle of the river where it narrowed to the width of a two-lane highway. The waves were tremendous, much larger than we ever expected."

Blackadar, surprised at the size of the waves, paddled forward in some of the larger waves to keep from sliding backwards. After about a half mile of the waves, he dropped over a large hole in the right center of the river. He rose up at a 45-degree angle on the large backwash of water, stopping him and entrapping him in recirculating water.

Just above, the river swept Hazelwood down towards Blackadar still struggling in the hole. Hazelwood turned his boat and paddled to the left of the hole trying to avoid a collision with Blackadar. Unaware of Hazelwood's move, Blackadar worked himself to the left, attempting to escape from the side of the hole. Fearing that he might hit Blackadar, Hazelwood lunged to one side and flipped upside down. The strong downward current of the hole sucked his boat underwater and underneath Blackadar's kayak. Blackadar had no idea what had happened until he and Hazelwood later discussed events of the day.

Rolling up, Hazelwood looked back and saw Blackadar still caught in the hole. He paddled furiously to the right side of the river and turned into a small eddy which surged up and down and slammed his boat back and forth against the rocks. Reaching out, Hazelwood held tightly to a crack in the wall, and under control for a moment, he stared downriver: "All I could see was whitewater in front of me and a diamond pointed rock in the middle."

The huge rock, now named "The Devil's Horn," almost entirely blocks the river. On either side of the rock, water cascades over into frothy holes below. Hazelwood could not see beyond the rock, but what he could see looked terrifying. It was a possible death trap, thought Hazelwood. A kayaker might be thrown against a pile of boulders just beyond the rock. He couldn't get to a position where he could see the bottom. While looking at the river disappearing below, he heard something.

Blackadar, in his kayak, swirled by and yelled at Kay Swanson, who had come out of his boat. Swanson, at the mercy of the monstrous waves, gasped for air. "Swim, Kay. Swim Kay," he yelled.

Swanson saw Blackadar frantically motioning him to shore. There was something very insistent in his wave. "Something was ahead of me that he could see and I could not," Swanson instinctively felt. "Something that might kill me if I didn't do as he said!"

What Blackadar saw was the Devil's Horn and nothing beyond. Swanson must not wash over it until they had a chance to look at it. He did not know what kind of treacherous water and rocks might block the river beyond. Swanson abandoned his kayak, and with his remaining energy, he swam against the potent current to the right shore: "Struggling, I rammed into a half-submerged boulder, then pulled myself slowly half out of the water, exhausted, my head spinning. There I lay puffing like mad, unable to move."

Blackadar saw Swanson reach the shore, but now the river dashed him toward the dangerous rock. There was no possible place to stop. He was irreparably committed. He had to run it. "I can't say I honestly was afraid—it came too fast," he said later. "But I was definitely worried." He, too, thought that he might be thrown into boulders at the bottom, but then he realized that with that much water volume rushing through any rocks below should be cushioned with rebounding current—at least his reasoning seemed logical.

The water shot him over the edge. "I dropped over fast thru the boiling mist trying to ride my boat by my hips— [I] began to tip [to] my right toward the rock cliff but caught myself with a desperate paddle brace which held me up. Immediately I was up & free, looking back at that huge . . . spire."

❋　❋

DEVIL'S HORN is the crescendo of the run through the gorge. Like trailing musical notes, the rest of the rapids quiet. The water flattens and slows. Within a mile, the walls slope back and the noisy dissonance of the gorge is overtaken by a stillness. Blackadar was out and was safe. Seeing Swanson's boat, he paddled over to catch it and towed it off to the side of the river. But where were Kay and Roger? He couldn't go back up the river to check for them. The current was too powerful and the walls of the gorge too steep. All he could do was wait.

Paddling to the shore, he scattered the boats and gear out on the shore to be more visible to his two missing companions if they had managed to climb out of the gorge above him.

❋　❋

MEANWHILE, back in the gorge, Hazelwood considered what he should do. He could not see Swanson, who was actually only a few yards below him but screened from his position by the cliffs. The ever crashing sound of the rapids, echoing off the canyon walls, prevented Hazelwood from hearing anything. He also did not know that the Devil's Horn marked the last of the dangerous water. For all Hazelwood knew, Swanson could have drowned, and he had no idea what had happened to Blackadar.

He decided that he had had enough. He lifted his heavy boat filled with his equipment from the river and jammed it in an upright position in the cracks of the rock cliff, and then for two hours he struggled to a ledge. From the ledge, he climbed carefully, over slick rocks and tundra and finally reached the top of the gorge. He had found a way out, but it was getting dark, and seeing no sign of his friends, he climbed back down to the ledge. Concerned that he might roll off at night, he tied a rope to himself and fell asleep.

*　　*

WHILE Hazelwood was climbing up out of the gorge, Swanson was doing the same. He knew that the river had washed Blackadar over the Devil's Horn, and although he hadn't seen Hazelwood since they entered the gorge, he believed that the river had swept him away also. He feared for his friends: "I began to wonder if I was the only survivor of this expedition. I knew that my kayak had been smashed to pieces on that rock [Devil's Horn] and that I would have to walk out of there with nothing but a small jackknife and some matches in a waterproof container."

He formulated a plan to try to climb up out of the gorge. Keeping close to the river, he would work his way down to the railroad crossing at Gold Creek. He had only the wet suit he was wearing and no sleeping bag nor shelter nor food. At least, with his matches, he would be able to build fires for warmth.

He began to climb. "I looked up at the near-vertical wall and saw a crack in it. Slowly, inch by inch I wedged my way up that crack to a narrow shelf about forty feet above the river." He continued climbing above the ledge, and two and a half hours later, he reached the top. "I sat on top puffing, bone weary and thirsty. I wondered if I really was the only survivor. I didn't see how anyone could have survived a passage around that jagged rock and the boiling hole below it."

Swanson continued and worked his way up and down steep ridges, over rocks, and through heavy bush and timber. He whistled, hoping not to surprise a grizzly. Looking downstream, he noticed that the river was slower, and only a few small rapids remained. He started heading down.

About this point Blackadar spotted Swanson. He shot several times with his .44, but Swanson didn't hear or see him. "At 9 PM," Blackadar wrote in his notes, "I collected his boat and paddled downstream, towing the kayak by a slip knot tied to my life jacket. Within a few miles I spotted the dazed Kay—totally unresponsive . . . ."

Swanson looked at Blackadar, unbelieving. The appearance of the shouting Blackadar seemed to him an hallucination. "But it was no mirage," Swanson wrote. "It really was Walt and he had my kayak. He came ashore where I was and we pounded one another's backs for a long minute."

Concerned about what had happened to the missing Hazelwood, Blackadar decided that they should continue, and paddled down to Gold Creek. It was late, but the lingering Alaskan twilight provided them with plenty of light to travel. Several hours later, around midnight, they reached the railroad bridge. Looking near the railway station house, they saw a light glinting out of a trailer house. At first, after hearing their story of the running gorge, the woman inside refused to let them in. But with further reassurances from the exhausted men, she opened the door and allowed them to make a phone call to Cliff Hudson, their pilot in Talkeetna. Responding, Hudson agreed to fly the canyon in the morning and look for Hazelwood. The two kayakers climbed into Blackadar's tent and fell asleep.

THE next morning, Hazelwood from his perch in the gorge waved to Hudson's plane flying over. He tried to indicate to Hudson that he was all right and that he could get himself out of the gorge, but he knew the pilot didn't understand and would return with more help. Hudson, after giving Blackadar and Swanson the welcomed news that their friend was alive, called Air Force Rescue in Anchorage and asked for a helicopter.

Once again the air above Hazelwood vibrated with the sound of aircraft, but this time it was a military helicopter flying through the gorge. The helicopter appeared to make a landing upriver, and Hazelwood started working his way in the same direction. Confused when the helicopter took off and flew away, he decided that his best bet was to climb back down in the canyon and remain at the location where he had been last spotted. After another break, the helicopter returned. This time it was obvious to Hazelwood the helicopter crew had sighted him and that they must be planning to pull him out of the gorge. Realizing that there was no way for the 'copter to reach him high on the gorge walls, he climbed down to the river.

The aircraft finally moved into position and hovered. Hazelwood looked up and a cable appeared, stringing down from the 'copter's belly. "Chips of shale were flying in the wind," remembered Hazelwood. "They had to swing the cable out across the river to get to me."

The cable swung out over the river and then swung back towards him. Hazelwood reached at the cable as it arched back towards him. He locked a grip on it, and immediately it flung him back out over the river and the torrent below. Hazelwood dangled in the air. Beneath him, the water pounded and frothed. Above him, the helicopter's motor roared.

"I closed my eyes and hung on as the cable went up," Hazelwood recalled. "Then this big arm reached out and swept me into the helicopter. I looked up to the front, and Walt was sitting up there, looking like he was Buck Rogers with headphones and microphone."

Grinning, white teeth showing behind the microphone, Blackadar turned and gave Hazelwood a thumbs-up.

VIII

Tragedy on the West Fork

JULIA ANN WILSON was one of Blackadar's young admirers. He had met her in Georgia in early 1973 when Don Wilson, a neurosurgeon and kayaker, had urged him to come run the Chattooga River. It was an enjoyable trip for Blackadar. Kay Swanson, his Susitna companion, came along and joined the party made up of a virtual Who's Who of southeastern boaters: Hans Carol, Claude Terry, Doug Woodward, Les Bechdel, Payson Kennedy, Cleve Tedford, David Truran, and Donald Sanborn. Julie was a good boater, and he had delighted in her smooth style as she adroitly paddled the difficult Section Four of the Chattooga. Her parents, both outdoor enthusiasts, had brought her up with a largesse of boating and camping trips.

Thirsting for the taste of western rivers, she came out to Idaho for a short trip later that summer and kayaked with Blackadar on a Selway run. "I truly enjoyed paddling with you," she wrote to Blackadar upon returning to Atlanta. "I feel ripe to learn lots and feel much more confident and competent."

In her letter she also described her trip back to Georgia. On the way she had stopped by the Little Big Horn and bought the book *Black Elk Speaks*. She romanticized about the book's descriptions of the Sioux and "their wanderings": "I got excited about the book and also excited that we'd be exploring this place where these Indians once roamed. One day we climbed up the canyon about 4 miles to a meadow. We spent the night there and explored a bit. I was feeling very 'Indian.'"

She wrote several more letters that fall and winter, chattingly describing kayak trips that she had taken on nearby rivers. She confided to him her discontent with the Atlanta urban area and her administrative work as a psychologist at the Georgia Mental Health Institute. For a change, she told Blackadar, she and her boyfriend, David Truran, might start looking around for a smaller community in which to live. David had recently built her a Prijon 400 kayak, she excitedly explained, and she had fitted the boat with a pair of thigh braces which Blackadar had shown her on the Selway. "I've never felt so comfortable and well braced in my boat. What a great idea you had." She also reported that she had convinced a number of her friends to write letters for one of Blackadar's conservation causes.

For some time, she had been thinking about quitting work and traveling, but the first energy crisis, the first wave of Arab oil price hikes, had driven up gas prices. She fretted over rumors of a recession in wake of the crisis and if she left her job, whether she'd find another. "I've finally made my decision to leave Atlanta and travel for a while," she wrote Blackadar in a letter just after Christmas of 1973. "I've been saving my money and planning to leave for three years now." She described her plans for an extended vagabonding journey, stopping at ski resorts, working for a short time here and there, and traveling on, seeing the sights throughout the west. She would be coming out with her friend, Boni Zucker. Besides skiing, she also told him that she would like to do some more kayaking and asked him how early she could drop by for a trip.

Blackadar had so enjoyed paddling the Chattooga that he had thought about returning for another run before Julie came out to Idaho. She told him that she would quit her job early and kayak with him if he decided to come to Georgia. However, he had been having some problems with pain in his shoulders, and at the end of January he had undergone corrective surgery on both shoulders. The trip to the Chattooga was out. "[I] cancelled at the last minute," he explained later, "because I was still short of breath." By late April, when Julie and Boni arrived in Salmon, he felt recovered enough to kayak again.

In Salmon, Julie and Boni met Ken Collins and Vane Jones, both Salmon teachers who Blackadar had interested in an early season kayaking trip. The small group drove out to a hot springs to practice their rolls. Everyone's roll being proficient, they discussed various options for trips and eventually decided upon the West Fork of the Bruneau. Since the West Fork was an advanced river, Boni decided to do the car shuttle.

On the way to the river, they stopped in Stanley and picked up Mert Stapleman, who rounded out the group to five experienced kayakers, a safe number for the type of whitewater they planned to run. The first night camped alongside the river was cold and threatening, and in the morning several inches of snow covered the ground and their boats, but any chance of turning around left with their shuttle car, which had been driven back to beat the storm.

BLACKADAR considered the West Fork of the Bruneau a safe river. The portages around unrunnable rapids made the run an arduous one, but he felt that its overall difficulty was not nearly as hard as the lower rapids on the main stem of the Bruneau. It was imperative, however, on the West Fork to be able to identify the location of the unrunnable rapids and stop beforehand to portage.

The group talked over the running procedure. Blackadar would kayak first, and unless the water was obviously easy, no one was to go ahead of him. At anything that looked suspicious, he would stop. Julie would follow in the second position behind Blackadar, replicating his moves in rapids and stopping when he did. Ken Collins would take the number three position, where he could see Julie and assist if she had any problems. Stapleman and Jones took up the rear or sweep position.

"After a hearty steak breakfast," Blackadar wrote later in an analysis of the trip, "we all paddled down starting at noon but all boated poorly and after a series of minor upsets I called an early halt for the night." Concerned over Julie's boat which, burdened with the weight of her camping equipment and food, was responding sluggishly for her, Blackadar removed 15 pounds. She was not used to paddling a fully loaded boat, and he hoped that the weight reduction might sharpen up her kayaking.

On the second morning they awoke to clear, sunny skies, but soon the clouds moved in, and it began snowing again. "We slowly and carefully worked our way downstream, carrying several times, usually only for a few feet, never over three hundred," Blackadar wrote. "Julie and my friends had smoothed out their paddling technique and we were doing superbly." Collins, who watched Julie from behind, could tell that she was a proficient boater as she easily followed Blackadar's moves and stopped where he did. Although this was only Blackadar's second time down the river, he recognized most of the major rapids and the places where they needed to stop for a portage. "After the toughest carry of the day I thought we were basically below all of the falls and had just a couple of easy stops for Class V rapids where most would have to carry but which I might possibly run," he reported.

Blackadar had employed a cautious approach. It is an approach that is nearly universally accepted by river runners. The leader proceeds only if the rapid viewed from the boat can be run. If the rapid looks difficult, the leader pulls off in an eddy, and takes another, more scrutinizing look from the stationary position. If the leader needs to look from a closer position and there is another eddy below, the leader may proceed to the next eddy. He or she may continue eddy hopping closer, all the while carefully looking at the rapids. If, by using this eddy hopping form of reconnaissance, the rapid is determined to be safe to run, then it's run. If it looks difficult or the rapid goes out of sight, the leader signals to the other kayakers behind to stop and look the rapid over from shore. What is essential in this approach is that the followers do not crowd the leader. When the leader catches an eddy, they must catch an eddy behind. When the leader moves to a new eddy, then they can move to the eddy just vacated by the leader, but they must never pass the leader.

Blackadar later wrote that the safety procedure on the West Fork trip "disintegrated." "We relaxed a bit because I thought we were below all the portages," he said. "Also I knew that there were no surprises on the river and all stops were easy to spot and to stop the group."

Occasionally, when the water was flat and there was no danger of being pulled into unrunnable rapids, Julie paddled alongside Blackadar. She was anxious to learn everything she could from him. She admired his type of kayaking, a different style than what she had learned in the Southeast. And although he had told her some wild tales about the rivers he had run, she trusted his judgment. She had told him the night before that she felt he was one of the safest kayakers she had been with. She was full of admiration and questions, and Blackadar, thoroughly enjoying the attention, was happy to oblige. He pointed out wildlife, a chukar partridge, and then three deer watching cautiously as the kayakers floated by. In a prior location he had delighted her by finding a pile of arrowhead chips left long ago by the peripatetic Indians of the area.

Midway through the second day, they approached the falls in which Al Beam had upset and had taken a dangerous swim two years earlier.* Initially, the falls wasn't apparent to Blackadar. In front of him a juniper tree had fallen and blocked three fourths of the river, hindering his view of what lay downstream. He looked to his right and saw a calm eddy, a good stopping place just above the tree. Below the tree, he saw another eddy on the left, but it was smaller and posed just above a drop from which he couldn't see any further. He decided to choose the lower, smaller eddy on the left to get a closer and unobstructed view of what was below. Stroking quickly, he pivoted into the eddy. The thin patch of quiet water was barely large enough to hold his boat, and to prevent him from being pulled away by the current, he held onto the shore.

He had made no mistake. He had stopped, and if Julie had followed safe boating procedure, she too would have stopped in the larger eddy on the right side above the juniper. But the tree complicated the situation.

No matter how carefully thoughtout and how universally accepted, safety procedures can never cover all the vagaries of nature. Experienced kayakers remain flexible, adapting to the circumstances. Safety ultimately boils down to judgment, examining the options, weighing the odds and making decisions, sometimes in a split second, based on the situation at hand. If Blackadar had thought of Julie's situation, that she might be screened from him, a warning bell might have sounded, telling him not to proceed until Julie and the rest of his party were stopped. He had not made an error of procedure—but what would haunt him later was his judgment.

As Julie approached the tree, she doubtless saw the eddy on the right. She probably realized that if she had stopped in the right side eddy, she would not be able to see Blackadar on the left side since the tree would hide him from her. The falls wasn't

---

*According to interviews conducted with most of the members of the 1972 West Fork trip, this falls seems to be the one responsible for Al Beam's swim. However, there was not complete agreement among the members, and it is possible that Beam might have swum a similar looking falls further upriver.

in sight from her location, and seeing no danger, she continued on. She had moved close to Blackadar on other easier parts of the river, and although a tree blocked her downstream view, it seemed no different than before.

Meanwhile, Blackadar looked below him, and now close enough to see part of what lay below, he immediately recognized it as the lower falls. It was not runnable.

"I looked around," he wrote, "to see which side we should portage . . . ." Julie edged around the tree. There was no room for her to pull into Blackadar's small eddy, no other place for her to stop.

Blackadar yelled. Julie's boat started for the edge of the falls. Collins, close behind, followed Julie around the tree. He heard Blackadar's shout but did not hear what he said. Reacting quickly, Blackadar turned out into the current and sprinted out in front of Julie. He knew she was heading into a dangerous falls, and he wanted to be in front of her to guide her along the best path he could pick "through the hell below."

The falls consists of four tiers, each dropping eight feet or more into tightly spaced boulders. When Blackadar dropped over the first tier, the force of the water capsized his boat: "I had to wait forever upside down until things were right before coming up. Thereafter I was so busy surviving as I plunged on down that I saw no one else."

Blackadar, now underwater, could do nothing to help Julie. As Blackadar struggled to roll, Collins also found himself swept towards the edge of the falls. He had no time to stop. He saw the ends of Julie's and Walt's boats tip in the air and then disappear, a sign of steep drop. "Oh, shit," Collins thought to himself. "I don't know what this is but I know we're getting into something that we shouldn't be."

Collins turned and tried to warn Vane. It was useless. The breakdown was complete. The inexorable sequence of events was like a house built with toy blocks. After the first block had been removed, all the other blocks collapsed into disarray. Next

Vane Jones and then Mert Stapleman kayaked around the tree, and caught in the current, each toppled over the falls.

As Collins plunged over the first tier, he saw Julie in an upside down position trying to roll. The current pushed her toward the second drop of the falls, which was separated by a large boulder. Collins caught one last glimpse of the young kayaker coming out of her boat and swimming, as she and her boat dropped out of sight on the left side of a large 10 foot high boulder.

Unaware of Julie's predicament, Blackadar rolled up and pulled off to the right, just below the second drop. The current tossed Collins by Blackadar.

"Get out. Get out," Blackadar shouted.

Collins, responding to Blackadar's frantic shouts, turned his boat and tried to paddle towards Blackadar: "I tried to turn into the eddy where he was, and I stuck my paddle out but he couldn't reach it." Unable to make the eddy, Collins desperately tried to straighten his boat out as the water carried him toward the third drop. He went over. His boat crashed against a rock.

"It held me there," said Collins. "I could feel the front of the boat collapsing on my legs." He had to get out. A boat crushing around a kayaker's legs is a death trap. Collins lunged out of his boat. Water poured into the cockpit, and as he pushed away, the boat snapped into two pieces and tumbled through the rocks of the last part of the falls. To Collins' right was a willow protruding from the shore. He grabbed for it. He held tight, and it swung him out of the current into the bank.

The last Collins had seen of Julie, she was in the water rushing over the second drop. On shore, he searched the rapids for her and then saw Blackadar, who was just getting out of his boat. He yelled back up to Blackadar, trying to make his voice heard over the noise of the river: "You gotta get back in the water. Julie's swimming."

Blackadar reacted immediately, yelling something to Collins about helping Mert and Vane, as he dropped back into his boat and hurriedly started down over the last half of the treacherous falls. Collins ran down the river for about a hundred yards, looking for Julie. Blackadar by this time had somehow run the rest of the falls, and Collins, figuring that Blackadar would help Julie, ran back up to find Mert and Vane.

Blackadar at first thought that she must have been carried by the current around the next corner. When she wasn't around the first corner, he checked the next corner and then the next and then the next. He worked his way down the river, searching for her, paddling mile after mile, looking, searching, hoping, clinging to the belief that she was just around one more bend.

FORTUNATELY, Jones and Stapleman had managed to stop before the current swept them over the second drop. Stapleman, however, had collided with a rock and knocked a hole in his boat. Collins quickly explained what had happened and helped Jones carry his boat around the remainder of the falls. Jones put in and ran down the river to catch up with Blackadar. Collins helped Stapleman patch his boat with duct tape, and once the boat was carried around the falls and by some rapids below, Stapleman took off to find the others.

Collins, left without a boat, began walking downriver. "I really believed that Julie was just around the corner somewhere with Walt, and she was safe," he said. Approximately two miles down from the falls, Collins found half of his boat along the bank with his gear still inside. Knowing that he would have to hike out of the river, he slipped into his boots and continued hiking downstream. He walked for 10 miles and finally reached the three others. There was no sign of Julie. He yelled down to Stapleman, who had been hiking on the other side of the river. "Is Julie all right?" Collins asked.

"We haven't found her," replied Stapleman. "We're pretty sure she's probably drowned."

Collins couldn't believe it. "It's real hard to accept that you've lost somebody," said Collins later. "You want to assume the best, and you want to think that everything's OK." With the slim chance that they might have missed Julie on the way down, Collins began hiking upriver on his side, the right side as one looks downstream, and Stapleman worked upriver on the left side.

It was now early evening, and Blackadar was emotionally and physically spent. His shoulder operation, three months earlier, had left him in worse shape than normal, and he was in no condition to begin hiking back. He and Jones set up camp, planning to walk back up in the morning.

Collins and Stapleman worked their way upstream in descending canyon dusk. They searched in and around the juniper trees which lined the bank in patches.

Then Mert saw something. "Look!" he yelled. "Look in the water."

"I ran up to the bank," Collins wrote in his notes, "and saw the orange of Julie's life jacket in an eddy on the far side. Mert ran up on the other side and stopped an arm's length from the jacket." Stapleman hesitated and then reached and pulled out the jacket. He was surprised to find only the jacket, inside out and still zipped and tied.

"I sank to my knees at the water's edge," Collins continued. "All at once the same thought seemed to come to both Mert and I. Maybe it's a signal. She's hurt but safe and she has thrown the jacket in to signal us to come back upstream."

In a gathering dusk, they continued their upstream search. "I would yell," recalled Collins, "and I'd swear that sometimes I'd hear someone answer me. It was one of those conditions you get into that you hear things."

When they got back to the falls, Stapleman, still on the left side of the river, and Collins on the right got out their flashlights and shined them in the water, looking for more signs. Part way down the last drop in the waterfall, Stapleman thought he heard something banging. Looking, he found Julie's submerged boat.

Pointing their lights into the water, they could see the hazy outlines of a black object in the cockpit. "We assumed at first that it was Julie's body," Collins said. Stapleman tied a line around the boat and began pulling it out, while Collins from the other side of the river shined his light on the boat. As the boat slowly came to the surface of the water, Collins realized that the black object was not a body but rather a flotation bag hanging halfway out of the boat. Eventually, Stapleman muscled the boat onto shore.

The time was about 3 or 4 in the morning, so the two kayakers finally gave up their searching and collapsed into their sleeping bags, remaining on opposite sides of the river. Blackadar and Jones started early and arrived back at the falls the next morning. The 10-mile walk had been taxing on Blackadar. "Walt was really tired," observed Collins. "I was worried that he was going to have a heart attack. He couldn't keep from crying. He had lost a lot of the confidence that Walt always had."

Collins talked to the group about searching more, but Blackadar stopped him. "No," he said, "we've got to accept the fact that Julie's dead. We've got to stop looking." It was a hard thing for Blackadar to concede, but he was a pragmatist and knew that they now needed to inform the authorities and get help.

Concerned about Blackadar's health, the others didn't want him to walk back down the river. Collins picked up his paddle and brought it back, so Blackadar could run Julie's boat to where he had left his own boat the night before. Without boats, the three remaining kayakers walked down the river, planning to meet Blackadar there.

While floating down the river, Blackadar thought about his next move. He met Collins at a slow stretch on the river, where Collins planned to swim across to walk on the easier left side. Blackadar outlined his plans: "When you get back down there,

I'm going to be gone . . . . I'm paddling straight through. I'll pick my own boat up. I'll leave Julie's boat for you. I don't want you guys to go any further than Indian Hot Springs."

Indian Hot Springs is the point where the main stem of the Bruneau starts and where a jeep trail comes into the canyon. Blackadar was planning to go out by himself and call friends to drive out to pick up his three companions.

Collins, concerned about Blackadar's fitness, didn't like the idea of him running the large rapids of the lower canyon alone. "Walt," he tried to reason, "I don't think that's fair to us or you. I don't think you should be boating alone."

But Blackadar was adamant. "No. I've already drowned one person. I don't want the responsibility of anyone else. I'm asking you as a friend to let it be this way. From Indian Hot Springs out, it can really get hairy, and in the condition I'm in, I don't want the responsibility of anybody following me."

"I don't agree with you," Collins replied. "But if that's what you want, I'll do it that way."

Blackadar then left. Anguished and guilt-ridden, he kayaked alone, his solitary form disappearing from Collins between the bleak canyon walls below.

HIS life had abruptly veered off course. For some time he had danced with danger on his river trips, playing the odds, and though stumbling now and then, he always managed through sheer drive to regain his step. He thrived on risk and delighted in balancing on the fine edge separating life from death, staying always an arm's length away. He had thought carefully about his own death, and writing about it, he had said that it would willingly but grudgingly be accepted.

But in the end when death came on the river it was not his own. It was somebody young, hopeful, just starting her life, someone who had looked up to him, sought to learn from him, trusted and depended on him. Her loss shattered him, and over and over again he relived those horrible last few seconds in which she disappeared in the falls.

When Blackadar reached the take-out point on Monday, April 29, he was met by Julie's traveling companion, Boni Zucker, and another friend of Julie's, Rodger Losier. Losier and two other friends had just driven out from Georgia to join Julie and Boni for part of their travels. Grief-stricken, Blackadar told them the news. After driving from the river, he then notified the authorities and Julie Wilson's parents, Ross and Elizabeth, and made arrangements to have Jones, Stapleman and Collins picked up. By the next day the sheriff of Owyhee County, where the accident occurred, had organized a small search party, which Blackadar, Losier, and Julie's other friends joined.

The snow left from the storm which hit the night before they departed now had melted, and along with it, more snow melt from the Jarbidge Mountains of northern Nevada caused the waters of the West Fork of the Bruneau to rise. Nothing was found the first day, and on the second day, Blackadar put his boat in below the falls and ran the river down to Indian Hot Springs where he was picked by Owyhee County Sheriff Tim Nettleton, Losier and others. When Blackadar was two hours late in coming, Nettleton was visibly angered by the delay. It wasn't the last time Blackadar and Nettleton would have their differences.

Blackadar returned to Salmon to rest for a day, planning to return and search. He had previously contacted Ross Wilson and discussed what should be done if they found Julie's body. If Wilson felt it was appropriate, Blackadar told him he would try to make arrangements to have Julie buried along the river. Wilson agreed and confirmed their oral understanding in a subsequent letter sent special delivery to Blackadar on May 2. Julie was the Wilson's only child, and they felt the loss deeply.

Even in his own pain Wilson must have sensed Blackadar's despair which he addressed in his first letter: "Sad as this expe-

rience has been to us, we recognize that any activity has its risk
. . . . It is not affecting our feeling about the activity [river
running] and my own personal inclination to continue partici-
pating in it. We know that all of you were using a normal degree
of care but that there are certain situations where even that is not
adequate."

To give Blackadar proper legal authority to make decisions
about Julie's burial, Wilson had provided him with Power of
Attorney: "We hereby constitute and appoint our friend, Dr.
Walt Blackadar, of Salmon, Idaho . . . to authorize, approve,
decide, and/or determine any and all matters or issues or questions which may arise in any manner in connection with the
death of our said daughter . . . ." Blackadar contacted the coroner of Owyhee County and secured permission to act as his
deputy, which allowed Blackadar to bury the body without removing it to a nearby morgue. The arrangement was formalized
in a letter which included the original Power of Attorney sent by
Blackadar to the coroner 10 days after the accident.

Blackadar didn't return to work. He immediately began
planning for a return search. Other kayaking friends had called
and volunteered to help, but Blackadar refused, repeating that
he wanted no responsibility for others. "He was really devastated," his daughter, Nan, said. "He even refused to allow me to
go, but I could tell he was troubled, and I told him 'I'm going to
go with you.' He looked at me and accepted my emotional
support." His wife had been off visiting friends and relatives in
the East, so before leaving Salmon, Blackadar sat down and
wrote a letter describing the last few days:

Shirl Darling   5-3-74

This has been a tough week! Julie Wilson drowned when I
wasn't able to stop her in time at the brink of a falls on the
Bruneau River. A huge juniper tree blocked the river on a bend
and leading I chose to paddle around the tree to scout which was

my right. I decided to go around the tree. I saw a tiny eddy where I could stop & stop I did for I saw the falls. Everyone else was supposed to be far enough back to stop at least one eddy above where I stopped but our safety broke down & Julie & the gang were on me with no place to stop so I led over the falls trying to pick a route . . . .

I've paddled the river 3X looking for her and I'm going back tomorrow but I have little hope . . . .

The memorial service will be May 17th in Atlanta at 2 PM. Please meet me there . . . . If I don't find Julie's body, I'll hurry home & continue weekly searches—

Her family is great—I have their permission and David's— her fiancee's—to bury her near the falls with a sign on her memorial (boat) saying "buried nearby"—The boat is already erected in steel brackets visible from the approach to the falls.

I'll be in Atlanta the night of the 16th. Please meet me there— DON'T COME HOME. I'm terribly broken up but the kids are great & you can't help me now since I'll be gone hunting for her . . . .

Love,

Walt

Blackadar, his daughter, Nan, and Rodger Losier drove back to the West Fork. By a rough jeep trail, they were able to reach a point about two miles upriver from what is now called Julie Wilson Falls. Blackadar searched for a while and then joined his daughter in locating a site for the grave. "He was really emotional, always on the brink of emotion," said Nan. "He had many tears. It was the first time I'd seen him cry except for when his mother died."

Viewing the pleasant spot found by his daughter overlooking the river, Blackadar said, "This is perfect for her. She deserves a perfect place." They dug into the rocky soil and about four feet down ran into a huge boulder which they couldn't move, so they excavated around the boulder, eventually making the grave six feet deep as required by law.

While they were digging, Losier, who had remained by the river, found a neoprene wristband. He recognized it as one of several he and a few other of Julie's friends had made the winter before. The appearance of the armband gave Blackadar some reassurance that the body was still lodged in the falls. Until that time, he worried that the body might have washed downriver, greatly reducing the possibility of a speedy recovery or finding it at all. Blackadar left the shovels and a Bible at the grave.

The water was still coming up. Nan Blackadar described it as "raging," but Blackadar wanted to run the river below the falls again. Putting his boat in the water, he made his fourth descent of the West Fork since the accident. After Nan and Rodger picked him up at Indian Hot Springs, the three drove back to Salmon. In the days before Julie's memorial service in Atlanta, he remained obsessed with finding her body and flew the river once with Dick Roberts and ran it at least one more time alone.

A DAY before the memorial service, Blackadar flew back to Atlanta, as he had arranged with his wife. It was now three weeks after the accident. While he was in Atlanta, Rodger Losier, JoAnne Comins, and another close friend of Julie's had hiked in to the West Fork for another search. Much of the snow now had melted in the Jarbidge Mountains, and the river was on its way down. Looking across the river near the bottom of the falls and along the left bank, they spotted the body caught on the branches of a submerged tree.

"We managed to get her off the log jam and into an eddy downstream," Losier wrote in a statement later. "Rep and I lifted her into a plastic bag and at this point a 'chai' (a Jewish Medallion) came off in my hand. I recognized it as the one Boni Zucker had given both Julie and I earlier that year as a token of her friendship. I brought it back to her folks and it is now in their possession."

The body was ferried across the river and placed in a zippered bag. The three friends then carried the bag up to the prepared grave site. "Walt had left a Bible," Losier continued, "and we held a small religious ceremony of prayers for her before closing the grave. That night we drove to Sun Valley and called Julie's parents and Walt (he had attended the memorial services). We notified them that we had found Julie 45 minutes before the memorial services and had buried her as they had wished."

IX

The Biggest Ride

IN JULY, Blackadar, his wife and two of his daughters, Nan and eight-months pregnant Lois, bumped across the Bruneau desert heading for the access road near Julie Wilson Falls. He wanted to visit the grave and leave the chai medallion which Elizabeth Wilson had sent to him. It was the same medallion which Rodger Losier had recovered and carried back to Atlanta. Elizabeth had sent the medallion with a note: "Enclosed is the friendship 'life' medal which Boni gave to Julia Ann and had requested that it remain with her. It is my desire that Boni's and Julia Ann's wish be carried out. I do hope that you can arrange to place it with her."

Throughout this disquieting time, the Wilsons had continued to support him. After the memorial service, Ross had written to him: "We are truly grateful to you for the care and love you exhibit toward those persons who participate with you in kayaking, and for the care, love and concern and effort you have made with regard to Julia Ann. We could have expected no more from anyone."

There was more than just Julie Wilson's death. The early season of 1974 had been a bad year. Above normal mountain snowpacks melted quickly as the temperatures rose, going as high as an unusual 103 degrees in Salmon for mid-June. The Salmon River flooded thousands of acres of pastured land, washed out the highway, and set an all-time record high of 8.70 feet at the Salmon City gauge on June 17. The raging waters of the Salmon and its tributaries had claimed six lives. Two lives were lost when a commercial float trip guided by a California company, American River Touring Association, ignored Forest Service warnings of dangerously high water conditions and put on the river anyway. Two rafts capsized on the second day, and two passengers unable to reach the shore perished. All 33 boatmen and passengers were evacuated from the river.

Another death was 6-year-old Carrie Prestwich, Karyn's sister. Sheriff Baker reported that Carrie's bike had been found upset at the downstream side of a bridge over the North Fork, and the youngster had presumably fallen into the turgid creek. When Blackadar saw Carrie's mother, Marsha Prestwich, he put his arms around her, and without saying anything, he cried. "He was a man with a heart," Marsha said later, remembering the incident. "What he felt, he felt."

The Salmon River claimed more lives. Al Beam, whose guiding business had been steadily growing after Blackadar's initial encouragement, was guiding a rafting group on the Salmon near Stanley. The boat hit a breaking wave and capsized, trapping nine guests under it. Beam repeatedly dove under the boat, pulling people out one by one. "The last time I went under there, I didn't think I was going to come back up. I was probably closer to buying it than the [West Fork of the] Bruneau swim." One of his fellow guides, Byron Caddy, caught up and helped him slice open the bottom of the raft, freeing more people who had been caught. Beam fought against frigid waters and mounting exhaustion to save most of his passengers, but in the end, he wasn't able to reach two in time. Both were drowned.

It might have seemed to Blackadar that river running, having grown exponentially over the last several years, was now on the verge of self-destruction. Certainly, his life had nearly self-destructed. Since Julie's death, grief had ruled his life. "For the first ten days," Blackadar wrote, "the loss of Julie was almost more than I could take. I quit boating a thousand times that week . . . ."

He fell into a prolonged depression. His daughter, Lois, observed that "he was devastated. It was like he was going to fall totally apart." Even through his busy professional schedule, he found no solace. "He was crying on and off for a number of days in the office and hospital," remembered Boyd Simmons, his partner.

In time, he began to look at the tragedy on the West Fork objectively. He wrote to Barb Wright telling her, "I'm sad & I can think of lots of things I might have done differently but at the time I did what I felt was safest." It was that point, that he had acted in a safe manner, which slowly began to lift him out of the depths of his despair. His own analysis of the accident, and that of those he was with, came to the same conclusion: he had made no gross errors, and what had happened was a terrible accident. "I'm going to keep boating & leading—Not for a bit but I will," he told Wright, "for I strongly believe this is a safe sport & I know how to make it safer."

After Julie's death, he met with others involved in the accident and discussed what could be done to minimize the risk in similar situations. He prepared an article which analyzed the accident in depth. Don Wilson, who had helped arrange the Chattooga trip, reviewed it for him. "Please publish the paper," Wilson replied to him. "I have said it before. It is a truth, unconditional and without exception, that without risk one cannot possibly win. Any risk, no matter how small, means you might lose. Julie risked—and lost. By her death, and your clear memory, others will profit, and survive."

The article did appear in two separate periodicals, *Down River*, a new whitewater magazine by World Publications out of California, and in *American Whitewater*. In the article, he did not try to evade responsibility. While for some reason the *Down*

River editor expurgated several key passages, including the sentence in which he accepted blame, *American Whitewater* maintained the integrity of his original typescript: "I was her [Julie Wilson's] leader and as such [I] must necessarily bear much of the burden of the tragedy." In a way, this very public pronouncement of responsibility helped him exorcise the burdens he carried and begin the process of healing.

In the article he detailed four "errors" which contributed to the tragedy. The first was Julie's life jacket. It was a light buoyancy jacket of approximately 13 pounds. Before the trip, Blackadar suggested to her that she wear a larger 30 pound life vest, but feeling more comfortable with her own jacket, she decided not to change. The perfect jacket didn't yet exist, but he knew that high buoyancy was important. In the article Blackadar urged that development should begin immediately on high flotation life jackets, that they should be constructed with extra cushion to protect a swimmer from rocks, and that they be built for a tight, secure fit to prevent the jacket from being pulled off a swimmer in violent water.* Secondly, he suggested that an obvious error which led to the accident was the crowding of the leader. The following boaters must give the leader adequate space and not pass.

In his third point, he admonished that when kayakers are knocked over in dangerous water, they must make every possible mental and physical effort to roll. Coming out of the boat must be done only as a last resort. "This sounds like I am critical of Julie for swimming," he wrote. "Not in the least. This was a real terror of a place! If any gal could have rolled up, Julie would have. But this was early in the season and we had just started getting our heads conditioned to the abuse one must accept to successfully roll in clutch situations. . . . I know Julie tried—but not hard enough!"

---

*Since then, high buoyancy life jackets have been developed for kayaking. Charlie Walbridge, a longtime proponent of safe kayaking equipment and technique, helped develop some of the first models.

Lastly, he said that if he could have done it again, he would have yelled to all the boaters to stop. He realized that all the kayakers with him were proficient, and even though it didn't seem possible at the time, perhaps Julie might have been able to stop after the first drop of the falls as did Jones and Stapleman if he had shouted loudly and emphatically to pull off.

✳   ✳

By the time he made his trip across the desert to deliver the medallion to the grave site, the nightmare was beginning to pass. The inordinately high waters of the Salmon had receded. Eager rafters and kayakers were again flocking back to the river. The sport would go on. His life would go on. His humor had returned, and he was even deep into plans for a Colorado River trip scheduled for late July. Perhaps another sign that his life had returned to normal was the event which turned his trip across the Bruneau desert into an adventure of the kind for which Blackadar was famous.

Driving at his usual pace over the rough, dusty road, he was forced to a stop when he heard the thumping of a flat tire. His daughters discussed with him whether it was wise to continue since they now would have no spare tire and were a long way from any gas station. Blackadar, after changing the tire, told them not to worry and continued on, kicking up a tail stream of dust as he resumed desert cruising speed.

As they neared the West Fork canyon, he scraped up against a rock in the road, cutting the sidewall and flattening another tire. Now he was in trouble. Located in a remote corner of the Bruneau area, it might be weeks before another vehicle would come by. After a few days, someone back in Salmon would sound the alarm and start a search, but the last thing he wanted was to be the object of a search, particularly one which would bring Owyhee County Sheriff Nettleton after him. His only option was to walk out, get the tire fixed, and borrow a car to drive back to his disabled truck. Nan wanted to accompany him, while his wife and the pregnant Lois walked down to the nearby river where they would have water and protection from the hot sun.

Blackadar gave his daughter one of his gloves, and keeping the other, he would push the tire in front and watch it roll until it wobbled and flopped over. Then he'd pick up the tire and roll it again. When he tired of the task, Nan relieved him, rolling the tire in front of her. All day across the hot desert they alternated, pushing the unwieldy black rubber object down the dirt road. That night, they camped next to the tire, sharing butterscotch candies, life savers, two cans of pop, an orange, and their one sleeping bag.

They set out again the next morning, and eventually at midday, hot and dehydrated, they reached Mary's Creek, where they found water and at which point they had hoped to stop a passing vehicle. They traded off standing alongside the road, while the other sought refuge from the heat in a small patch of shade against a cliff. For a couple of hours they waited for someone to pass by. When a truck finally came, Nan was not bashful: "I ran directly in front of the truck. I was not going to let the truck pass because we needed to get the hell out of there."

Blackadar and Nan got the tire fixed and borrowed a vehicle to get them back to the river. It was now later the second day, and concerned about his wife and pregnant daughter surviving alone in the desert, he hurried back. The rush had been unnecessary. Upon returning, he found that the resourceful women were quite prepared to spend a long time if need be: his plucky wife had set up a comfortable and sheltered camp, and Lois, well trained from her childhood, had caught fresh fish to supplement their meals. After a visit to the grave, where Blackadar left the medallion, and with no further troubles, they returned to Salmon.

The Biggest Ride

✳   ✳

BLACKADAR had always derived great pleasure from watching and showing films of his trips. His own collection of eight millimeter films of hunting and rafting went back as early as the fifties. When kayaking became the focus of his life, he made it a point to get copies of Klaus Streckman's films or those of others who had been filming on trips. He loved performing. In front of an audience gathered along the side of a major rapids, he was always the showman. Considering his growing reputation in the sport and his love of being in the spotlight, it was only a matter of time before television and Walt Blackadar would discover one another.

Kayaking was not new to television. Competitive slalom kayaking, which had first made its appearance as an Olympic event at the 1972 games in Munich, received widespread coverage along with the other popular events. Also in 1972, Barb Wright had appeared in a television program in which celebrities tried a new sport—in Wright's program, William Shatner of "Star Trek" kayaked through Pine Creek Rapids on the Salmon under her tutorship. Blackadar planned to watch Wright's program, but Salmon's unreliable television reception spoiled it. "I heard it was great," Blackadar wrote to Wright. "But we were blacked out at the last minute! Our relay translator broke the Sunday morning of the [show] & Shirl and I cried! Had we known soon enough we would have driven to Missoula—we'll catch the reruns!"

Indirectly, the program served as Blackadar's introduction to national television. The producer of Wright's program, Bob Duncan, was involved in filming for the American Broadcasting Company's *American Sportsman* series. The content of *American Sportsman* centered on fishing and hunting, though the show's producers were beginning to branch out into other sports. Kayaking was one of those sports.

Duncan knew of Blackadar's reputation in the kayaking

world and had contacted Blackadar prior to Wright's program. In fact, it was Blackadar who had suggested that Barbara Wright do the program. But Blackadar was not one to pass up future opportunities, and he began testing the waters, suggesting to Duncan that *American Sportsman* do a future program on running the Grand Canyon in kayaks. What Blackadar proposed was a new way of portraying the sport. Television audiences had primarily seen kayaks slipping between slalom poles and maneuvering between the rocks of small rivers, but they had not seen Blackadar's brand of kayaking through big whitewater.

The genre sounded like it was made to order for television, and Duncan eventually bought the idea. In late June and July of 1974, Blackadar busied himself with lining up the group on which the program would be centered. He wanted a mixed group of talented kayakers so he chose several national competitors: Linda Hibbard, who had been on his 1970 Colorado trip; Lynn Ashton of North Carolina; Jamie McEwan, a handsome C-1 boater who had been a medalist at Munich; and rounding out the group, Blackadar's good friend and experienced big water boater from Montana, Kay Swanson.

On July 22, Blackadar drove to Salt Lake with John Dondero, a young boating friend from Sun Valley. Dondero had recently started Natural Progression, a kayak manufacturing business and was supplying some of the kayaks for the Colorado trip. A proficient kayaker himself, he had managed to wrangle his way on the trip by suggesting to Duncan that he ought to have a boat repairman along.

On the way to Salt Lake City, Blackadar talked with Dondero about Julie Wilson. Dondero remembered that "he was still very shaken about it. He had thought that he would give up kayaking, but when the ABC deal came through, he decided that he couldn't throw in the towel and that he had to keep on living." They arrived late in Salt Lake and spent the night in a gas station parking lot. At noon the next day they met Hibbard and McEwan, who had flown in, and the four drove down together to meet the rest of the group at Lees Ferry.

On the way, Hibbard and Blackadar sat in the front and Dondero and McEwan in the back. "Walt and Linda were talking about handguns," said Dondero. "She didn't know much about them and Walt said, 'Hell, you don't know anything about handguns? Let me show you.' And he pulled off the road, walked off a short distance, and started firing his .38." Dondero, and to some degree Linda Hibbard, was used to that sort of thing from Blackadar, but Dondero wondered what McEwan must have been thinking about this wild character with whom he'd soon be running the river. McEwan would see plenty more.

Walt Blackadar, poised and comfortable before the camera, clearly dominated the segment which was eventually cut for *American Sportsman.* "We have a very good group of boaters on this trip," Blackadar begins. He easily flows into the next sentence by saying "I," and then he unconsciously pauses, just for a moment, and by doing so he effectively emphasizes that *he* is in charge here. "*I* invited the boaters because *I* knew they had varying styles, and *I* wanted to learn some new techniques from many of them." His slow careful pace and the low tonal quality of his voice are confident, reassuring.

"Jamie and Lynn are really going to enjoy this big water," he continues by introducing the boaters that he chose to go on the trip. "Linda, who was here before, is very good in huge water, and she looks pretty out there . . . . Kay has been a paddling friend of mine for many years. We go all over the country together and Alaska. . . I really love kayaking, because it allows me to get away and get into the wilderness, and this makes a super highway for wilderness for the experienced boater."

John Dondero, eager to help on the trip while they floated down the wilderness highway, ended up assisting with some of the filming. In Hermit, a rapid known for its very large waves, he boated through with a camera mounted to his helmet to present a view of a ride down whitewater from the kayaker's perspective. Dondero had just finished filming Hermit, when at the bottom, he came across two women and a man sitting nude on the beach. "One of the women had blond hair and beautiful breasts," Dondero remembered. "It was like a dream."

Dondero started his helmet camera, thinking that the ABC editors back in New York might enjoy some of the footage. Dondero's newly found friends came back up the river, and he introduced them to Blackadar. "Walt was trying everything he could to get them to float down with us," Dondero said. Unfortunately, Blackadar couldn't convince them to join the party, but the doctor was fascinated by a scar on the chest of one of the women, which he reasoned might have been from open heart surgery.

The party continued down the river, without—much to Blackadar's disappointment—the alluring women from Hermit rapids. In time, though, they were forgotten. The delightfully warm days on the river blended into one another. Periodically, they stopped and filmed, and in the evenings on sandy beaches they relaxed, the boating and filming gear scattered about, while above them, the ancient walls of the canyon pinched together, leaving a narrow strip of the night sky.

As they approached Lava Falls, a more serious tone came over the party. Lava Falls is a rapids that demands respect. It is big, raw, and powerful. Blackadar had been bothered by Lynn Ashton. Throughout the trip, she had been wearing a low buoyancy life jacket. Now that they were at the Colorado's biggest rapid, he tried to convince her to wear the large Mae West life vest. "He turned away from Lynn and walked toward me," Dondero remembered. "He had big tears in his eyes. They were tears for Julie. He had been really moved by that experience." Ashton was moved, too. She agreed to wear the life jacket.

❉   ❉

AT Lava Falls, the ABC crew caught on film a spellbinding

performance by Blackadar.

Paddling over to the right side of the river, he turns his boat around slowly, facing upstream away from the falls. The smooth brown water begins to pick up, and his boat slides faster towards a large V-shaped wave at the top of the rapid. Reaching back over his left shoulder, he drops faster and faster, hits the first boiling brown wave and breaks through.

He's now moving faster, at the pace dictated by the descending current of the falls. A wave knocks him over. He rolls easily, but without warning he is slapped backwards by a mammoth wave rebounding off the large rock on the right side of the falls. Completely at the mercy of the river, he is engulfed in a hole, one of Lava's most violent, bubbling and boiling, the brown water like a seething cauldron of oatmeal. All that can be seen is an arm and paddle and a red flash of his boat.

And then nothing.

After a few moments, a palpable nervousness begins to spread among those watching on shore.

Still nothing.

He has disappeared. There is no boat. No paddle in the air. Nowhere is there a sign of him.

"Come on, Walt," one of the boaters says.

"Come on, Walt," someone else repeats, this time in a louder, more urgent voice. Then a cameraman cries out, "Where is he?"

The camera pans quickly, searching the rapids for any sign of him or his boat, then it jerks downstream far below the hole where Blackadar disappeared. He pops to the surface of the river, still in his boat.

McEwan says, "God bless!"

For a second or two, Blackadar is disoriented, and then paddling to the shore, he says in a grainy, excited voice, "What a ride! That pulled me out of my boat."

His voice becomes more agitated, and he exclaims, "Pulled me clear out of the boat even with these thigh hooks." He takes a breath and slows, emphasizing each word of his next sentences: "I had to crawl back in. That's the biggest ride I've ever had!"

＊   ＊

A few days after Blackadar's biggest ride in Lava Falls (he later admitted that the Alsek was really *the* biggest), a worn and defeated Richard Nixon announced his resignation from the presidency. As Nixon's star tumbled, Blackadar's had been rising. The Colorado trip, his most exciting run of Lava Falls, and the subsequent nationally televised program of his Colorado trip on *American Sportsman* had revitalized his life. He could never forget what had happened on the West Fork, but at least he could now live with it.

The chapter on Julie Wilson's grave, however, had not yet been closed. In mid-September, while Blackadar was at a medical meeting, he learned of a shocking development. Owyhee County Sheriff Tim Nettleton had obtained a permit and exhumed the wilderness grave along the West Fork.

According to the Twin Falls *Times-News*, reporters learned of the event two weeks after the grave had been opened. Nettleton said that he acted to comply with an Idaho law that requires the sheriff to conduct an investigation in any death in his county that results from causes other than natural. Since no law officer had ever seen the body and the body had not been properly identified, Nettleton undertook the disinterment. The body was removed and stored in a funeral home in Nampa, near Boise.

Blackadar was stunned. From the beginning, he had been careful to seek legal advice from his county prosecutor and obtain the necessary permission for Julie's burial. Upon returning from the memorial service in Atlanta, he had phoned Coroner Goetz of Owyhee County giving him details of the burial. Goetz gave Blackadar permission as a physician to file the death certificate, which Blackadar signed on the 20th of May and was received by the local register on the 26th. Goetz said that as far as he was concerned, the case was closed.

The doctor's initial shock turned to anger. He remembered the chai medallion which he had left at the grave and wondered if it had been tossed to the side somewhere. He had not been notified of the exhumation, nor had Ross and Elizabeth Wilson been informed. Worse yet, the Wilsons had been planning to come out to Idaho to visit the grave site with Blackadar. Since neither Blackadar nor the Wilsons were aware of what had transpired, it might have been entirely possible that he would have led the Wilsons to an open grave.

When asked by reporters, Coroner Goetz termed Nettleton's interference "underhanded." In fact, Goetz felt the whole incident was politically motivated, and, indeed, it appeared that way. Goetz was a Republican, and he was running against Hank Acosta, a Democrat who had worked for four years as a deputy sheriff under Nettleton, also a Democrat. Timing is everything in politics. The news of the exhumation broke when the election was only two months away.

"He [Nettleton] wanted to get me out of office," said Goetz. It was no secret that Nettleton and Goetz did not get along, and the need for the exhumation made it look like Goetz wasn't doing a proper job as a coroner. Blackadar immediately picked up on the political sensitivity of the situation and decided to withhold any public statements until he was sure that the body had been reinterred. He knew that Nettleton held the upper hand as long as the body remained out of the grave. He was particularly bothered by rumors that Nettleton might try to block returning the body to its resting place in the wilderness. To keep from exacerbating an already delicate situation, Blackadar held his tongue, but privately he fumed.

The process of identification went on for more than a month. Finally, Blackadar learned that the body had been identified from dental records and reburied in its original grave along the river on October 12. He wasted no time in drafting a letter, parts of which were printed in at least two Idaho newspapers. On October 17, Idaho's largest paper, *The Idaho Statesman* in Boise, made Blackadar's story the headline article in its regional section.

In the *Statesman* article, entitled "Leader of Kayak Trip Assails Exhuming of Bruneau Victim," Blackadar called Nettleton's actions "inhumane" and "barbaric" and labeled him a "grave robber." He excoriated the sheriff for finding a "loop hole" in the law. "Never once were Julie's parents phoned or contacted by Idaho authorities. How inhumane can we become even if we act legally?" Blackadar asked.

Blackadar continued: "The first weeks that Sheriff Nettleton possessed Julie's body he made no attempt at identification. Never once did he request its examination, nor did he check to see if she was a girl or a man; he never looked into the sealed nylon sack. Instead he phoned the Bureau of Land Management and requested them to file documents requesting that Julie's body not be returned to her wilderness grave. However, the exhumation order and Idaho law emphatically states that no place of burial can be changed without permission of the next of kin." Once Julie's parents were "belatedly notified of this heinous act," they refused to change the place of burial.

In his letter to the newspapers, Blackadar left no question that he felt politics were behind the exhumation. But here Blackadar stumbled. For some reason, the doctor was under the impression that Nettleton was up for re-election. Nettleton's next election, however, was several years off. In the letter, the doctor encouraged all residents of Owyhee County to "show their support to these brave parents at the polls November 5th by voting these rascals out."

Thankfully, from Blackadar's standpoint, editors both at the *Idaho Statesman* and *Times-News* saved Blackadar an embarrassment by leaving out all of the political references. They also left out Blackadar's request that the voters of Owyhee County "show their strong support to a . . . true humanitarian Coroner

Goetz." Goetz could have used the help. After all county election returns were in, Goetz had lost his bid for re-election to Nettleton's deputy, Hank Acosta.

When interviewed later about the affair, Nettleton conceded that politics were involved. "Coroner Goetz and I had problems," Nettleton admitted. It hadn't been the first time the two had locked horns, and it came to a head in the Julie Wilson case. Nettleton felt that Goetz gave Blackadar bad advice and exercised poor judgement and was sorry that the doctor had been "caught in the middle."

Moreover, Nettleton's side of the story is distinctly different than Blackadar's. The sheriff first became uneasy about the burial when he learned through a newspaper report that Julie Wilson's body had been found and buried by "friends" while Blackadar was in Atlanta. Then, as the summer wore on, he received requests from the Wilsons' insurance company for a report on the death.

Nettleton wrote Blackadar for information. "Two requests were sent to Doctor Blackadar to send statements," Nettleton said. Blackadar sent the sheriff his write-up on the accident which appeared in national kayaking magazines, but Nettleton needed more. He needed sworn statements from witnesses at the time of the accident and the burial. "All we had was a verbal statement and a short written statement," Nettleton said. "It was a short, arrogant statement and it was the statement of one man. He had given me the names of the witnesses, but I had no addresses."

Ostensibly, it was about this time, in mid-summer, that Blackadar was busy with his first filming project for ABC on the Colorado River. If there was one crucial point which influenced later events, it occurred here. Either Nettleton did not make himself clear, or Blackadar, preoccupied with his practice and the ABC project, did not understand exactly what Nettleton needed.

Sworn testimony was critical for Nettleton to establish some important facts: "When the second and third request for insurance came, I talked with the prosecutor. We weren't sure that, number one, if there was a person in the grave; and, number two, if that person was Julie Wilson." Nettleton never suspected foul play and "agonized" over the decision. "I knew how I'd feel if it was my daughter or a friend's daughter. But I knew that two years later that rumors could start circulating. If a rumor comes up two years later, then it's too late."

Nettleton, then, did what he felt was necessary. By the time Blackadar understood the importance of the sworn statements, it was too late. In late September after he had learned about the disinterment, he belatedly asked all the witnesses to the accident and burial to prepare notarized statements and send them to Nettleton. If the statements had come prior to September, Nettleton said he might not have then requested the exhumation order.

Blackadar never understood the reasons behind Nettleton's actions. Blackadar's own anger and personality clash with Nettleton removed any possibility of reasonable dialog between the two. And even if he had been able to listen to Nettleton, he was too emotionally close to the situation to fully grasp the sheriff's side. To Blackadar, Nettleton was a contemptuous, self-serving, county politician who had disturbed the resting place of someone who had been lovingly buried. He detested Nettleton and never forgave him for the loathsome deed.

✳   ✳

A MONTH after the reburial, a shocking development on a conservation issue had him back on his feet, fighting once again. Gerald Ford's administration, which had changed little from Nixon's since his summer resignation, announced its recommendations for the lands surrounding the Middle Fork and Main Salmon Rivers, at the time called the Idaho Primitive Area. If approved by Congress, the announced proposal would forever change the character of central Idaho as Blackadar knew it. The administration mapmakers, under directive of top Department of Agriculture officials, slashed away half of the existing prime roadless land in central Idaho, and in one area alone, the Chamberlain Basin—an area which, wrote *Field and Stream* editor Ted Trueblood, "could very well be the best elk range in America"—386,000 acres would be open to road building and timber harvesting. Blackadar's Clear Creek area was opened for development, with only the upper part of the drainage to be protected.

To Blackadar the proposal was appalling and shamelessly catered to well-heeled moneyed interests. The timber values of primitive country in central Idaho were negligible when compared to the rest of the United States. To sacrifice wildlife habitat, endanger streams and destroy the beauty of the Salmon River country was pure greed on the part of Idaho's timber industry.

From the beginning Blackadar had been involved in efforts to expand the size of the existing Idaho Primitive Area to include important areas like Clear Creek which were contiguous to the area. He hosted the key meeting at his Salmon home in which conservationists put together one of the most important proposals ever fashioned to save Idaho wilderness.

The newly-developed River of No Return Wilderness proposal created a 2.3 million-acre wilderness which protected much of the drainage of the Middle Fork of the Salmon and parts of the Main Salmon. Blackadar had sent letters out to lists of his kayaking friends, asking them to write supporting the proposal. "To win," Blackadar wrote, "we need a vast number of letters from all over the country. Now your letter is not going to be enough to win this fight. You must take this proposal, as I have, by the teeth and write or get a number of your friends to do the same . . . . I'm counting on each and every one of you to generate ten letters for this proposal."

Blackadar, his conservation friends and the newly formed River of No Return Wilderness Council were successful in generating a large number of letters supporting their proposal. "An analysis of the responses showed," according to Forest Service documents, "strong public support for Wilderness classification . . . . In addition, the response reflected a strong recommendation for enlarging the areas proposed for wilderness by the addition of a number of contiguous areas . . . ." With that kind of support, conservationists expected a reasonable proposal out of Washington.

The devastating final result came after the public hearings and was linked by conservationists to a meeting that representatives of Boise Cascade and the Idaho Mining Association had with Earl Butz, Nixon's Secretary of Agriculture. The industry representatives had no trouble getting their point across to the development-oriented Secretary. Their political influence was written all over the final administration's proposal.

BLACKADAR knew that the battle wasn't over. Congress would make the final decision on the area. Though Idaho Republicans in Congress deprecated the River of No Return proposal, both Governor Andrus and Senator Frank Church vocally supported a reasonably-sized wilderness for central Idaho. During the remaining years of his life, Blackadar would continue to support and campaign for the River of No Return Wilderness proposal. His involvement in conservation issues, however, began to lose the intensity of his early work. It was the same with community work. His time spent in Chamber activities and local service organizations dwindled.

He simply had become too busy. Kayaking was now occupying large amounts of his time. Work on his ranch kept him busy with irrigation, maintenance and improvement projects. Indeed, kayakers who stopped to visit or camp in his backyard might find themselves awakened early in the morning to help him move sprinkler pipes which watered his alfalfa. And his practice continued growing. Even with the hard working Simmons, the demand on his time was great. To relieve the load which both Simmons and Blackadar agreed had grown inordinately unmanageable, they would eventually bring in a third partner.

Of all his years, 1974 was a pivotal year, one of highs and very deep lows. For the country, it had been a dismal year, the year of 14 percent inflation, of CIA admissions of illegal invasions of privacy, of abuses of presidential power and of a loss of American confidence in government. For Blackadar, it was the year of Julie's terrible accident. But it was also the year of Blackadar's big start in films and television, becoming a sport personality. More films would follow this first ABC appearance, firmly establishing his role as kayaking's *celebrité*.

It was also the year that destiny brought him together with another showman who, like him, gained fame through risking his life. It was a rather unusual and brief meeting with the archetypal stuntman himself, Evel Knievel.

X

On the Edge

THE RED, WHITE AND BLUE rocket sits listless at the bottom of the 108-foot steel ramp. Straining to see, watching for any movement, the noisy, impatient crowd of 15,000 onlookers and 130 journalists gathered at the edge of the Snake River Canyon stare at the sleek, silent form. Inside, sits a man in a white leather jumpsuit with diamond cufflinks.

He pushes a button. Now . . . .

White steam hisses and pours out the back. The 5,000 pounds of thrust flatten the man against his seat. The lump of metal hurtles up the ramp. Then, something appears in the steam before the rocket reaches the end of the steel launcher. It is difficult to see at first, but as the rocket rises higher, the white object taking shape in the steam is unmistakably the rocket's parachute!

It is far too soon for the parachute. Straining against the chute, the rocket slows, and its fuel is quickly spent. With its forward motion stopped, it dangles from the chute, the spear-like nose points down. The crowd reels. The rocket may fall into the canyon. This is part of the reason why they have come to watch. Someone might die here.

177

Overhead the rocket drifts in the wind, sinking languidly over the 600-foot-deep canyon below. The white steam is gone, but decorative red smoke spews from the tips of the two small tail fins as the nose slips beyond the canyon rim. The crowd jostles toward the edge. The wave of bodies pounds against the chain-link fence, straining against the 11-gauge wire and finally toppling it over. The lifeless rocket crashes against the side of the cliff, bounces and scrapes against black rock and falls further into the canyon.

Part of the crowd breaks through the last of the retaining fences. Miraculously, no one is pushed over the edge of the cliff. The last that most of the crowd sees of Evel Knievel's Sky-cycle is the half-deflated parachute disappearing into the deep fissure beyond.

Those sitting in their kayaks on the river below have the best view now. Blackadar, directly under the launch site, watches the swinging object settling into the canyon. The wind is blowing the rocket, and anticipating where it will fall, he charges upstream.

"I knew," he wrote later, "Evel was going to land in my lap!"

KLAUS STRECKMAN had a lot of news to tell Blackadar over the phone. He had just returned from attempting to run the Alsek River with Dick Tero and Dee Crouch. Their late summer trip in 1974, the first try of the river since Blackadar's 1971 trip, was stopped by the advancing Tweedsmuir Glacier. It was the continuation of the surge that had started when Blackadar had run Turnback Canyon. "The Tweedsmuir," Streckman said, "was broken into ice pinnacles and more crevasses and jumbled ice than you could imagine. We realized that there was no bloody way we could cross. It was just impossible."

What they saw while on their reconnaissance was unforgettable. Massive icebergs from the glacier blocked and pushed the river up and over the east bank. With its normal channel altered, the river reworked its way around the ice and poured back into Turnback Canyon, creating a terrifying rapid of foaming grey water and shredded ice.

Their escape from the canyon was, in itself, a remarkable journey. The three men left their boats and started out on foot, climbing up 1,500 feet across steep slippery slopes and back down 1,500 feet, crossing swollen glacial streams, and slogging through bogs, tangled alder thickets and ignominious devils club—a chest high, broad leaf plant covered with thorns from the stem base to leaf tip. Nearly a week later, wearing torn and shredded clothing, wet and hypothermic and infected with cuts from the interminable battle with insects and devils club, they stumbled upon a road which led them to the Alaskan highway.

After his survival march out of the Alsek, Streckman was looking for a milder trip. He told Blackadar that he had heard about Evel Knievel's jump of the Snake River Canyon near Twin Falls and had thought about coming down to take films of it.

Blackadar was already way ahead of him. He was planning the same. "Oh yeah, I'm going to be right there underneath," Blackadar confidently declared on the phone. "I'm going to pick him [Knievel] out of the river."

He had friends in Twins Falls with whom they could stay, he said, inviting Klaus to join him. What's more, he had figured out a way to slip past all the security checkpoints to view the jump without paying the $25 admission fee.

Streckman, amused at Blackadar's boasts about plucking Knievel from the river, recognized immediately that it would be a fun time, just what he needed after the marathon journey he had endured in Alaska that summer. He drove from Vancouver to Salmon shortly before the jump was scheduled in early September. Arriving, Streckman was struck by Blackadar's fascination with Evel Knievel. His daughter, Lois, noticing the same about her father, said that he had an "Evel Knievel toy," a motorcycle, and that "he used to take it down to the hospital and run it down the hall." He also bought one of the toys for her son and gave at least one other away to another boy. While in Salmon, Streckman heard Blackadar repeatedly tell others over the phone that he was planning to go to Knievel's canyon jump and pull him out of the river.

The two drove south from Salmon and went first to Jackpot, Nevada, just south of Twin Falls. Blackadar gambled, drank, and won some money, and before leaving, Klaus took over the wheel since Blackadar was too drunk to drive to Twin Falls. On Saturday, the day before the launch date, Blackadar and Klaus met Dick Roberts, who knew the property owner whose land Knievel had leased for the affair. They had some drinks and drove on to check out the pre-launch preparations.

At the launch site, the black lava canyon of the Snake is 1,600 feet wide and 600 feet deep. On top, a level grass and sagebrush plain rolls outward from the canyon edge, and on the bottom, broken blocks of basalt that have crumbled off from the upper walls are intermixed with twisted sage and lie in sloping talus fields near the water's edge.

The canyon is not nearly as deep as the Grand Canyon, where Knievel originally thought about staging his jump, but when the Park Service gave him a thumbs down to that idea, he chose the Snake River Canyon as an adequate substitute. Private property was available on the rim for the launch site and for spectators, and it looked deep and formidable enough to attract the kind of publicity and big money that he desired. Successful or not, Knievel would be paid $6 million before the jump and pick up a 60 percent cut of the post-jump take from closed circuit television hookups.

Security prevented Blackadar from getting close to the rocket launcher at the canyon's edge. Extra heavy precautionary measures—a double row of fencing, 150 private security guards, and 600 national guardsmen on standby alert—could prove to be warranted by the looks of the numbers of party-seeking motorcyclists arriving in Twin Falls. From a distance, the rocket appeared small compared to the long beams of the steel launcher which steeply angled above. In fact, it would have been smaller yet if the Sky-cycle had been based on Knievel's original idea of using a motorcycle with booster rockets attached. A rocket expert, Robert Truax, whom Knievel had hired, convinced him otherwise and developed the small missile which would carry the daredevil aloft.

Knievel would be strapped in the seat of the open cockpit of the rocket, which had no steering mechanism nor ejection seat. Nor did the Sky-cycle have much of a landing system. When the rocket reached the end of its arc over the canyon, Knievel was to pull a lever to release a drag chute. The chute, in theory, would cause the rocket to drop from the sky nose first, and when it hit the ground, a shock absorber in the front would cushion the fall. If it remained upright, it would bounce again and again, like a pogo stick, springing through the sagebrush. Truax wasn't quite sure how well the pogo stick landing would work since the two previous test flights had not made it across the canyon, dropping the rocket in the lava rocks below.

That night, Dee Crouch drove in from Yakima, Washington, and joined Blackadar and Streckman at Dick and Muff Roberts' house in Twin Falls. After a late night party which included films and slides of past trips, they all rose early, driving down to Blue Lakes Country Club, which is located downstream from the launch site in an open area along the Snake River. A few nearby golfers, already out on the course, paused and looked on with surprise as the small band of wet suit-clad people slipped their kayaks into the river and began paddling upstream.

"We were well equipped with food, booze, ice cubes—everything for a party," said Streckman. They paddled three miles upriver to Pinnacle Falls, where they portaged up to the top of the rapids to play in it for awhile. To avoid being thrown out by any security people within the canyon, they waited at the falls until shortly before the time of the jump. The wait proved to be unnecessary. Few people were in the canyon.

As they approached the jump site, Streckman looked for a good angle for filming. "I positioned myself 300 yards downstream so I could see the arc of the jump," said Streckman. Blackadar, however, wanted to be right under the trajectory.

"You take the film. I'll get the guy," Blackadar announced to Streckman.

"He had an obsession," said Streckman. "He was going to pick Knievel up. He was so sure of himself that it was amazing. I asked him how he could be so sure, and he said, 'I just know I'm going to pick him up.'" Streckman, shaking his head, set up the camera, and Blackadar moved under the launch site.

F ROM within the canyon, they could hear the boom when Knievel's rocket left the launcher. "It looked as though he was stalling," described Streckman later. "Then I saw the bloody parachute. Orange smoke was pouring out. It looked like the guy was burning. I kept rolling my camera as he was blown back towards the canyon rim. He crashed on a ledge, the chute folded some, and then it fell again."

Blackadar described later what he saw: "The rocket then careened down the steep vine covered slope and came to rest on the bank. I was directly under the ramp at blastoff and approximately 100 feet away as the Sky-cycle landed. However, I was overtaken by an outboard, which arrived a few seconds before I did."

Blackadar caught up, went immediately for Knievel, and yelled, "I got him. I got him. I got him!"

Streckman paddled up to the site, and as they finished unstrapping Knievel, Blackadar announced, "I'm a doctor. I'll take care of this."

"He was bleeding but O.K.—unhurt except for scratches but in shock," noted Blackadar. "He had no knowledge of what had happened or where he was, although he was glad to be alive."

The small group moved Knievel into the outboard boat and powered off to reach a helicopter landing site. Blackadar stayed close to Knievel in the boat. "During this ride I found out what he was made of," wrote Blackadar. "In spite of his shock and mental trauma he grabbed a Sky-cycle aileron away from a youngster in the boat and said, 'What's your name?' Then he graciously pulled out a pen and wrote 'To Mike from Evel Knievel' and handed the precious souvenir back to the over-whelmed boy."

When they reached the copter, Blackadar, still very much in charge, had planned to fly directly with Knievel to the hospital. But Knievel wanted to go back to acknowledge to the crowd that he had survived. Checking his pulse, which was a healthy 78, Blackadar agreed.

"It was two or three minutes before the people would clear a way for our landing," Blackadar wrote. "Immediately we were crushed and crunched by an insane mob which tried to tear him apart, some grabbing for souvenirs, though most were try-ing to wish him well. One burly hand reached across my face to his helmet and received a well-earned bite—to the bone."

It was a scene out of a surrealistic film: Knievel in his red, white and blue leather flight suit, greeting his fans, Blackadar in a black wet suit, red nylon paddling jacket and white helmet, clamping his teeth into a menacing arm. Blackadar held tightly onto Knievel while they pushed their way through the mass of humanity squeezing in upon them like a great fist.

At one point, a young man who had worked his way through the crowd, reached them and yelled, "I'm a doctor . . . . I'm a doctor!"

Blackadar glared at him: "Well, so am I, sonny, and I got to him first."

✻ ✻

THAT night in Twin Falls, Blackadar and his friends held another party, and the doctor was the cynosure as he retold his story of Evel falling into his lap. The similarities between the two men, of course, are plain. "He is a braggart," Blackadar wrote, describing himself as much as he described Knievel. "But he is as courageous as they make them and a hell of a good guy . . . . I salute Evel Knievel and will forever be a staunch admirer of his."

At the celebration party, he pulled Streckman aside and told him that his film of Knievel from inside the canyon was worth a lot of money, and he could help get it to the right people. The next morning, Blackadar called ABC and made arrangements to send Streckman's three rolls of unprocessed Super 8 film to New York.

"That was the last I ever saw of it," said a disappointed Streckman. Repeated inquiries by both Blackadar and Streckman with ABC failed to locate the missing film. At the end of March of 1975, Blackadar was still trying, sending a letter to Knievel, asking if anyone had tried to sell him film footage of the canyon jump. Margaret Meagher, Knievel's secretary in Butte, responded, telling him that they had no knowledge of the film.

While he was making this last unsuccessful attempt to locate Streckman's film, plans were well under way to make a film of a more familiar topic. Blackadar had been invited to kayak the Grand Canyon for a part in a movie under preparation for the theatrical circuit. The invitation was an indication of how meteoric his rise had been. Only a few months had passed since his first nationwide appearance on ABC's *American Sportsman,* and he was already being sought to appear in another film, this time one that involved plot, characters and a combination of fiction and true drama.

The film was conceived by Coloradans Roger Brown of

Summit Films and Tom Hubbard of Crystal Productions. Brown and fellow cinematographer, Barry Corbet, who had been on the first successful American Everest climb, had just finished making a hang gliding film for Hubbard's educational film business. Hubbard was interested in similar films for other sports like kayaking, climbing and skiing. Brown, a veteran in the outdoor film business, suggested a larger project: "Why not go for the big market," Brown told him. "Combine all the little films into a feature? Maybe make some real money on your money."

"OK," said Hubbard, "I'll put up half."

Brown wanted a 90-minute film portraying several high-risk, high-adventure outdoor activities, but he knew that to capture and hold the typical moviegoer's interest for an hour and a half, he needed a story to tie together the diverse sports into one smoothly-flowing unit. In time he developed a script which centered around two adventure-seeking individuals—a man and a woman—who meet and end up traveling together, immersing themselves in adventurous sports: skiing, hang gliding, kayaking, and rock and ice climbing. Through shared excitement and exposure to danger, the two end up falling in love. But their life on the edge has consequences, and the film's climax comes when it appears that one of the characters steps too far over the thin edge and dies on a climb.

The dramatic story thread was to be woven around actual sport personalities, creating a mixture of theatrical and documentary subject matter. The two characters would seek out the help of well-known climbers and kayakers, and with their help, they would learn about and immerse themselves in each of the sports.

Brown at first was reluctant to experiment in the fickle field of theatrics. He preferred to work solely from a familiar documentary standpoint. But if he wanted to produce a feature which he could sell to the largely conservative moviehouse distribution network, he was told he must have a film with a theatrical basis. "I was really forced into putting the actor and actress in the film [by investors]. I wasn't sure that was a good idea," he recalled.

For the leading actor, Brown chose Tom Babson, whom he had met at a hang gliding school in Aspen. For the actress, he interviewed more than a hundred hopefuls before settling on Greta Ronnigen, a petite blond who he felt would be able to handle the adverse conditions of making an outdoor picture. Documentary characters included Yvon Chouinard and Mike Covington, two big names in American climbing; John Totman, John Deahl and Tom Hamilton, respected hang gliders; and for kayaking, Fletcher Anderson, a friend of Brown's and a cinematographer from Colorado—and Walt Blackadar.

Fletcher Anderson and Walt Blackadar couldn't have been more different. Anderson was young, wore his long hair tied back in a ponytail, and kayaked with a careful, calculated style that had come from his experience in competitive kayaking. (In 1964 he beat out the field in the junior kayaking nationals, and in 1965, he won the U.S. team senior trials in the slalom.) Blackadar, now reaching 53 years old, had never competed and never planned to. Yet, if they were different, they were also similar in one respect. "At that time, both Walt and I suffered from excessive egos," reasoned Anderson.

From the beginning, it was obvious that the two personalities would conflict. "A couple of days before the trip," Anderson said, "all the kayakers [except Blackadar] had arrived early." Others who were kayaking on the trip included three more experienced boaters, Will Evans, Will Perry and Ann Hopkinson, who is now Anderson's wife. It was evening in the desert and quiet and peaceful. Anderson continued: "We were sitting around and watching all the rocks turn orange. All of a sudden the airport limousine drives up. This guy comes screaming out of the limo: 'Hey, land lovers, I'm Walt Blackadar. I'm king of the river.' 'Oh God, [I thought] is this guy for real? What's his problem?'"

Making the entrance along with Blackadar was his daughter, Nan. Taking Roger Brown up on an offer to allow guests to come on the trip, Blackadar had invited Nan for the first half of the trip, and Sue, one of his other daughters, would hike in and join him for the second half. Neither of them had done any kayaking, and he had brought an extra boat along, planning to give them a few lessons.

Nan had heard other people talk about her father's fearless kayaking, but seeing it was another thing. At House Rock Rapid, the first rapid selected for filming, he came to her and said, "I'm going to paddle those holes, and I might drown." She was taken aback. He really was doing dangerous things on the river. As if to underscore the point, he handed her a letter which she was to give to her mother if he died on the trip.

Looking over House Rock Rapid, Fletcher Anderson and the three other kayakers discussed their routes with the cameramen. Blackadar, joining in, explained that he planned to run through both holes, a route which was not technically difficult, but certainly more gutsy than what the other kayakers had planned. Blackadar ran it as he had said, crashing through the giant holes and coming out triumphantly at the bottom, waving his paddle. To the cheering cameramen, his run had been terrific stuff for the film. Anderson, on the other hand, wasn't impressed. "To us [the other kayakers], it looked like one big long mistake." That event did little to improve the worsening relationship between the two.

At the same time, the two co-stars, for all the coziness called for by the script, weren't getting along well, either. Although they never fought outwardly, Ronnigen had no love for Babson. She was the more adventurous of the two, willing to try much of what was necessary to make the film believable, while Babson vacillated. Their parts in the Colorado River portion of the film included one scene where the two go for a nude swim, another segment which shows the actress flipped from one of the rafts, and an instruction session where Blackadar teaches the actress how to roll a kayak.

The stars, however, were being upstaged. The strong personalities of the documentary characters solicited by Brown outweighed the performances put on by the actors. In their own environment, people like Yvon Chouinard and Walt Blackadar ruled. In Blackadar's case, not only did his presence upstage the thespians, but that of his fellow kayakers as well.

It was a fact that was becoming painfully clearer to Fletcher Anderson as the trip went on. More and more, Anderson found himself pushed into an uncomfortable role of playing second fiddle. "I felt I was being pressured to take risks and pressured to do things I didn't want to do," said Anderson. He placed the blame for this competitive atmosphere squarely on Roger Brown's shoulders, saying that the *Edge* director played his two main kayakers against one another. Anderson said, "By doing that, he could convince us perhaps to take risks we wouldn't ordinarily take." Consequently, Anderson rebelled, rejecting the taunts: "I actually ended up taking far fewer risks than I normally would on the same river—than, indeed, I did on other trips."

Brown, who rejects the idea that he was asking anyone to take unnecessary risks, needed not worry about Blackadar. As his past experiences showed, the doctor needed little encouragement. When the cameras were rolling, Blackadar was ready to put on a show. For the filming at Crystal Rapids, Blackadar again successfully ran the threatening hole on the left side of the river which he had first run in 1970. Anderson elected not to run it. "The competition never stopped," said Anderson. "We'd get up in the morning, and there'd be competition about what we're going to eat for breakfast. Every rapid we came to, there'd be competition on who was going to do the hardest run. After we ran it, then we had to sit down with Roger Brown and rehash it—and try to determine which thing that who did was the hardest or the most dangerous."

Brown feels that the conflict between the two resulted because of jealousy on the part of Anderson and young boaters like him: "A lot of the young kayakers resented Walt because they couldn't believe that he was that good. They didn't like his style. That's typical of young people in general looking at older people. It's hard for an up-and-coming young star to give recognition to the old veteran." Brown felt the clash between the two was even more pronounced because of Anderson's "antagonistic" personality.

Whatever the basis for the derision, that the two looked at the river from two separate perspectives was obvious. Anderson pointed to an incident in Marble Canyon which illustrates their philosophical differences. Marble Canyon, early in the river journey down the Colorado, is a lovely stretch where the river runs placidly through sheer, polished red limestone walls. There are few rapids. Anderson had been looking forward to this part of the trip from an aesthetic standpoint, desiring to take in the canyon's quiet beauty and ancient, moving ambiance.

"Blackadar looked at his guidebook," remembered Anderson. "In huge writing across the top of Marble Canyon was written 'DULL, DULL, DULLSVILLE.'" With no big rapids showing, Blackadar hopped up on the motorized raft, and as they began floating through the lovely canyon, he laid back and started reading a two-week-old copy of *U.S. News and World Report*. To Anderson, the sight of Blackadar reading a news magazine amidst the beauties of Marble Canyon was a sacrilege.

❊　　❊

"WALT always had to be one up on every other kayaker along," said Anderson. "In not just boating, but in camp and everything else." In particular, Anderson pointed to Blackadar's drinking. He had brought along a number of plastic bottles of what Anderson thought was pure grain alcohol—others say vodka—and he would mix it with lemonade powder to make his favorite drink. "By God, I wasn't man enough to drink that," said Anderson. Anderson referred to the volume of alcohol carried by Blackadar on the trip as a "rather staggering amount."

It seems his drinking, which had always been prodigious while on outdoor trips, had increased substantially. His daughter Sue who had now joined the river trip, said that her father's "grieving [for Julie Wilson] had taken on the form of drinking more." "Walt," Sue said, "would retire to the tent in the late afternoon and drink, becoming drunk before anyone else."

❊　　❊

BECAUSE of its reputation in the whitewater world, Brown planned to spend at least two days filming at the Colorado's largest rapid, Lava Falls. Three cameramen were positioned at the falls: Barry Corbet with an Eclair ACL camera from a high location at the head of the rapids, while Jim Emerson shot with an Arriflex camera and Brown with a Miliken camera at a low angle, near the water level. With the cameras rolling, Blackadar led off as usual, taking a route on the far right side. An upper wave caught him by surprise and threw him into a churning eddy located dangerously above a place where the water piles up against a large rock midway down the rapid. The currents here are powerful enough to flip 30-foot-long pontoon rafts.

"I knew behind me and just a little further down I'd be in real trouble with that rock, so I wanted out," he said later. From Anderson's view on the side of the river, it looked as though Blackadar could be jammed in a void between the shore and the great cushion of water recoiling from the rock. "It looked to me," said Anderson, "like the chances of being killed were awfully good. I was really terrified then because there was just nothing I could do . . . . I couldn't scream out any directions or jump in or anything. All I could do was just watch somebody else right on the brink, and for me that was pretty frightening."

Blackadar, in trying to escape from his perilous position, was turned around backwards and flipped over. "I was definitely in the mix master," he said. "And once I flipped, I made no attempt to roll because I would have been in trouble rolling up into the hole [above the rock]."

The current tossed Blackadar and his boat up against the rock with a glancing blow to his shoulder. Unhurt, he floated free. The wild ride excited him. "It's great, you know," he said. "You can feel everything . . . . Every part of you is working . . . . Your mind works. Your body works. . . . It just all goes together the right way." For a few glorious moments, Blackadar seemed able to turn back time: while in the midst of the fury of the rapids, all his senses became youthfully sharp and keen, and his muscles reacted like those of a fine-tuned athlete.

Remaining upside down, he rolled at the bottom of the rapid. It was a good take, and the gripping drama of his run would appear in the final film.

Anderson, Will Evans and Will Perry also ran the rapids. Evans had a particularly spectacular run when his boat stood on end and flipped over—an "endo," in kayaking parlance. Another set of runs was made, and then a stop was called. All the boaters had made good runs, and the group returned to the camp above the falls.

In facing and running something as intimidating as Lava Falls, the challenge itself often transcends personality differences. At camp, Blackadar separated off from the larger group, and sitting with the other kayakers, he settled into a conversation about their runs of Lava. It didn't matter what anyone's idea of proper technique was, he said. "All that matters is that you made it or you didn't. And by God, all of us made it." Anderson felt that he was reaching out for some common ground. His comments lessened the tension between the two for the afternoon. "It sounds really trivial," said Anderson, "but at the time it didn't. He was quite sincere." Nonetheless, any good feelings Anderson might have had for Blackadar were elusive. Afterwards, the animosities returned. Overall, Anderson simply couldn't stand Blackadar—"on or off the river."

❆　❆

ON March 12, 1976, Roger Brown planned a sneak preview showing of *The Edge* in Sun Valley. Blackadar sent invitations to friends throughout Idaho, and describing the movie, he made frequent use of the adjective "spectacular": the movie is "Summit Film's spectacular" ("they of course filmed the 'Outer Limits'"), the movie "puts you in the boater's seat," the film includes "hang gliding in the Bugaboos and spectacular surfing and climbing as well as skiing," all in all the movie is a "spectacular 35 mm wide screen show on dangerous sports." To fete the occasion, Muff and Dick Roberts planned a spaghetti meal for Blackadar's out-of-town guests before the showing and a wine party for all afterwards.

The word had gotten around fast in the outdoor-oriented community, and all the seats in the Opera House, Sun Valley's movie theater, quickly filled before the 7 p.m. starting time. Looking for other available space, the talkative audience continued to stream in through the doors, standing along the back wall or sitting on the floor along the aisles. When no more could be packed in, latecomers waiting outside were turned away. With Brown, friends and family, Blackadar sat near the rear of the theater, on the right side.

As the movie flickered on the screen, the audience stayed quiet during the performances put on by Babson and Ronnigen, but began stirring as the acting led into action scenes of freestyle skiing, hang gliding and climbing. When the action finally moved onto the kayaking portion of the movie, clapping broke out.

"Most kayakers will tell you that they are not going to drown," says Blackadar at one point in the movie. "I will tell you I will never drown. I know I could paddle Niagara Falls and not drown. I just can't drown."

The audience loved it, and the cheers and clapping became more enthusiastic. "Every time I have come close to dying,"

Blackadar continued in the film on a more serious vein, "I value my life more. And I value everything around me more. I just love life more, and I think that I will love my old age more."

Then the scenes of his run through Lava Falls splashed across the wide screen, his small boat battered by the towering brown waves which fell upon him. When he rolled up at the bottom, the house erupted in whistles, shouts, and more applause.

He stole the show. Everything left in the movie that night was anti-climactic. To the Sun Valley audience the Idaho doctor had put on a virtuoso performance. The response of his kayaking friends and youthful crowd must have been one of his most satisfying moments of public recognition.

The enthusiastic reception in Sun Valley was far different than the one in Salmon. At a showing in his own town, the atmosphere was more reserved and quiet. In Salmon he was appreciated for an entirely different reason than in Sun Valley. Moreover, his rise in the kayaking world and appearance in films was looked upon with disfavor by some fellow Salmon residents. "We feel that because of his responsibility to the community as a surgeon and a doctor, that it is unfair of him to take chances with his life and physical well-being," said a former Salmon mayor in an interview. "We don't take unnecessary chances, we do things on the safe edge. We are a little resentful that he might take something from us that we have enjoyed, utilized and appreciated." Conversely, in Sun Valley, he was a celebrity because he had taken chances with his life. His medical practice built over his lifetime gave him recognition around Salmon, but the singular fact was apparent: in less than 10 years kayaking had vaulted him to national and international prominence.

The level of his fame never seemed more glorious, nor more temporal, than in the applause of the Sun Valley audience. In order to stay at the top, he needed to continue boating at a level equivalent or greater to what he had done in the film. But how long could he maintain his position at his age? He knew that he didn't have the technical ability of people like Fletcher Anderson or Olympians such as Jamie McEwan, yet what he lacked in ability, he could make up with the force of his personality. As long as his body would hold up, he could continue to lead the sport. That night while his wife retired early in their Sun Valley condominium, he drifted from party to party, drinking heartily, and lingering noticeably in the company of admiring young women.

Brown took the film around to several other ski towns. The response was similar. "Everywhere I went, the film was sold out and there were lines around the block." Impressed with the film's showing at sneak previews, Cooper-Highland Theaters of Denver invested in the film for the purposes of distributing it nationally. The film's first major test was Denver where it played for 10 weeks to receptive audiences. *The Edge* was then booked in Minneapolis for the important Thanksgiving film season. At the last minute, however, a ploy from a large Hollywood distributor caused the Minneapolis theaters to bump *The Edge* for *The Last Tycoon*.

Time was short. The film's promoters did not want to lose the film's building momentum, and a new deal was quickly arranged with Indianapolis and Kansas City theaters. As Brown feared, audience preferences in Indiana and Missouri were a world apart from Colorado. The film flopped. The considerable sum of advertising money expended by Cooper-Highland in an attempt to salvage the film failed. None of the investors was anxious to expend any more. Net revenues on the $300,000 film were well into the red. "It was a major disaster financially after [the Kansas City and Indianapolis showing]," said Brown. "It showed great promise, and then it died."

Besides a financial loss, the film failed in its attempt to amalgamate documentary material with a theatrical story line. Brown had foreseen problems but hoped that they might be able to come upon the right formula. The story portrayed in the final cut of the film is fatuous and supported by weak and artificial acting. Where the film shines is in the action scenes and in the performances put on by the documentary characters. The financial and public fortunes of the movie might have been entirely different if it had been produced solely as a documentary work.*

❊   ❊

WHILE enthusiasm remained high for *The Edge's* prospects, Blackadar met with Brown in New York 12 days after the Sun Valley showing. Brown was on a business trip, and Blackadar was attending a medical convention. Over fillet of sole washed down with Pouilly Fuisse, they started making plans for another film project. Blackadar proposed making a film of running Devils Canyon on the Susitna River. Devils Canyon is "the Mount Everest of kayaking," he told Brown. He had run all of the canyon's rapids except for one, Devil Creek Rapids. It is far bigger and more dangerous than anything in the Grand Canyon. He said: "It makes Lava Falls look like a mill pond." With a strong team of kayakers, he felt it could be run for the first time in front of Brown's cameras.

For Brown, it was an alluring proposition. The Everest of Rivers, its difficult rapids, Blackadar's strong presence, and the chance to film the first-ever run of Devil Creek Rapid gave Brown a highly saleable package to wave in front of ABC.

For possible boaters, Blackadar suggested that at least one member of the team be a nationally known racer such as Eric Evans or Jamie McEwan. His first choice for the next position was Alaskan John Spencer. After Blackadar's initial 1972 run, Spencer had made a solo journey on the Susitna, portaging Devil Creek and Hotel Rock rapids, but running the rest.

---

*In Brown's view, the film is "still the best, most exciting sports photography that anybody's ever seen. It still stands alone and way ahead of anything that's been done like it." In fact, the acceptance of the film seems to have altered in the changed lifestyles, said Brown, and it is regularly shown by college groups and clubs.

Blackadar greatly admired Spencer's adventure on the intimidating Susitna. From Blackadar's perspective, if anyone should be invited on the filming trip, Spencer should. "He certainly deserves the right to go again with a group if he decides [to]," he wrote to Brown.

In addition to Spencer, Blackadar suggested Keith Taylor, a fellow physician from Boise with whom he had made several trips and who had been with him when Al Beam had taken his bad swim at Julie Wilson Falls. Roger Hazelwood, Blackadar's companion on the 1972 trip, was also on the list. For potential woman kayakers, he suggested Donna Berglund or Mary Nutt, both boating companions from past trips, or Terry Goss from San Francisco. One person glaringly absent from Blackadar's list of boaters was Fletcher Anderson.

As Brown came close to cinching the deal with ABC, Blackadar went to work in the spring of 1976 sending out letters to friends in Alaska and prospective kayakers. He wrote Barb Wright, asking for suggestions for an expert woman kayaker who might want to join the party. By early June, Brown had a budget approved with ABC, and the team had been decided. Two of the five-member kayaking team were selected by Brown. Cully Erdman and Billy Ward, two skillful kayakers from Colorado, were to join the team. That reduced Blackadar's choices to two. He chose John Dondero, who would supply any boats needed, and Roger Hazelwood, who had been with him in 1972. John Spencer was not able to make the run.

No more kayakers could be accepted, nor could a woman be invited to balance out the team. Additional kayakers meant greater expenses and more time required to set up shots, and Brown's budget wouldn't allow any extras. There was a little more leeway on rafters, but even the numbers of raft riders had to be kept to a minimum since all would have to be carried via the expensive helicopter portage around the canyon. Blackadar planned to have his son, Bob, now a proficient raftsman, handle all the food and raft support arrangements.

The date for all to meet in Alaska was set for July 26. During

June and early July, Blackadar busied himself with trip logistics. The word had gotten out among kayaking circles, and other hopefuls were calling him. "Getting a lot of inquiries from boaters," Blackadar wrote Brown. But Brown's budget simply wouldn't allow for any more, and Blackadar was forced to tell them no. Any persistent ones he referred to Brown.

Dick Tero, helping with trip logistics in Alaska, put Blackadar in touch with Lori Kincaid in Anchorage, who wrote telling him that his group could use her home as a staging area. That in itself helped keep their Anchorage expenses reasonable, but she also further assisted Brown and Blackadar's project by lining up friends who would do some flying for the party: "Have lined up a 172, 180 and possibly a 206 for aerial work," she wrote. "There may be a nominal charge on the airplanes—gas, costs, etc."

Before Blackadar left in mid-July, he stopped in to see Bill Baker, still Lemhi County sheriff. Blackadar planned to take a .44 pistol with him, and if airline personnel or law enforcement officials stopped him, he wanted an out. Baker prepared a short letter typed out on his stationery:

TO WHOM IT MAY CONCERN:

The proper proof having been shown to the Sheriff of Lemhi County, Idaho.
PERMISSION IS HEREBY GRANTED: WALTER L. BLACKADAR M.D. of Salmon, Idaho to carry concealed, upon his person, his weapon, to-wit:

Pistol of his own choice.

Date this 13th day of July, 1976.

William Baker
Sheriff Lemhi County
Salmon, Idaho 83467

Shortly before leaving, he dashed off a letter to Brown on one of his kayak business "Message-Reply" correspondence forms. "It's all falling into place," he wrote. "I'm so high I know I'll run that bastard."

XI
I'll Be Back

ONE MORNING in late May of 1963, Blackadar gave his good hunting friend, Joe Nebeker, a call. He had just bought a new horse, he told Joe, and he needed some advice and help pulling the tail. Later that morning, Nebeker showed up at Blackadar's, and together they pushed the horse towards the fence. While Nebeker started working on the tail, Blackadar held the agitated horse in position, backed against the fence, with a wooden pole. The horse suddenly lunged towards Blackadar, knocking the pole out of his hands and smashing it against his face.

The blow threw Blackadar backwards to the ground, and he collapsed, unconscious. Nebeker dropped to his side and, not sure exactly what he should do, started artificial respiration. Eventually, Blackadar came to, sat up and spit out three teeth.

"It looks like you've lost some teeth, Doc," Nebeker said, relieved that his friend had come to.

"I don't give a damn," said Blackadar faintly, "they're no good anyway."

Shirley took her husband to the hospital where X-rays showed that he had fractured his jaw and his left clavicle. The jaw was wired shut, and for some time he fed himself by taking liquid nourishment through a straw. He also had two subsequent surgeries to pin the broken clavicle, and with his left arm in a sling much of the time, he found himself relying on the help of others around his office. Hazel Dean, his nurse, remembers one incident shortly after the accident when she got a frantic call from the bathroom. "Hazel!" he yelled, "Hazel!" She went into the bathroom to see what the problem was and found that he couldn't get his pants zipped back up. Amused at his predicament, she gave her helpless boss a hand.

As a result of the accident, he started wearing partial denture plates, but more importantly, the event marked the beginning of a series of problems with his shoulder. Three years after the horse accident, he started having pains in his chest which later were attributed to the two clavicle procedures. The pain kept him awake at night and affected him in kayaking and in surgery. Sue Blackadar remembers watching her father perform a surgery and stopping midway through to shake his hands, complaining of numbness. To help correct the problem, he had several more surgeries, including an operation on both shoulders before Julie Wilson's accident on the West Fork. The 1974 surgery helped temporarily, but as time passed, shoulder problems continued to hound him.

IN 1976, he probably wasn't thinking much about his shoulder as he and the other kayakers climbed along the slippery slopes above Devil Creek Rapids. Through a break in the trees, they stood looking down upon some of the most formidable whitewater in the world.

Devil Creek Rapids is a powerful stretch of whitewater. Above Devil Creek, the Susitna River seems to lumber with the slow, deliberate movement of a grizzly. Then, at the top of the rapids, it lashes out in raw, explosive fury. Devil Creek enters on the north side (right side as one looks downstream), and for several feet out in the river from the mouth of the creek, the gray glaciated waters appear dyed in the shape and shade of an azure ink splotch. The clear waters are no match for the great silt load of the Susitna, and within 30 feet, the waters have mixed and the entire river is gray again.

At the top of the rapids, several large boulders divide the river. The right-hand channel drops over a series of three major ledges. Each ledge in itself is a drop of six to eight feet and looks dangerous enough that most river runners would opt to portage around. Combine all three, add the huge 15-foot waves just above the nozzle, and you have an exceedingly difficult run on the right side of the rapid.

But the right side of Devil Creek is the sneak, the easy run. The middle and left sides, where the majority of river current goes, are where the real action is found. The middle channel is strewn with holes that could swallow Volkswagens, and it is a nasty piece of territory for a kayak. The left entrance is better, but about 200 feet down, the river, which has collided against the left-hand cliff, creates a deep hole, then a large wave and then an even larger, sharply peaked wave that could easily break over the top of the windshield of a city bus. This second wave (Blackadar called it the Roostertail) breaks into a chaos of foaming water. These waves are followed by more huge, 20-foot swells of gray water, each a little higher than the previous one.

About 400 feet down, the river narrows between low granite shelves and floods through in a series of haystack waves, finally squeezing through one last final pinch, which Blackadar named the Nozzle. After the Nozzle, the river immediately widens into an hourglass with two very large circulating eddies; the one on the left is the most powerful, and it is this one which gave Blackadar and Hazelwood trouble on their first trip down the river.

Blackadar and Hazelwood, looking over the rapid, were seeing it for the second time, while Erdman, Dondero and Ward were seeing it for the first. Nobody was disappointed. Blackadar had not been exaggerating about the rapids. For the next few days, they would attempt to run the canyon's biggest rapid.

❄   ❄

PREPARATIONS for the journey to Devil Creek Rapids had begun a week earlier in Anchorage. Kayakers, cameramen and onlookers gathered at Lori Kincaid's natural wood home set within a birch forest. One of the onlookers present as the kayaking team readied for a warm-up run was an 18-year-old Alaskan kayaker, Barney Griffith. He wanted to run Devils Canyon and asked Brown and Blackadar if he could join the party.

There was no room, he was told. The trip was already too full as it was, but he was welcome to join them for the warm-up run on nearby Six Mile Creek. While kayaking with the team on the Six Mile, Griffith continued to press to go on the trip, but after he was unable to roll up after a spill, Blackadar firmly told him no.

Blackadar, however, wasn't dealing with an ordinary 18-year-old. He was dealing with the son of Dick Griffith.

Although Dick Griffith and Blackadar were close in age, Griffith had started running the big western rivers earlier than Blackadar, and in particular, he had run the Colorado River in a small wooden boat 19 years before Blackadar. Dick Griffith moved to Alaska in 1954, and soon after arriving, he started making long solo journeys across the vast wilderness of the interior, fighting off swarms of insects, brushing closely with grizzlies, and living off the land as he went.

With this kind of paternal background, Barney took up kayaking. From outward appearances, Barney just didn't look like a serious kayaker. He was "an excellent boater," Blackadar wrote, "but he wore a space helmet and had used an unfeathered paddle." Boating with an unfeathered paddle was almost un-heard of in whitewater kayaking, and was looked upon as unso-phisticated. Blackadar and those he kayaked with always used a feathered paddle in which the blades were offset to one an-other by 90 degrees. By offsetting the kayak paddle blades, wind resistance is cut down: as one blade digs into the water on a paddle stoke, the other blade planes through the air.

After Blackadar's refusals to have him on the trip, Barney stopped at John Spencer's house. It was obvious to Spencer that Griffith planned to run Devils Canyon one way or another.

"Barney," Spencer said jokingly, "why don't I fly you and your kayak up to High Lake." And Griffith replied in all seri-ousness, "That sounds great."

THE film crew and boaters took four days to float down the upper Susitna to the head of Devils Canyon. Bob Blackadar had been placed in charge of doing all the support work, including feeding the group. To help him, he brought along his girlfriend and future bride, Janice Judson. Running one of the rafts was a friend of Bob's, John Petit, and oaring the other raft was Victoria O'Laughlin, whom Blackadar asked to join the party at the last minute when it was realized that a third boat would be needed to carry all the people, supplies and food. Riders included wives, cameramen, and Brown's son, bringing the total to 15.

Once the party reached the canyon, a helicopter, by pre-arrangement, flew in to a small heli-spot that had been cleared several hundred feet above the river. Three additional camera-men, one of whom was Fletcher Anderson, were flown in from Anchorage to High Lake and transported by helicopter to the team's base camp near the heli-spot.

Additional food, alcohol, and supplies had also been flown in and were all shuttled to the camp close to the river. On one of the helicopter shuttles, the pilot handed Blackadar a note. It was from Barney Griffith:

> Walt, I am up at High Lake with the rest of the people. I have my kayak and am going to run the river. I need to know if I can run it with you guys. If not I will run it today. John [Spencer] will fly me in 3 miles above your camp, and I will float down from there. I scouted the river this morning with John from the banks. Please send answer.
>
> Barney Griffith

Blackadar was angered. It was clear from the letter that Griffith was serious. He was prepared to run Devil Creek Rapids—and he would run it before Blackadar and the rest of the team. Part of the attraction of the film was the fact that the team was making a "first"; Griffith could spoil it all. Griffith's approach was clever, and Blackadar and Brown felt they had no other choice than to invite the pesky kid.

But there was another reason for having him join them. "I had a long serious discussion with Walt," said Brown. "We felt it would be a lot safer for him to go with us because we had rescue methods and protection . . . . If the guy got killed and was somehow connected to us it would sour the whole project." Although Blackadar felt blackmailed by the teenager, he very much admired Griffith's pluck. Blackadar tore off a piece of a Summit Films package label, wrote a short note and gave it to the helicopter pilot:

> Barney
>
> Join us—Land upriver & boat down to my yellow & red boat across from Devil Cr. & climb up to camp. [A]nd we'll send chopper for Spencer if he wants to eat steak with us—
>
> Walt

Some of the other kayakers thought that Griffith's tactics were in poor taste. "Barney was in for the ego," said one. "He was a son of a bitch for doing that. It was an act as low as you can get and a sad commentary on his sense of ethics." Griffith, when asked about his stratagem, said, "In one way it was blackmail, but in another way it's a free river. Anyone can run it any time they want." Any differences were soon forgotten, and Barney settled in as an integral member of the kayaking team. "A common adversary as big as Devils Gorge," wrote Brown, "brings people together."

Some time before the kayakers started running the gorge, Blackadar had a talk with Fletcher Anderson. "You probably heard that I vetoed you on this trip," he told Anderson. Anderson said that he had. "Well, the reason I did it is because I want to get along with you, and we couldn't do that on the last trip. Also, you look better in a kayak than I do, and I want to be the hero." Anderson wasn't sure if Blackadar had meant his flattering words, but the tête-a-tête seemed to clear the air between the two. Although Anderson would later take jabs at Blackadar in print, he also, when asked, would defend Blackadar and, in particular, Blackadar's accomplishments on the Alsek.

When Anderson wrote about his impressions of the 1976 Susitna trip, he described Blackadar as two people: "Walt the hero kayaker" and "Walt the human being." Anderson immensely preferred the latter. But the latter hadn't made Blackadar famous, and even some of his old friends felt that the new media attention he had attracted had changed him. "Kayaking is a team effort," said Hazelwood, "but something different was happening here. It seemed that each kayaker was pitted against each other. Walt was really into making movies. He was turning into an actor, yelling 'Quiet on the set' and being perfectly serious about it. It just didn't seem like he was the same guy."

Hazelwood didn't like the atmosphere, and he didn't like what he saw in Devil Creek Rapids. "It was the kind of rapids you can die in . . . nasty holes, a bad run out, really a mess." The next day, Hazelwood decided not to run. Blackadar called Hazelwood's decision an "agonizing" one, but "I respected him for it," he wrote, "and I still do!"

The weather was perfect. Brown was delighted. Early in the morning, he had the helicopter move the cameramen into position. Fletcher Anderson was dropped off on a small rocky island on one edge of the rapids. Another cameraman was positioned above and another below the rapids, and Brown would shoot from the helicopter. The first descent of a rapids had never had such complete film coverage.

"Even more perhaps than the others," Blackadar wrote, "I felt committed and somewhat trapped. I had to run it no matter what! As the tension mounted I knew that I would head down the center of the biggest wave." Blackadar carefully scouted out the rapids. "The entrance is vast," he described. "With few landmarks in the huge river, one could become lost, but by weaving a route through the big rocks I knew I could stay oriented. Beyond that was the roostertail which plunged into the abyss."

Blackadar pushed off. From above in the helicopter Brown watched: "His boat was tiny in the big river, a beautiful red projectile that would carry his mind into his body and his body into the biggest 'Maytag' of his most horrible dreams."

Blackadar seemed to lose sight of his entrance in the rapids and hesitated. "Walt's loneliness must have been excruciating," Brown continued. "He eddied in behind a rock, paddled upstream, looked down, searched, hesitated, searched again, and moved back into the current, and off a drop between two larger rocks. Now he was committed to the line down the center between the giant waves."

"A piece of driftwood in an ocean storm" is the metaphoric expression that one of his boating friends liked to use when describing the feeling of paddling a kayak in big whitewater. The images recorded by Brown's camera show just that. As Blackadar in his kayak hits the Roostertail, as the gray water rains down from above, and as he is tossed into the deep abyss beyond, one thinks of the fragility of his craft and the helplessness of his position under the grip of a power far greater than he. He is, indeed, tossed like a derelict ship in a fierce ocean storm. "I thought my boat would punch through . . . how wrong I was," he wrote later.

Blackadar rose up toward the top of the Roostertail. His boat pointed nearly vertically as it climbed the mammoth wave, and still the wave was higher than his 13-foot-long boat.

The wave stopped his momentum and collapsed on top of him, throwing him over backwards. The wave, fortunately, did not hold him, and he slipped through and rolled up easily. Then, caught in a strong current, he wobbled through a series of haystacks, and his mind reeled.

"Rollups and rollups, flips on flips, blurred my mind into a drunken stupor from which thought ceased and reflexes died," Blackadar wrote.

From Brown's position, he could see that the terrible ride was sapping Blackadar's energy. "Each successive roll weakened [him]," said Brown. "He stopped completing his stroke, and then he began pulling his head out first to get air. He came up on his side, sculled and sucked in air; but he didn't have the strength to get all the way up. Suddenly a big wave knocked him upright, but he was too dizzy to take advantage of it."

The weakened Blackadar capsized again. The current swept him into the Nozzle, and facing upstream, he came through a few last waves and washed into the right side eddy.

"I tried every roll I had," he said later, in a voice laden with weariness. "I just couldn't make it. And I used every breath I had, and I couldn't make it." Finally, totally exhausted, Blackadar came out of his boat.

"Watching from the helicopter," wrote Brown, "I saw him, and then I didn't. Something was pulling him under, Mae West [life jacket] and all. Whirlpools. I panicked and threw down the rope. The rotor blades seemed to clip foliage from the cliffs as we hovered over him. He grabbed the near vertical shore rocks, then reached for his boat, broke loose, and sucked under again. Finally, he accepted the rope, and we lifted him out of the water and onto the shore." Blackadar managed to hang onto his paddle, but his boat was caught by the current and disappeared down the river.

Blackadar had barely survived his run. Alarmed at what he had just witnessed, Brown thought it too dangerous for the others to attempt any further runs. "I radioed the ground crew that I didn't want anyone else to run it, that it was suicide . . . ." Despite Brown's message, the four others had been mentally preparing for the run all that morning. They were poised, ready, and intended to kayak it. Cully Erdman, disregarding the warning, pushed off.

Erdman took a different route than Blackadar, entering on the left side. Once into the rapids, he used a technique in which he approached the big waves sideways, as he had learned to do on the ocean surf. The technique worked. Erdman rolled twice, the last one in the Nozzle, but he maintained a reserve of energy and paddled off to the shore. Blackadar had been the first to run the rapid, but Erdman had been the first to run it and not swim.

John Dondero ran next, following a route similar to Blackadar's. He hit the Roostertail and went over. "'Oh, my God, how did I get over here,'" Dondero remembers thinking to himself. "The hole started to windmill me, end over end inside the wave. People from the outside couldn't see. It was pinning me back up against the deck of the boat, then it would slap me forward on the deck." He rolled up and was knocked around and finally capsized again in the Nozzle.

John had trained for weeks before going on the Susitna trip, but when he reached the Nozzle, he was exhausted. "A whirl-pool opened up [on the left eddy line]. It sucked my boat under water. I reached up with the paddle and couldn't feel any water. By then I was starting to black out." Dondero came out of his boat, but a favorable current washed him and his boat over to the safer right shore. Slowly and weakly, he pulled himself up out of the water and onto the rocks.

Billy Ward followed Dondero in what was nearly a flawless run with no rolls. Elated, he pulled off onto the left. Brown, from the helicopter, waved him across the river. Dondero, who was still recovering and sitting along the bank, saw Ward start to paddle across. The left eddy line harbored the whirlpool which had caused Dondero's swim.

Dondero yelled to him not to cross. Ward, not hearing him, neared the eddy line, and then a whirlpool appeared, sucking his boat under like it had suddenly become a lead weight. Ward's boat completely disappeared under the river, out of the sight of the others. Then Ward popped up, and the boat, several feet away, also bobbed up. "I threw the line," Brown said, "but before it reached him he disappeared over a drop. When I saw him again he was motionless. Then he was sucked under again. Luck saved him at that point. He popped up against the shore, grabbed hold and pulled himself out." His boat was swept away, disappearing as did Blackadar's down the river.

Next up was Barney Griffith. Concerned about Barney's safety, Brown asked Blackadar whether they should rethink allowing the 18-year-old to run it. Blackadar went back upriver and carefully checked Barney's life jacket and harness. Like the others, he knew that Barney wanted to run the rapids. "I knew he had the right to go. He had earned it . . . ."

Most of the day had been taken up in filming the previous runs, and the sun was low, shining into Barney Griffith's eyes as he started his run. "He looked more vulnerable," Brown wrote. "Knowing about his lack of experience, his youth and his possible guilt, my stomach knotted. He is only a child, I thought, only five years older than my son."

Griffith, the most inexperienced boater of the group, approached Devil Creek Rapids with much the same kind of spirit that governed Blackadar's kayaking. What he lacked in technique, he made up with determination. With his motorcycle helmet and unfeathered paddle, Barney Griffith dropped into the rapids. His style wasn't smooth or pretty, and he missed a couple of rolls, but he made it, paddling to the right side of the Nozzle and avoiding the whirlpools. He was at the end, said Brown, "frightened, exhausted, and happy."

❋   ❋

"When I got out of that water," Blackadar said, describing the end of his run, "I was all done paddling. I wasn't going to paddle again. I couldn't cross over there. I was just . . . just completely beat." Despite being completely drained, Blackadar wanted another try at the rapids, and he and Ward enlisted the help of John Spencer and the helicopter pilot in locating and recovering their kayaks. Blackadar's was located washed onto shore a couple of miles below Devil Creek and retrieved by the helicopter. Spencer located Ward's boat near Gold Creek, 25 miles below the rapids. Tying it to his float, he flew it back up to the group.

"I'm sure glad to be back with my boat," Blackadar said, the tape recorder picking up his slow, deliberate voice, "and I'm sure glad to have the chance to run it tomorrow. And I'm going through the same damn place."

The next day, the weather deteriorated, and not being suitable for filming, the time was used to helicopter all the equipment and non-kayakers to a camp just below the Pearly Gates at the end of the canyon. The sky remained clouded following the camp move. The budget was nearly spent (in fact, Brown wrote Blackadar later saying the trip expenses had exceeded what was allocated), and if any more runs were going to be made, they had to be done that day.

Although Blackadar had taken a beating in Devil Creek, he was willing to risk another. He had nothing to be ashamed of in his first run. Two other young men, fit and in their prime, swam at the bottom of the rapids as he did. Nonetheless, Blackadar had to try it one more time.

That he might not get another chance was one of the reasons why he returned to the canyon in the first place. "I know I'm getting a little older," he says in the film version which appeared on television, "and I know I won't be able to do it too many more years."

He also may have wanted a second chance as a matter of pride. He had organized the trip. He was the first one to run the canyon. He wanted to put on a good show for ABC, and perhaps he thought he could make a run without the blemish of a swim. Perhaps, too, he yearned for that feeling of sharpness of mind and responsiveness of body that he had felt and described in his last run of Lava Falls. Whatever it was, the cameras were readied, and he pushed off again, pointing toward the "same damn place."

He had better control at the top of the rapids on this run, he later wrote: "[I] hit the big roostertail to the left and rode safely over the biggest of all of the waves. This plummeted me into the only wave that I had missed on the first run and unfortunately I hit this head-on and was pinwheeled mercilessly. My roll brought me up on the crest where, on a perfect surf, I scooted across the river like an express train."

The suddenness of his rapid surf across the river disoriented him, and he flipped over. "From there the old familiar pattern took over, with each roll up followed by an equally quick flip back in. At the Nozzle, my spray skirt was half off, and I went in backwards."

He knew that he wanted to be in the right side eddy. He had seen enough whirlpool action on the left to know that it was a poor place to be. He lunged towards the right eddy as he flipped over again. With his spray skirt partially off, his boat began filling with water. He reached out to the surface with his paddle and made a sweep. The boat rose a little, but then fell back over to its upside down position.

In the relatively calm right side eddy, the wild ride was

over, and his boat floated, slowly turning in the gentle currents and swirls. But Blackadar was again drained, and as his energy ebbed away, he again reached to the surface of the river and swept his paddle.

Brown's film captures the agonizing struggle of an exhausted man in a small boat in a large gray river. Trying again, from his upside down position, Blackadar slowly sweeps his paddle and then falls back down. Again and again he makes weak attempts to roll. The scene which appeared on television is terrifying and stark: a lonely struggle with a harsh, powerful foe.

Although he never made the suggestion, it is possible that his injured shoulder weakened his roll. Indeed, if the shoulder wasn't adversely affecting his roll it would have been surprising, for over the next two years he would have increasing problems with it, and he would even, for a time, lose the ability to roll. What is sure by viewing the film is that his rolling technique is poor. The weakness in his technique which Barb Wright had recognized at the very beginning of his kayaking is exaggerated in the film. He does not allow his hips to bring the boat under him; instead he makes long sweeps, his hips move little, and, as a consequence, neither does the boat.

"I took one little feeble stroke," says Blackadar in the *American Sportsman* program, "because I was out of breath completely. I was rather surprised when I didn't roll up. And when I missed my fifth, sixth, seventh or eighth roll . . . either get out . . . or die in my boat."

Finally, he pushed out of the kayak. The eddy swirled him and his boat towards the shore. John Dondero, along the river, helped him out of the water. His ordeal was over.

Cully Erdman also tried a second run at Devil Creek Rapids. His spray skirt came off, and he flipped over in the boiling water on the left Nozzle eddy and swam. The currents were in his favor, and he was safely swept to the side of the river. Clearly, from the performances of the kayakers, Devil Creek Rapids is a humbling stretch of whitewater, but Bob Blackadar and John Petit, who had watched the runs, wanted to try to oar their raft down the far right-hand sneak.

Their run, though not without its share of excitement, went as expected for the first raft attempt of Devil Creek Rapids. At the beginning, the raft barely fit through the slot between the rocky island and the ledge along the right shore. Slipping through, it dropped over each of the six-to-eight-foot falls, and as it bumped over each falls, the boat filled with more and more water. By the time the boat reached the large haystack waves above the Nozzle, it was so full of water that Bob struggled with the oars to keep it under control. Pulling hard on one of the oars, it snapped out of its oarlock, and the boat spun out of control through the Nozzle. Replacing the oar and regaining control, they lined the raft up and ran smoothly through the next rapids, Hotel Rock.

While these runs were being made, Roger Hazelwood had been sitting in his boat at the bottom of Devil Creek Rapids ready to paddle out in the river if one of the kayakers ran into trouble. Although he had decided against running the first rapids, he planned to run the rest. Blackadar watched him paddle out of the Nozzle eddy into the current.

Still tired, Blackadar had nearly abandoned plans of running any more of the river. "I had lost my self-confidence, not only in myself, but in my roll," he wrote. A year before, Blackadar on the Colorado trip talked about fear on the river. He said that while in a rapids, he never felt fear. It was after running a particularly stressful rapids, after he had a chance to think about what he had just done, that the full realization of the danger struck him: "When the actual fear sensation sets in I'm all done and I may be done for three or four days before I'm calm . . . ."

But as he watched Hazelwood leaning into his eddy turn, something quickly snapped him out of it. Hazelwood was in trouble. His spray skirt had ripped, and his boat began filling with water. The boat, now unresponsive with its heavy load of water, carried Hazelwood toward Hotel Rock. It was almost a repeat of Hazelwood's 1972 run with Blackadar when they both had been washed over the giant rock.

Blackadar, who had been lying on the ground, jumped up and yelled to Dondero, "Let's go get him." Leaping into his boat, he charged out into the current and after his friend.

Hazelwood tried to paddle to the right side of the hole, but his ponderous boat remained on its course in midstream. Falling upside down, Hazelwood dropped into the hole. Coming out of his boat, he swirled around in its foamy depths and then washed out below, finally swimming to the side. Blackadar followed, ran the hole successfully and paddled to the side of Hazelwood. The emergency was, according to Blackadar, "the best thing that ever happened to me . . . from then on my fears were gone and my self-confidence restored."

Roger, who was unhurt, floated off to the side into the calm water following Hotel Rock and was greeted by the waiting rafters and the rest of the kayakers who had planned to run the lower canyon. Because of his ripped spray skirt, Hazelwood could go no further in a kayak, and he disappointedly joined the two oarsmen in their raft. The raft, however, offered little security. At the next major rapids, Screaming Left Hand Turn, John Petit was at the oars of the raft when they hit a hole near the top, throwing the bow of the raft up and over. As the boat tumbled upside down, it flipped Bob Blackadar into the air, and Hazelwood did a back somersault over the stern.

Hazelwood, now in the cold river for a second time, came up under the capsized raft. As it washed through several holes, he managed to swim out, climb on the derelict boat, and hold on as it careened down two or three more miles of large waves, finally to be stopped by the kayakers.

Because the more difficult Pearly Gates Rapids remained, the helicopter was called to carry out the raft and its passengers. Bob Blackadar, the only missing rafter, was found on a ledge alongside Screaming Left Hand Turn and was also helicoptered to the lower camp.

Together all the kayakers ran through the last wild stretch of the gorge. They floated out of the canyon screaming in delight: "Walt said it was big. He was right, it *was* big in there." "It was some of the biggest stuff I've ever run." "I'll never forget it." When the five kayakers reached the lower camp below Pearly Gates, the tension was off, the filming complete, and they and the rest of the party celebrated late into the night.

※   ※

SOMETIME after the Susitna trip, explained Cully Erdman, Blackadar was sitting in a car with several of the other kayakers: "We were passing around joints, getting loaded, partying and telling stories. A mosquito was flying around in the car and Walt said, 'Wait, I'll get it.' He pulled out a bottle of Raid and doused the mosquito." The car was so filled with insecticide that the doors were thrown open, and everyone poured out.

"Walt, isn't this bad for our health?" Cully asked.

"I got the mosquito, didn't I?" Blackadar replied.

Cully Erdman, who had probably impressed Blackadar most with his kayaking style in big water, enjoyed his style. "He was on our level," Erdman said, "He was always a personable, fun-loving guy."

Although the fun-loving Blackadar had not been pleased about swimming in the Nozzle eddy twice, any lingering wounded pride passed quickly, and two and a half months after he returned from Alaska, he was already thinking about new filming possibilities. The Susitna, he realized, had been an expensive project, and Blackadar suggested a much cheaper idea to Brown. How about the first run of Selway Falls in Idaho? Blackadar proposed. Brown replied that it sounded interesting, and that he would talk to the series producer at ABC about it. Actually, it would be a year before another film project would come through, and in the meantime Blackadar would return to the Susitna for one last shot at its implacable rapids.

*   *

IN February of 1977, ABC aired the segment of running Devils Canyon on *American Sportsman*. Blackadar already had seen a version prepared by Roger Brown, but ostensibly because of time limits, the original version was cut in size. "All of us were very chagrined at the final cut of ABC's show," wrote Blackadar to a friend. "When Summit Films turned it over to ABC it was a fantastic production. But it got into a mixmaster, came out with a series of bits and pieces which really treated all of the boaters very shabbily except for me . . . ." The little time given to the other kayakers bothered him. "It was a team effort," he wrote to Dee Crouch, "& should have been recognized as such."

In order to fit in 10 to 15 minutes of air time, however, documentary film editors had to pare down the extraneous material. Having too many personalities at the center of attention muddles the film. Rob Lesser, who has been in a number of documentary kayaking films, agrees: "You don't want a whole bunch of people there because it complicates everything. It just does not get a clear message across."

Blackadar, because of his background and strong film presence, was very much the center of the show. Even in "bits and pieces," as Blackadar put it, the show was a graphically visual depiction of the great natural forces involved in big water kayaking. Moreover, running throughout, side by side to the major theme that Blackadar and his companions are risking their lives, a less obvious secondary theme gives the film more compelling, emotional substance: it is the struggle, mental and physical, that Blackadar wages at 53 years of age to stay at the top of the sport and run the world's biggest whitewater.

At the end of the segment he is talking, facing the camera alongside the river. He has a smile, but it is not his characteristic wide grin which curves broadly across his face during genuine moments of joy. His raised cheeks are tan and wind burned.

He speaks, shaking his head now and then: "I'm coming back, but I hope I'm younger. She's a big one. And I don't know. I gave her everything I had. I haven't got anything better than that. I tried and tried and tried. And I can't try any harder. And I think . . . I'll be back."

He will be back.

XII

Through the Night

DURING THE FIRST PART of 1977, Blackadar began putting together a team of kayakers for another Susitna attempt. There would be no cameras this time, no helicopters, no large support group. It would be Blackadar and a few friends, just like his first attempt in 1972.

His need to return may have come from a feeling of unfinished business or a simple compulsion to make a clean run of Devil Creek Rapids without a swim. He may also have felt obligated to return because he had claimed on national television that he would, though it seems far more likely that he was drawn back to the Susitna for more personal reasons. At the time, the rapids had taken on symbolic proportions, looming as his life's greatest obstacle, and if he could only overcome it completely, as he had overcome Turnback Canyon, he would taste again of that sweet wine of true accomplishment.

Kayaking, the culmination of all of his outdoor sports, always presented one more challenge. His life's other great passion, medicine, was like kayaking in that respect, with one difference: surmounting the great challenges of medicine wasn't always so clear-cut. In kayaking, he either ran the rapids or he didn't. Medicine's pathway, however, was littered with ambiguities; no matter how hard he might work, some patients lingered with incurable diseases. With Devil Creek, the pathway was clear: all he had to do was to make one good run.

Blackadar's third journey down the Susitna might not have even taken place had it not been for Rob Lesser. Lesser, the son of a Boise physician, had been working in Alaska the last several summers. He had boated with Blackadar just once in 1970 on Pine Creek Rapids, but along with other Idaho and Alaska boaters, including John Spencer, he had slowly been putting in an apprenticeship. By 1976 he was ready to begin his own ascent in the kayaking world. Eager to join Blackadar in the 1976 Susitna trip, he stopped by Lori Kincaid's house in Anchorage while the group was making trip preparations, but there was no room for any extra kayakers, and he hadn't been invited in the first place. Not discouraged, he decided at the time that he would organize his own, small, self-contained group and attempt the river the following year.

As the summer of 1977 went on, Blackadar experienced difficulties organizing parties for both the Susitna and the easier Tatshenshini River. He had heard about Rob Lesser's trip, and shortly before Lesser was to leave, Blackadar called him. Could he join Lesser's Susitna group? he asked. Lesser said yes and agreed to pick Blackadar up at the Anchorage airport later in July.

✳   ✳

LESSER'S party consisted of two others, Al Lowande and Ron Frye. Lowande was a strong kayaker from New Jersey who would eventually move to Coeur d'Alene, Idaho, for a teaching job. Ron Frye, also a teacher, lived in New Meadows, a small town on the west edge of the central Idaho wilderness. He paddled a covered canoe (C-1) and was, at the time, Idaho's only C-1 boater. Coming from a strong whitewater canoeing tradition in the East, Frye was a confident, reliable canoeist and among the top boaters living in the state. Frye, with his wife, Jill, left early, making the trip into an extended boating holiday and eventually rendezvousing with Lesser and Lowande near a Canadian river called the Stikine.

One stretch of rapids, the Grand Canyon of the Stikine, had been on Blackadar's mind for some time. Kay Swanson had first written to him about it in the summer of 1973. Swanson and Blackadar discussed making an attempt on the Grand Canyon of the Stikine in 1974, but it was early in that year that Julie Wilson drowned, and any Alaska plans were quickly forgotten. Film projects kept him busy the next few summers, but Blackadar's continuing interest in the canyon was evident in a letter he sent to Klaus Streckman in the early summer of 1977: "The more I think about the Stikine River the more enthusiastic I become. Also, Kay Swanson was here and shows real interest in the area and of course owns a Piper Cub [plane]. If he were to fly up he would probably fly our boat in gratis. This might solve some of our transportation problems. We will keep in touch."

Lesser had heard about the Stikine, and, together with Frye and Lowande, flew the canyon. What they saw put to rest any ideas of running it. It was an exceedingly dangerous stretch of whitewater.* After deciding against the Stikine, Lesser's group then worked its way north, running rivers here and there. At Anchorage they stopped at the airport to pick up Blackadar, who obviously had drunk too much on the flight over.

That was the last Blackadar had to drink until getting off the Susitna. "He took the Susitna damn seriously," said Ron Frye, who was Blackadar's tentmate for the trip and who was in a position to see if the doctor was drinking. All three of Blackadar's companions were sure that he had not taken any

---

*Lesser eventually did run the Stikine with a team he had organized for an ABC *American Sportsman* segment aired in 1981. He feels it is more difficult than the Susitna or Alsek.

alcohol along. Certainly, it was obvious that at this point in his life Blackadar had problems with alcohol. Some of his hunting friends in Salmon described trips in the fifties and sixties where the wild doctor drank until he would throw up. When he visited his daughter in California, he retired to the house for a drink after splitting wood and "in no time he'd have a stiff on and be out." Alcohol was a means for him to unwind, he told his worried daughter, and he could give it up when he wanted. "If I ever say I can't stop," he said, "then I'll know I'm in trouble—and then I will give it up." For the Susitna, at least, he had given it up.

The small party took four days floating down to Devils Canyon. Blackadar, who had always been the life of the party on past trips, seemed reserved and distant to Lowande: "It was almost like he had some fatalistic attitude towards boating at that point. He didn't seem real confident—and with good reason. His shoulder had been hurting him, and he'd been taking cortisone shots." Blackadar's shoulder bothered him enough that he even carried a supply of cortisone with him on the trip.

"He was real enthused about the possibility of seeing a bear," remembered Frye. On the way the group did come across a bear in the river while they were floating. Blackadar paddled over towards the bear while the others moved a safe distance away. "The big difference between him and us," said Frye, "was that he wanted to get close to the bear, and we wanted to make damn sure we didn't get close to it." The other thing that Frye remembered vividly about Blackadar was trying to sleep in the same tent with him. "He snored like a son of a bitch. We'd always sleep feet to head so I could get as far away from the noise as I could."

Finally they reached Devil Creek Rapids. The water was as high as Blackadar had seen it. His three companions, awed at the sight of the intimidating rapids, started investigating possible sneak routes on the right. But even the right side looked dangerous. The ledges cutting across the route formed symmetrical holes which could entrap a kayak. Blackadar made up his mind. He would go right down the middle of the big current on the left side of the rapids.

After looking at the rapids, Ron walked above their camp looking for Jill, who had flown in to High Camp to watch and take movies of the group. Jill, hiking alone down through two and a half miles of the bear-inhabited tundra and spruce forest, reached the cliff band near the rapids, but not seeing Ron or the other kayakers, she decided to return to the safety of High Lake. The next day, Ron still had not located his wife. Concerned about her and not anxious to run the rapids, he decided not to run any further.

He taped up the cockpit of his boat, sealing it from water leakage, and pushed it off above the rapids, hoping to pick it up someplace below the canyon. He then left for High Lake, still uncertain about what had happened to his wife. When he reached High Lake, he found her, sitting comfortably in one of the warm cabins.

Meanwhile, back at Devil Creek Rapids, Al Lowande pushed off. He had planned to run the far right side, the same route taken by Bob Blackadar and John Petit in their raft the year before. At the top of the run, he intended to stop and get off on the slender rock island for a second look at the route and possibly carry part of the rapids if necessary. Lesser and Blackadar waited above.

Blackadar had decided that since each of the boaters could do little to help the other, they should run about 10 minutes apart. But this wide spacing didn't make any sense. Even though there was little one could do in the main part of Devil Creek Rapids, someone still upright in the Nozzle eddy might be able to help tow a swimming companion to the shore and save a terrifying run through Hotel Rock.

Lowande, thinking about it later, called the plan "stupidity" which he attributed to everyone's nervousness: "We were so psyched out that we just weren't thinking."

"[Devil Creek Rapids] is a situation where you are so preoccupied with the enormity of the rapids, it tends to dominate your mind," said Lesser. "You don't see the little things." Lowande, entering the rapids, planned to cut into a small eddy in order to stop at the island and climb out, but he misjudged the entry, missed the eddy and dropped into one of the symmetrical ledge holes. The hole caught Lowande off guard. Suddenly he found himself trapped and tossed around like a wobbling toy top.

"I was half out of my boat from being thrown around in there," Lowande described. "I got out [of my boat]. I was exhausted." Lowande then started a swim which, up to that time, was the worst anyone had taken in Devil Creek Rapids. The big waves poured down on top of him, forcing him under the water: "I was trying to figure which way was up most of time. I didn't know where the surface was. I was head over heels. By the time I got through the Nozzle I could not get air. I didn't have any strength left at all. I couldn't even move my legs. The only time in the whole swim I remember being above water for a noticeable period was in the glassy tongue leading into the Nozzle. It was amazing. I came up and saw that thing, clear as the day."

Neither Blackadar nor Lesser could see below the top part of the rapids and had no idea of the perilous swim that Lowande was taking. He was a strong boater, and they figured that he would run the sneak and wait for them at the bottom.

Lesser took off next, heading for the right side. Surprised at how quickly the current propelled him towards the ledge drop which had caught Lowande, he paddled quickly and managed to catch the small eddy and climb up on the island. He had planned to take pictures of Blackadar, but the more he thought about it, the more he realized that if Blackadar had trouble he could do little to help him from shore. Returning to his boat, Rob ran the right-hand channel, barely missing the last dangerous ledge drop. He paddled off to the side just above the Nozzle and waited in an eddy.

Blackadar started off, staying with his plan to run down the middle of the rapids. "By the time he got to me," said Lesser, "he was rolling or trying to roll. He was not doing very well. He went into the Nozzle, still in his boat, but it threw him over. He didn't try any more rolls in the Nozzle."

Lesser saw Blackadar eject from his boat and grab hold of a rope which he had tied to a small life jacket. Apparently Blackadar had tied the spare life jacket to the grab loop of his kayak as a means of staying close to his boat. But it caused more trouble than it was worth. The boat swirled around behind him, pulling against the rope and jerking his arm and his shoulder back. The force injured his shoulder again, and the rope burned and cut into his hands. The rope connected to his boat snapped, and Blackadar spun away from his kayak and flushed down the river towards Hotel Rock.

This was his third swim in the Nozzle. It seemed that he, like a Jack London character, the old fighter Tom King, had only a finite number of fights in him and only a finite number of challenges in big water. When he had fought them all, that was it. No one could fault him, though. He had fought this one as he had the others, with exceptional courage. He said he would come back, and here he was, at it again, "going through the same damn place."

He had also said that when he came back he hoped that he was younger. But it didn't work that way. He wasn't any younger, his endurance not any better, his shoulders not any stronger, and his swim not any less frightening as the current pushed him over the swells of gray water and into the great crashing hole of Hotel Rock.

Fortune had been on Lowande's side. Sometime before Blackadar's swim, the current washed him up on a rock ledge below Hotel Rock. He lay on the shore, panting and throwing up water, half in shock from his swim. "I turned around and saw Walt silently float by," said Lowande. "He wasn't yelling for help. He wasn't making any movements. He was floating on his back face up. I thought he was dead."

There was nothing Lowande could do. He had no boat, and even if he had, he was in no condition to try to reach Blackadar. Prone and exhausted, he remained on the shore as Blackadar disappeared downriver.

While Blackadar had been swimming, Lesser had portaged around the last part of the Nozzle, and, upon finding Lowande's, Blackadar's and Frye's boats all floating around the Nozzle eddy, he realized that all of his companions were in serious trouble and that he was the only one still in a boat. He pushed the loose kayaks out of the eddy and into the current and maneuvered quickly down through Hotel Rock, finding Lowande on shore.

Lowande told Lesser that Blackadar was probably dead and that he should go downstream to try to find him. Lowande, recovered enough to walk, started slowly hiking up out of the canyon, hoping to regroup with Ron and Jill Frye at High Lake.

Continuing for another mile, Lesser came upon Blackadar, laying half in and half out of the water. Fortune had been on his side also. He was alive. He had survived another bruising fight. "He was wheezing on the shore," said Lesser, when he arrived. "He was almost comatose." Staying with Blackadar for a couple of hours, Lesser waited as he began to regain his strength. When he seemed adequately rested, Lesser gave Blackadar his map, some of his clothes and insect repellent in a blue plastic bag. The weary Blackadar left Lesser and began to climb out of the canyon heading for High Lake, just as Lowande had done earlier.

❋   ❋

RON and Jill Frye were sitting in one of the cabins when they thought they heard someone yell from the landing strip. Looking outside, they didn't see anything and thought it might have been a noise from the sow bear that they had heard earlier. Actually, the noise came from Lowande. He had reached the landing strip. Hot and sweating in his wet suit (which he kept on to save himself from the mosquitos), Lowande had collapsed from a leg cramp and laid on the runway, hidden from the Fryes in the tall grass. Finally, his cramp subsided, and he limped to the cabin. Explaining what he knew, Al told the Fryes the grim news that Blackadar had probably drowned.

The pilot who had flown Jill Frye in earlier began to fly each member of the group out of High Lake to Talkeetna in his small Super Cub. On one of the runs he spotted Lesser, and, upon landing on the river, he learned that Rob had successfully run the rest of the canyon. The pilot reported the good news to Frye, the last person left at High Lake, that both Lesser and Blackadar were fine and that Blackadar was climbing out of the canyon. Frye waited for Blackadar, and every so often he fired a .44 pistol that the pilot had given him to help guide Blackadar to High Lake. At dusk, Frye looked out and was relieved to see Blackadar's form walking stiffly across the airstrip.

Going out to greet him, Frye was immediately taken back by the doctor's face. It was blue and luminescent.

"I wondered if he was having a heart attack," Frye said, "I didn't know if he knew that he was blue, and I didn't know whether to tell him or not."

Blackadar's blue face, they both discovered later, had come from the blue dye of the plastic bag, leached out by the leaking bottle of mosquito repellent. As Blackadar wiped his face with repellent, he had been painting himself blue.

Lesser collected all the boats at Gold Creek and took them back to Talkeetna where he rejoined the rest of the party. After a celebration at the Fairview Inn at which Blackadar broke his drinking ban, having a few drinks "for medicinal purposes," the group went their separate ways.

Even though his shoulder had been reinjured, Blackadar wasn't planning to leave Alaska yet. He had one more wilderness trip to take. Catching a plane, he was off to Juneau to start yet another journey, which would include a midnight raft ride across the stormy seas of the Gulf of Alaska.

❊   ❊

SOUTH and west of the Gulf of Alaska lies the great curving dome of the Pacific Ocean. For thousands of miles, there is nothing but salt water. Even traveling at speeds of hundreds of miles per hour, jet passengers sit for monotonous hours flying over the expansive ocean on the flight between Anchorage and Tokyo. Where the Alsek River enters the Gulf of Alaska at Dry Bay, there are no protecting islands to block the weather which rolls across the northern seas, and, in fact, the mainland coast of southeast Alaska is exposed to the full force of the Pacific storms except in the south where it is protected by the series of large islands making up the Alexander Archipelago.

The hundred miles of open ocean extending south between Dry Bay and Cape Spencer, which marks the beginning of the protected waters of the Alexander Archipelago, is not a place to be in a small raft. Throughout a good part of the stretch, the seas break into a broken, rocky shore, and there are few safe places to land. It was, nonetheless, across this hundred mile stretch that Blackadar wanted to try to take rafts.

Blackadar had no seafaring experience in his background, but the idea of floating down a river and boating back to civilization by way of the ocean appealed to him. His idea was to run the Tatshenshini River which flows into the lower Alsek. At Dry Bay, Blackadar planned to have Layton Bennett fly in two outboard motors which would be used to propel the rafts, following a course close to the shoreline, around Cape Spencer into Cross Sound, past the spectacular Glacier Bay area, through Icy Strait, and on to Juneau, a distance of 175 miles. It was a circular journey, starting in Juneau with a ferry ride, and ending in Juneau, with the St. Elias wilderness and the great glaciated

228

coastline of southeast Alaska in between, traveling on land, river and sea. It was ambitious, adventurous, aesthetic, and dangerous. Just the perfect combination.

From the appearance of his early correspondence, Blackadar did not understand the full nature of the undertaking. In March of the year, he had written to Doug Wheat, a teacher and avid kayaker from Colorado, telling of his plans: "We are now contemplating using the raft on the open ocean and touring back by way of Glacier Bay National Monument . . . . There is probably sixty miles of open, unprotected ocean that would have to be boated. But the shoreline is kind and there is sand beach most of the way and if a storm comes up, I feel we would have no problem in beaching the rafts and kayaks and going ashore." As Blackadar would find out on the trip, however, there were few safe sandy beaches and practically no place to take refuge on shore.

Wheat was planning his own trip on the Tatshenshini, and Blackadar suggested that they combine groups. Having the same trouble as he did for the Susitna trip, Blackadar had only interested one other person in his trip, and combining with Wheat bolstered the size of the group. When Blackadar arrived in Juneau, he joined a party consisting largely of Colorado boaters put together by Wheat: Gary Young and John Wilhelm, who were both involved in a river guiding business out of Colorado; Tom Johnson, who kept a detailed diary of the trip; and Dieter Weck, who was the only other member of the party close to Blackadar's age. Weck, a German baker living in Colorado Springs, was planning to prepare donuts, cake, pizza, and other delectable pastries, not a simple task on the wet banks of an Alaskan river. Several others from Colorado joined the trip, bringing the total to 10.

The group took the Alaska Ferry to Haines and hired a driver to take them to the start of the Tatshenshini off the Alaskan Highway. Since the put-in is on Canadian soil, they stopped at a customs entry port on the Haines Road. The customs official, looking over the group which appeared particularly ragged in their outdoor wear, called for a thorough search. Packs were emptied and sleeping bags unrolled.

"Walt was indignant," said Wheat. "He was telling him [the customs official] off." Everyone was tense during the search, and Blackadar certainly had reason to be concerned. After nothing was found and the official let the group continue, Blackadar reached into his gear and pulled out a book with a false center. Inside was his pistol and a bag of marijuana. "If you guys need anything," he told his stunned companions staring at the book, "I've got it."

It wasn't Blackadar's only disregard for Canadian authority. He had also brought along a gill net, which he would use to catch salmon for dinner while on the river. The procedure was and is illegal, but Blackadar was a curious mix: an ardent environmentalist with disdain for authority. At one point on the trip, a helicopter flew low overhead as the gill net was in place. The helicopter was thought by the party to be returning to pick up some Fish and Game officers they had passed earlier. Again, the group was tense and "unnerved," for the distinctive floats of the net could easily be spotted by an observant game officer. The helicopter moved in closer and started to settle down for a landing.

"I had no affection for going to jail," wrote Tom Johnson, describing the experience. After hovering for about a half minute, the copter inexplicably took off, and, to everyone's relief, disappeared. The net was removed from the water and hidden in the bottom of a waterproof bag. But the next morning the net had again found its way back out in the water, and an eight-to-nine pound silver salmon was caught, filleted and broiled for breakfast. Salmon continued to supplement their meals throughout the trip.

Blackadar told the others that if the helicopter had landed he would have gone out with them. He was terribly sore, he said. His shoulder ached, his hands hurt, with the deep cuts of rope marks still showing from trying to hold the line attached to his boat in the Nozzle eddy. To top it off, early on the Tatshenshini trip, he had banged his knee trying to free a boat caught on some rocks, and it was now sore and swollen.

Despite his physical ailments, he rowed the raft and traded off in the kayaks as they made their way down the river. At night while Dieter prepared pastries, Blackadar entertained the group with stories of his most recent Susitna trip. "It was the Susitna that really obsessed him," said Gary Young. "It consumed the conversation the whole time [early on the trip]. He wanted to go back and try it again. It was one river that was not going to beat him."

Blackadar also bragged about his prowess with a pistol. Rising one night early on the trip, he seized his .44 and told the others he would prove his skill to them. "Reeling around, he tells us to throw beer cans up in the air," said Wheat, "which we did obediently, cautioning him to please go easy. Here he is— the perfect Lee Marvin, Cat Ballou-type drunk—weaving and bobbing. Everyone [else in the group] is hiding and crouching down. And he hit every one of those beer cans. He hit them in midair . . . ."

As the party neared Dry Bay, the current eased into the large lake that has formed below Alsek Glacier. While they drifted around the lake and marveled at the silent, blue icebergs released by the glacier and floating like giant chips of broken china, they collected pieces of ice to replenish their coolers. On the way out of the lake, Blackadar climbed from the raft onto one of the small icebergs and stood on top of it, riding down the river for several miles. "I'm having a blast," he yelled to the others before he was picked up. The real blast was yet to come.

❊   ❊

By coincidence, Klaus Streckman was also on the Tatshenshini that week, coming upon Blackadar and his group on the lower

231

river. When hearing of Blackadar's plans to motor out across the ocean, Klaus was enthused and asked to join them. Blackadar democratically cleared it with the others, assuring them that Streckman was good in emergencies and a strong addition to their party. Already, some members of the group were realizing that traveling across the open ocean would not be a picnic, so Klaus was welcomed in.

The fishermen working at the small Dry Bay fish camp scoffed at the plan, warning that the trip was foolish. One of the major problems, the fishermen told them, was the winds which come from the southeast, sometimes appearing as frequently as three times a week. A raft with a small outboard trying to make its way south could not travel against such winds and would be blown in the opposite direction. Doug Wheat said later that at the time he "was very apprehensive about the ocean and I voted against it." On the other hand, the majority wanted to try it, and from the fish camp, Blackadar radioed Layton Bennett to fly in some extra supplies and the two 20-horse Mercury motors which had been left at the airport.

When the plane arrived, Gary Young remembers being perturbed when they started pulling out the supplies which consisted of "mostly booze and Wyler's lemonade and very little food. That was about the only time we got pissed at him," Young said. They were counting on having plenty of rations for the trip.

Blackadar continued to tell the group not to worry, and if they had any problems, they'd just go to the shore and beach the boats. Blackadar had even brought a crab pot along, which would help supplement meals. The two rafts were lashed together and the motors mounted in place. With a favorable weather forecast—winds from the west—the eight people climbed on board the two 16-foot-long rafts, crowding in among cans of gas, food, beer, waterproof bags, camping gear, Blackadar's crab pot, and three kayaks.

They carefully motored out of the bay through fog, rising

up and over large rolling waves, and then, happily, upon leaving the bay, they broke out of the fog into sunlight and calm seas. The sun illuminated the snow and ice-covered peaks of the Fairweather Range as they traveled south. It was a beautiful southeastern Alaska panorama, but several members of the party weren't able to enjoy the view, having become seasick in the swaying boats. The ocean never seemed to bother Blackadar, though. "I was jealous of Walt, watching him put down beers," wrote Tom Johnson, who was one of those who felt ill, "when I could not even drink one . . . all the while Walt is yelling that he was having a great time."

They made good time with a breeze pushing them south. As evening came on, a decision was made to continue through the night. The weather looked favorable, the seas were right, and according to Wheat, in reality, they had no other choice. "We could not go to shore," he said. "Imagine rocks from car size up to house size on the shoreline. There was no beach at all. Walt said there'd be a beach. He said, 'Ya, we'll just pull in and do some beachcombing. We'll probably find those glass balls from China and all kinds of treasures along the beach.' Well, that was completely out of the question. We were completely committed to the ocean."

Darkness settled on the coast. Blackadar lined up the boat with the stars, and Wheat and Streckman used the compass. Overhead, the northern lights flamed elusively and outlined the Fairweather Range. The waters under them glowed with a fluorescent plankton, particularly showy in Alaskan waters.

With nightfall, the temperature dropped, and the wind came up. Chilled, the raft riders crouched down between gear bags, seeking places out of the wind. As the waves picked up, Klaus Streckman watched anxiously for any signs of breakers. He had some ocean experience and, perhaps more than the others, knew how vulnerable they were. As the night went on, the sea built. The rafts undulated nauseously, providing little relief to those who were sick, and on occasion, one would hang his head over the edge, throwing up.

Approaching Lituya Bay, which was approximately 50 miles south of Dry Bay, the swells were reaching 15 to 20 feet in height. Lituya Bay's narrow 1,000-foot entrance at low tide is known for its hazardous tidal currents. In 1786, when the bay was first discovered by French explorer La Perouse, 21 men drowned when three small boats surveying the entrance were swept into a tidal bore.

The tidal currents at the entrance of the bay bothered them, so unsure of their position in the dark night they decided that they would pass it. At approximately 1:30 in the morning, just before the opening of the bay, they had their closest call.

Klaus, still wide awake and keeping up his vigil, looked through the darkness for any signs of breakers or rocks. Then he saw it. Outlined in the glowing fluorescent plankton, he could see the breaking sea plainly, pounding against rocks. "We were perhaps two swells away from crashing," said Streckman. "It was a major emergency."

Streckman yelled to Wheat, who was running one of the motors, to turn away. Blackadar, waking, wondered what the excitement was about. Streckman and Wheat quickly explained, but Blackadar told them to relax and to remain on the same course. It seemed to Wheat that Blackadar had no concept of the danger. Ignoring the doctor, Wheat pointed to the right, and the rafts swung around. Since the boats were now exposed sideways to the waves, water splashed over gunwales, wetting the already cold occupants. Blackadar grumbled and wanted to return to prior course, but with more of the party realizing their danger, he was outvoted. "We were concerned enough with the situation that we didn't pay a whole lot of attention to Walt," said Wheat. "We were trying to save our skins."

Sideways in the waves, the two boats started separating. Streckman leaped to the front of the boats, trying to hold them together. Waves crashed over the top of him, and afraid that he might wash away, somebody in the dark nearby held his feet.

Streckman had been doing fairly well up to this point, but bouncing up and down on the bow, trying to relash the boats together was too much, and he got seasick.

Once the boats were secured, the nauseated Streckman returned to his watch. Blackadar fell asleep, woke once, looked around and said, "I'm having a blast," and then drifted off to sleep. Another time he woke up to a conversation in which the others were concerned about their position. "No problem," he said. "I've got Gary's head lined up with the moon. We're right on course."

As they motored along, with the rafts bucking in the waves, the shadowy outline showing off the Fairweather Mountains to their left, and the stars and northern lights overhead, Blackadar, with his eyes wide open, looked over at Wheat. "Doug," he said solemnly. "This is a night that you will never forget."

"He was right," said Wheat years later. "None us will ever forget." Finally around noon the next day, after the long, unforgettable night, the tired group reached the safety of Dixon Harbor, just north of Cape Spencer.

They dragged the boats up on the beach, dropped their wet things, scrounged a quick meal, and scattered about, most of them falling asleep. Three days later, traveling between the islands of the Alexander Archipelago, they reached the Gustavus Lodge at Glacier Bay. Blackadar called Idaho to talk to a colleague to schedule surgery on his ailing shoulder. The next day, while the rest of the group continued their raft journey to Juneau, Blackadar caught a plane flying out of the lodge and returned to Salmon.

❋   ❋

BLACKADAR'S sadness over the death of Julie Wilson lingered. Doug Wheat and Gary Young on the Tatshenshini trip remember him being "remorseful" and "unhappy" at times, and tears still came to his eyes when he talked of her. On other trips, he would carry on about dying of cancer or talk about how he would some day kayak off Niagara Falls. At times his preoccupation with death was annoying. "We were getting tired of his laboring on and on, and his talking about death," said one kayak companion. Yet, the mood would pass. The next morning, he'd be up, shouting out, "Let's go boating," booming out his laugh and galvanizing everyone around him.

Another winter came on. The winter of '77-'78, from nearly everyone's standpoint, was better than the previous winter which had left paltry amounts of snow for skiers and resulting low river flows for farmers and river runners. Snowfall on Lost Trail Pass reached six-and-a-half feet in January, 1978, hardly a record, but better than the previous year when snow depths were half as much. At Thanksgiving time, at the start of the rejuvenating winter, Blackadar and Doug Wheat had driven in the doctor's Volkswagen Rabbit out to Vancouver to build Eskimo kayaks with Klaus Streckman. They had seen Streckman's boat on the Alsek, and both, impressed with its storage capacity and reasonable maneuverability on whitewater, wanted one for themselves.

"It was a heavy snowstorm most of the way to Seattle," said Wheat, "and he [Blackadar] was roaring along at about a 75 to 80-mile per hour clip." Wheat remembered sliding up behind the back end of trucks hidden by a cloud of blowing snow, then once the taillights came in view a few feet ahead, Blackadar accelerated around: "It was a terrifying ride. I was scared to death." Wheat talked to Blackadar about his driving and asked him whether he ought to slow down. "Naw," Blackadar said, "no one's ever been killed in a VW Rabbit."

That January temperatures in Salmon dropped to 19 below and ice clogs along the river were a familiar scene. The steelhead run had improved over the last year, and with the season open again, fishermen eagerly returned to the river as soon as the ice went out in February. Temperatures surrounding Salmon's latest environmental controversy had also dropped that winter after a hot summer. While Blackadar had been in Alaska, the Forest Service held "workshops" throughout the state to solicit information on a study of roadless lands. Outside the Idaho Falls workshop, which had been well-attended by logging industry representatives, an anti-wilderness demonstration was staged with picketers and signs attached to a snowmobile and logging truck.

In February of 1978, Frank Church, as a matter of courtesy for Idaho conservationists, introduced the River of No Return Wilderness proposal which Blackadar had helped formulate. It did not mean that Church was lending his support to the proposal, but it brought the conservationists' plan for central Idaho out in the open and into the congressional forum.

The year 1978 was also a good year for the town. The new library, opened the previous year, had brightened the looks of downtown. Construction on a badly-needed new Salmon High School building got under way, and replacement work on the infamous old water line on Main Street was undertaken after years of multiple breaks.

The overall tone of the community remained conservative, but a small and growing number of young residents had moved in from the outside and added some new variations to the old harmonies. They were about the same age, late 20s and early 30s, as were many of those who kayaked with Blackadar. In fact, some of them were his boating friends, having come to Salmon to be near kayaking, skiing, and the wilderness activities that the area provided. They, like many before them, had sought an independent lifestyle, and some built their own log homes on drainages outside the town.

To the longtime residents, the liberal-minded newcomers were like Blackadar, not fitting in too well, seemingly loose in morals; marriage, it appeared, was not a prerequisite to living together, and stories were heard of nudity and marijuana on their river trips, and some of them spoke up at hearings supporting wilderness. It wasn't a passing phenomenon. They were there to stay, building homes, starting businesses, some raising families and finding their own place in the rural West.

While some greeted the counterculture element suspiciously, Blackadar enjoyed their company. He respected their beliefs. He attended their parties. He enjoyed their river trips and shed his clothes as easily as they did on a hot day on a river beach. At the same time, he could fit in just as comfortably with his old Salmon friends. He was, it seems, a man of two generations and of two lives.

For his life in kayaking, the accolades came in with increasing regularity. Editors from *American Whitewater* and *River World* magazines wanted him to write columns. He wrote back telling them that he wasn't a good writer and didn't have much time, but he might send an article or two. Don Wilson, his kayaking friend in the East, started working on a profile to submit to the *New Yorker* on a speculative basis.

Kayakers from all across the United States wrote to congratulate him on recent television appearances: "Saw you . . . impressive . . . exciting show," "a terrific boater," "[you give] me motivation to continue on with excellence." He was surely intrigued by a letter from a woman in Utah: "You might be the answer to my dream. You['re] a very exciting person . . ." Others wrote asking how to get hold of copies of his films, or prying for information about rivers, water levels, and where to obtain equipment.

Dave Sumner, a well-known outdoor photographer, wrote to him inquiring whether he might be interested in helping with a publicity "event" to help protect a river canyon in Colorado. The canyon, Cross Mountain Gorge in the northwest part of the state, was to be the site of a hydropower development. "I'd like to get you down here," he wrote, "(paying your way if apt) to take a crack at the Gorge. I'd like to quite deliberately stage an event, with you as 'star,' in an effort to get some publicity for Cross Mountain Gorge." Blackadar replied, expressing interest, closing his letter with, "Sounds like fun." Sumner, because of marital problems, would bow out of the project, but the idea would soon be picked up by Roger Brown.

To approach kayaking from a new angle, Brown decided to make a comparative study of river running for *American Sportsman*, showing the difference between a river in low water and high water. The first filming of the kayak descent of Cross Mountain Canyon would be made in the early spring of 1978 before the mountain snows swelled the river. Then the kayakers would return for the second part, a run of the canyon during the height of the runoff.

Brown's plans called for Blackadar once again to be the focal point of the film. However, because of events on a river in Idaho, the plans for the second part of the film would have to be drastically altered.

XIII

River of No Return

BLACKADAR'S SHOULDER CONTINUED to hound him
in early 1978. During the winter he had slipped on some
ice, and the resulting fall had aggravated it. By now both Boyd
Simmons, his partner, and Keith Taylor, an orthopedist in Boise,
agreed that he had arthritis in his shoulder. For the pain, he
asked his nurses on occasion to give him shots of cortisone or
novocaine.

Yet despite his escalating shoulder problems and his three
swims in the Nozzle, he continued to make plans for more expeditionary and exploratory kayaking. He had hoped to join a
team planning to parachute into a South American river, the
Orinoco, which the British kayaker Mike Jones had first suggested at Everest Base Camp to Dee Crouch and adventure cinematographer, Mike Hoover. In the end, the trip never came off,
but Blackadar intended to attempt the venture. He also continued his interest in kayaking the Grand Canyon of the Stikine,
telling one friend that he hoped to get up to reconnoitre the river.
Running Selway Falls in Idaho still remained on his list, and the
newest film project, Cross Mountain Gorge, was coming up soon
in April.

He had two major obstacles in his kayaking at that point. The first was his endurance. In poor shape, he couldn't paddle for long days as he had in the past. He started on a fitness regimen, but his cluttered schedule at his practice and his never-ending ranch work left him tired and worn in the evening and with little time or motivation for exercising. In his last attempt of Devil Creek Rapids, the difference in endurance from the year before was obvious. In 1976, he hung in his boat longer in the Nozzle, trying to roll as many as eight times. In contrast, in 1977, Lesser did not observe him making any rolls once he reached the Nozzle. All the same, Blackadar's endurance in kayaking had never been impressive and had been made up for by his powerful and reliable roll. He might have been able to get along relatively well then in 1977 and 1978 if it not been for the second obstacle, a deteriorating roll technique.

He went back to the pool in the spring of 1978, trying to sharpen up his roll. Instead, to his alarm, he found that at times he could not roll at all, and at other times when he did, the roll was weak and ineffective. Incredible as it seems, his kayaking technique in his later years did not include a good roll, and he was left to face the great challenges of kayaking on spirit and determination alone.

THE kayaking season came early in 1978. He had little chance to run any pre-season warm-up jaunts before leaving for the first filming trip of Cross Mountain Gorge. He, Rob Lesser and Linda Hibbard drove to Craig, Colorado, which served as the staging area for the runs on the gorge. In Craig, he greeted his friend and the field producer, Roger Brown, the small film crew and Eric Evans.

At the time, Eric Evans was the United States' top competitive kayaker, having won the nationals in men's slalom for 10 years. Evans, the kayak racing champion, had never met

Blackadar, the legendary kayaker of big water. "The stories I'd heard of him were as diverse as they were humorous," wrote Evans in his column for *Canoe*. He summarized several characterizations from others: "the Jim Taylor (former fullback of the Green Bay Packers) of kayaking," "today's version of the Western cowboy," and "a deeply sensitive person." "After hearing all the stories about what he was like," wrote Evans, "I wanted to see for myself."

What Evans found was a "man of tremendous energy, but with a sort of swashbuckling bravado about him that tends to turn me off a little bit." Beyond the bravado, Evans also found someone who loved free-flowing rivers. "He genuinely enjoyed being outdoors and breathing the air and riding the rapids," said Evans, "[with] how do the French call it, *joie de vivre*. I came away thinking that he really liked nature and wild places."

Brown had hoped that the film would portray the plight of wild places like Cross Mountain Gorge. The area certainly has all the elements of a whitewater and natural attraction: difficult rapids dropping steeply, 60 to 80 feet per mile, between a rocky and beautiful carved defile. It's dry and barren, a scene of vivid chiaroscuro, standing in stark contrast with the green opulence of the Susitna, where Blackadar had spent much of his time the last couple of years. Ensconced within the walls of the dry canyon is the Yampa River which is charged with the snows melting on the west slope of the Colorado Rockies. Located just above the boundaries of Dinosaur National Monument on the Colorado-Utah border, Cross Mountain Gorge is one of several canyons along the course of the Yampa drawing the attention of whitewater devotees. Of the whitewater on the Yampa, Cross Mountain Gorge is the most difficult.

Unfortunately, Brown's original intention to show the river at two diametrically different levels was stymied some when he learned that recent rains had increased the Yampa's volume considerably. Although the early season takes would not be as low as Brown had hoped, he decided to go on with the shooting.

As the runs were made, Lesser, observing Blackadar, felt that his physical conditioning had declined even more than the previous year's. It didn't appear that Blackadar was "physically paying attention to himself."

At one point when the kayakers were readying themselves, Blackadar had fallen asleep in the car. He woke, finding himself alone and hurried down to the river where the others were busy. "Where'd everybody go?" he asked. Left to sleep in the vehicle while the others worked, he must have felt left out. "I'm sure his ego was bruised by that," said Lesser.

They did two days of filming. Evans described the river: "The water was a good Class IV with some nasty holes and demanded critical maneuvering at times." It was clear that Blackadar's shoulder weakened his boating when maneuvering was needed, and he was, said Evans, in a "great deal of pain." "Yet," Evans continued, "even with one wing I could see the confidence which enabled him to get through the big water. Technically, there are hundreds of boaters with more skill, and he'd be the first to admit it. Most importantly, although running hairy whitewater is what he's famous for, Blackadar seemed more concerned with enjoying himself and the scenery in a river environment. The beauty of the canyon was what he talked of, not its whitewater." Evans picked up on what might have been a subtle change in Blackadar's approach to rivers, that the challenge of whitewater was starting to take a second seat to an introspective appreciation of the beauties of the river.

In two months time, the boaters would meet Brown again for the high water filming, the second part of the film. Lesser had grave concerns about whether Blackadar would be up to the demands that Cross Mountain Canyon would present in flood conditions. "It was obvious," said Lesser, "the message was, 'Walt, there's no damn way that you're going to be able to boat this TV thing at high water if you don't get in shape.'"

Blackadar was aware of the problem, and not long afterwards he left for a two-week trip to North Carolina and West Virginia in late April for some medical study combined with some kayaking with his friends in the area. While on the trip he swung through Watchung, New Jersey, his hometown, for a family visit and stopped to see Barb Wright in Boston.

"He said his roll was terrible," Wright said, "and he needed some lessons." Wright worked with him in her pool, trying to get him to use his hips as she had when she first taught him how to roll a decade earlier. Even with Barb's help, Blackadar didn't feel like he had made much progress: "I did get to Boston for a few hours to practice in Barbara's pool," Blackadar wrote to Don Wilson, upon returning, "and was sorely tempted to bag it all. But perhaps sometime later."

Wright said that he was complaining about his shoulder. His talk worried her, and she felt "premonitions." "I will admit that he was a little fatalistic," she said. "He was out of shape. He was getting fat. I think that if he was coming up on a big hairy thing, he would just go ahead and drop into it just to see what the hell's down there—not because he wanted to, but because he just didn't have the energy to avoid it."

For the first time, Blackadar was talking seriously about giving up. "Sorely tempted to bag it," he had written. To Joe Nebeker, he talked about taking up bird hunting again. Nebeker used to stop by his office and was occasionally stopped by Blackadar's nurses who told Nebeker that the doctor was busy. "I don't give a damn what the nurses tell you," Blackadar told Nebeker, "just come on in." In late April, after Blackadar's return from the East, Nebeker stopped for a short chat.

"Joe, I'm just getting about where I'm going to have to give up running the water," Blackadar told Nebeker. Blackadar had a bitch bird dog and wanted Nebeker to find a male to breed her with. He just had a couple more rivers to run, Blackadar told him, and then he was planning to hang it up. When he finished kayaking, he would concentrate on bird hunting.

Blackadar's plans to raise some bird dogs did not appear to be a passing whim, for Nebeker later picked up Blackadar's dog and took it down to Idaho Falls for breeding, paying the $200 stud fee. Nebeker, who had known Blackadar since the late fifties, felt that he was serious about quitting and that he simply couldn't physically keep it up much longer. "He had to have shots in his shoulder," said Nebeker. "His arms were locking up on him. His hands sometimes would turn white because of his shoulder problem." Whatever the reasons, Blackadar, it appears by now, had accepted the inevitability of relinquishing his position on the top of the sport and began laying other plans for his future.

Nevertheless, even while he was telling Nebeker that he was through with kayaking, the fight was still in him and he was making arrangements to boat "one more river." He and Doug Wheat planned to use their Eskimo boats on a trip on the South Fork of the Salmon that summer. He was lining up another Grand Canyon trip in the fall. In a letter to a film producer, he discussed running the North Fork of the Payette, and, of course, the second part of the Cross Mountain Gorge project was coming up in June. As his letter to Wilson seems to show ("sorely tempted to bag it. But perhaps sometime later"), he was torn between ending his kayaking career and extending it. Kayaking had meant too much to him to put it neatly away; there were just one or two more rivers he had to do first.

WHEN Blackadar returned from the East, he paddled with Rob Lesser on a river near Boise. Lesser noticed some improvement, but he was only "getting by." Besides Blackadar's physical problems in kayaking, Lesser said that "there was probably a mental aspect in which he felt that he was losing his edge. Kayaking is a mental game. Walt controlled the circumstances because he was so confident. I think he was beginning to lose that confidence." He told Lesser that he had only one more weekend in his schedule left free to kayak before returning to do the Cross Mountain high water filming. The free weekend was May 13 and 14, the weekend of Mother's Day.

For a couple of weeks before Mother's Day weekend, Shirley Blackadar had been visiting relatives in the East. Since her father was batching it, Lois invited him to dinner. First, he told his daughter that he was on a diet, but then, a few days later he called to say he'd take her up on it. The house had just been cleaned by a maid in anticipation of Shirley's return, and he didn't want to disturb the kitchen by doing his own cooking. On May 9, he and his daughter had dinner, and afterwards he strolled outside with her, talking easily, noticing the newly-leafed trees, and mentioning that he was planning to go boating with friends over the weekend.

He had mentioned the kayak trip to Berniece Bennedict while she assisted him in a gall bladder surgery. "I could see that his shoulder was really bothering him," she said, and, upon hearing of his plans, she told him "Boy, you are in some shape to go kayaking." But physical conditioning had not stopped him before, and now that it was warm and well into the spring, Blackadar was becoming more enthused about kayaking. He was having a new kayak made for himself by Jeff Bevan, a kayaking friend living in Salmon.

Bevan, in his 20s, had moved to Salmon in 1975 and would, in time, expand this early start in building kayaks into a small Salmon manufacturing business. Every so often, Blackadar stopped by to see how Bevan was progressing on the boats. "He'd come cruising in, 90 miles an hour," said Bevan. "We'd be dragging our butts from working with the resins and fiber-glass. He'd throw out a few bits of advice, and then he was off again, on to something else."

On Friday, Sue, who was living in Salmon at the time, saw her father and asked what they ought to get for Shirley, since

Mother's Day was coming up. "Honey," Blackadar replied, "she's not my mother. I'm going boating." Later that evening, he and Bevan worked on repairing Blackadar's Lettmann, Mark IV kayak for their weekend trip. They worked until 1:30 or 2 the next morning putting fiberglass patches in place and attaching a set of thigh braces. The braces, which draped over the top of the thighs, made it more difficult to get out of a kayak in an emergency, but they also helped give Blackadar a secure fit and enabled him to "wear the boat," which helped his rolling technique.

The next morning, Blackadar, after three hours of sleep, rose early and was nearly ready to leave, when Jeff and Woo McLean arrived around 6 a.m. Stopping at the Ranch, Woo went into the shop to find Blackadar and watched as he finished giving himself a shot of cortisone in his shoulder. They loaded all the gear and tied the boats on top of the camper of Blackadar's red 1976 Ford truck. Starting off, Blackadar realized that he had forgotten his toothbrush, and they drove back to his house to get it.

The destination was the South Fork of the Payette, about a three-hour drive away. Blackadar had invited John Dondero, John Petit and some other Sun Valley kayakers to join him, planning to meet them at a cafe in the small town of Lowman along the South Fork. Blackadar had also phoned Keith Taylor, inviting him on the trip, but Taylor told Blackadar that he was busy and that he and Tullio Celano had just run it. He cautioned Blackadar to watch for a tree caught in a rapids just below Big Falls. When they had run the river, the water was coming up because of the spring runoff. The tree blocked much of the river, and Tullio had just squeezed around the end of it.

It appears that Blackadar had never run that portion of the South Fork of the Payette. He had run the lower South Fork, but there is no evidence in his papers nor did any of those interviewed for this book mention that he had run it. The put-in for this section of the South Fork is at the confluence of a tributary

248

stream called the Deadwood. From the Deadwood downstream, the South Fork is a small, lively stretch of whitewater of intermediate difficulty (mostly Class III+ or Class IV-), which flows in a westerly direction. A road runs along the north side of the river, but for most of the run the road is hardly noticeable to river runners since it is situated a couple of hundred feet above the river. The South Fork canyon is like many in central Idaho, with open or sparsely forested south facing slopes and dense fir and pine covering on the cool northern slopes. Apparently because of what Taylor had told him, Blackadar planned to do a little scouting before they ran it.

EN ROUTE to the river, a deer jumped from the side of the road, hitting Blackadar's truck, falling to the ground. Blackadar stopped. He couldn't allow the dying deer to lie there, and using his pocketknife, the doctor bled and gutted the deer while Bevan watched, awed at the speed at which the doctor went about the task. Blackadar left the deer propped up visible from the road and drove on to a store where he called a Fish and Game office. If the meat is useable—and in this case it would have been since Blackadar promptly cleaned the animal—the department gives road-killed game to charities.

Bevan overheard part of the conversation. From Blackadar's end of the conversation, it appeared that the Fish and Game officer on the other end of the line thought Blackadar responsible and wanted him to stay with the deer. "Look, you've got it wrong," Blackadar said emphatically. "The damn thing jumped into me." Blackadar told the officer pointedly that he was busy, gave him directions on how to find the gutted deer, and hung up, in a hurry to meet Dondero on time. A few miles down the road, a Fish and Game truck sped by in the opposite direction. "Well, there he goes," Blackadar told Bevan and kept on driving towards the South Fork.

Blackadar complained to Woo that he was hungry. She suggested that he stop and eat something, but Blackadar, anxious to keep moving, ignored the advice. When they arrived at Lowman to meet the handful of boaters from Sun Valley, he went into the store and bought a box of cold cereal and a candy bar, but still in a rush to get to the river, he threw them behind the seat and drove on.

After reaching the Deadwood River, the put-in place, Blackadar, Jeff and Woo drove down the river, scouting as they went, from high up on the road. They drove by Big Falls, an unrunnable falls a couple of miles below the put-in, which the group had planned to portage around, and continued a short distance further, where they stopped to look down on a small rapid. Woo remembered that from their high position they couldn't see clearly the obstacle in the middle of the rapids. It appeared to be a large rock. Blackadar remarked that it looked like a boater could run on either side of it, but, he said, they'd take a closer look once they were on the river.

It was cold in the late morning, and Blackadar put on a full wet suit. Still not stopping to eat, he slipped into his boat and pushed off with the others. Woo, who had originally planned to kayak, decided that since it was cold and early in the season that she would shuttle Blackadar's truck. As the kayakers worked their way down the river, she followed along the road, watching their progress.

They reached Big Falls, pulling out on the left and making the steep portage up and around the obstacle. While the group gravely looked at the treacherous falls, Blackadar suddenly announced: "It's paddleable."

No one expressed any agreement; the idea of running the falls was ridiculous.

"No," Blackadar said. "You can make it through there."

Jeff Bevan thought it was just Blackadar being himself, always delighting in trying to shock people. "Whenever he came across the ultimate paddling risk," said Bevan, "he would say that it could be run."

The kayakers put their boats back in the water below the falls and started down. John Petit was in the lead, followed by Jeff Bevan and then Blackadar. A half mile below Big Falls, Petit came up on the rapid which Blackadar had scouted from the road. He pulled off on the right. Bevan caught an eddy on the left.

Looking downriver, at what at first appeared to be a wave, Bevan briefly saw the outline of a log under water. The hidden log was 12 or more inches in diameter at its smallest end and thicker at its base. It extended out from a cliff on the left, reaching nearly two-thirds of the distance across the river.

It was approximately 2:45 p.m.

Looking to his side, Bevan saw Blackadar floating past. "He smiled at me," remembered Bevan, "and floated as nonchalant as hell."

Bevan's mind was still processing what he had seen below, and as he realized the danger of what lay below, Blackadar was well past him.

Blackadar drifted towards the log.

"He hit the log hard with his bow, jarring him badly," said Bevan, who watched. The bow slipped all the way under, so the log ended up resting on his lap and against his large life jacket, which stopped him from going further. He was trapped.

No one really knows what Blackadar saw in front of him and whether he recognized the dark line under the wave as a log which could entrap him. It seems far more likely that what Blackadar saw ahead appeared as a wave with a boulder in it. That's what he had observed from above when he had scouted it from the road. He may have come upon the wave thinking that he could easily slide around the right or left side of the cushion coming off the underlying rock. Water broke over the top of the hidden log, and only in surges could the kayakers coming down upon it from their low upriver position see that a long dark object was under the water.

Jeff Bevan's first impression when looking downstream was that it was a wave. Blackadar, once past Bevan, might have finally seen the log, but he had very little time to make the sharp cut to the right. Getting around the log which blocked most of the river took some quickly executed strokes. Petit and Bevan barely missed the end of the log when they paddled beyond it.

Blackadar's continuing shoulder problems and his lack of energy, complicated by the fact that he had had no food all day, certainly must have dulled his ability to react. He might have believed that in the last split second before hitting it that he could lean against the wave breaking on the upriver side of the rock or log with a bracing paddle stroke and the water would carry his boat around to one side. That tactic might have worked had the log not been angled toward the middle of the river.

Held fast by the log, Blackadar reacted quickly. "Walt got into a high brace," said Bevan. "He was trying to pull up over the log. But as he tried, the log was slanted, and it pulled him left into deeper water."

The current bounced the boat, moving his body deeper into the faster water. Blackadar didn't show any sign of panic, he just kept hanging on to his high brace, reaching out, pulling, pulling, pulling . . . .

Then his head disappeared under water, and the back end of the boat, caught in the strong current, rose up in the air, bent and stood vertically. Blackadar did not let up. He pulled on the high brace, trying to escape.

The onrush of the water continued bending the stern until it wrapped tightly against the top of Blackadar's body. It was a complete entrapment. The boat and Blackadar were both immersed under the rushing water.

❄   ❄

ALL of the kayakers pulled off. They scrambled onto the shore, looking for some way to help. But there was nothing they could do. Pinned in the middle of the river, Blackadar could not be reached from either the right or left banks. The river was deep and the current powerful, and anybody trying to wade out would have been swept away. The left side of the river, where one end of the log was caught, was the most difficult problematically because of a sheer cliff preventing access to the river.

Even a rope rescue was impossible. If there had been enough time for one of the kayakers to get out of his boat before Blackadar went under, it was unlikely that the doctor could have seen or grabbed a passing rope. But the accident happened quickly. There had been precious little time to react. All they could do was to watch helplessly from the banks.

"I've spent a long time thinking about all the options available," said John Dondero. "The only possible way to help would be to ferry out on the back of someone's boat into the current. Let go and swim and try to grab his boat as you rushed by." Such an attempt, as John knew, was foolish and could result in a second person becoming entrapped. Downed logs with protruding branches are often called strainers by river runners because the current strains through. A body or boat can easily get caught against the branches, just as a strainer in a kitchen sink catches food particles. It is one of the most dangerous obstacles on a river and extremely dangerous from a rescue standpoint.

The boaters watched, hoping that Blackadar would float free, but both he and his boat remained under water, affixed to the log. His life jacket swirled past below the rapid, apparently stripped off by the force of the current, but nothing else was seen. After some time, it was obvious that Walt Blackadar had drowned.

The shocked kayakers began pulling their boats up the steep hillside to the road 300 feet above the river. Woo McLean, who had been watching from above, and Jeff Bevan notified the Boise County sheriff and called Bob Blackadar.

✳   ✳

IT was late afternoon when Bob received the call. He went up to see his mother, who was sitting at the kitchen table. "Jeff called," he said. Shirley Blackadar looked up at her son.

"There's been an accident. They think dad's dead." Her mouth dropped open. She didn't cry; she sat quietly for a while, and then Bob explained that he, Janice and Sue would drive up to the river.

Before leaving, he called Jean Tomita, his father's office manager, and she delivered the letter in which Blackadar had outlined instructions in the event of his death. His wish to be "buried by the roar" of a river was well-known among the family and friends and came as no surprise to Bob when he read its content.

It had become a pleasant May day, and as the afternoon blended into evening, the warm temperatures accelerated the melting of higher elevation snows. The water on the South Fork of the Payette rose. Looking down from above, the rescuers which had been assembled by Boise County Sheriff Stan Jensen, could barely see the boat caught on the log below. The only evidence of its existence was a rare flicker of color. Later in the evening rescuers tried dislodging the log with 11 sticks of dynamite, but the position of the log and difficulty of reaching it from the cliff made their efforts futile. Nightfall precluded any further search work.

After hearing of the accident, Tullio Celano, with his friend Dale Stubblefield, arrived early the next day to offer their help. The kayakers from the day before were emotionally drained, and they were relieved when Celano volunteered to float down, searching the banks of the river. As more attempts were made to loosen the log with dynamite, Celano and Stubblefield "nervously" put their kayaks in the flooded river which continued to rise higher each hour.

Approximately 15 miles below the log, on a shoal in an area where the South Fork Canyon opens into the lush Garden Valley, they found the body. Laying it across the decks of their two boats, they paddled across the river. Laboring under the load, they zipped the body, still with helmet and wet suit on, into a body bag and carried it up to their pickup. Celano knew of Blackadar's wish to be buried near the river and convinced his friend, Coroner Mike Johnson, to allow the family to keep the body while burial arrangements were worked out. Celano then turned the body over to Bob and Sue, who laid it in the back of the red Ford truck.

Early the second morning after the accident, Blackadar's brother, John, arrived after flying in from the East. His presence and calm manner helped dispel tensions, and he followed up on work initiated by Bob and Sue to obtain permission from the Forest Service to bury the body on government land near the river. John knew he must get the body in the ground that day, but several problems were encountered with their request. Forest Service officials were concerned about a possible dam proposal for the river, about new road work alongside the river which would pitch debris over the grave, and, most importantly, the legalities of burial on government land could not be worked out in the short time available.

Eventually, the caretakers of an old pioneer cemetery in Garden Valley, which had long been closed, gave the family permission to bury the body there. The cemetery wasn't next to the river, but it overlooked the valley, and the idea of having their father buried along with Idaho pioneers appealed to the children.

A special exception had been made for Blackadar's burial, and no more would be permitted in the old cemetery.* It is

---

*Even his wife, Shirley Blackadar, was not permitted a grave next to her husband. She, nevertheless, desired his company and made alternative plans to share his plot in Garden Valley. When she was suddenly taken ill and died of a brain tumor in 1982, the family, acceding to her wish, inurned her ashes beside her husband's grave.

fitting that his was the last grave amidst those of the early pioneers, men and women who forged their own place in the western frontier and who had lived a life so admired and emulated by Blackadar; it was an auspicious place to end his life's eventful odyssey.

*　　*

WALTER Lloyd Blackadar's burial was scheduled for the evening, Monday, May 15. In the afternoon, Bob, his sisters and friends dug the grave. Bob remembers it being therapeutic, and although somber, he felt lightened and accepting of what had happened. It was "almost a relief," said one of the daughters of the manner of her father's death. Kayaking companions and friends who learned of the circumstances of Blackadar's final fight in a South Fork rapid were similarly philosophical about his death. One of his patients summed up the feelings of many: "[death on the river] was the right way for him." Another friend wrote that drowning on the South Fork was in reality "a natural death" for somebody like Blackadar.

The word of Walt Blackadar's death spread quickly, and friends arrived with flowers, food and drinks for those at the grave site. The food went faster than expected. Bob's dog, Juneau, crawled up on a table and ate most of a bucket of Kentucky Fried Chicken before being shooed away. Along with the family members, many of Blackadar's boating companions were there, including Tullio Celano, who had been with him on his first wild run of the North Fork of the Payette, and Roger Hazelwood, John Dondero and Ron Frye, who had been with him at one time or another on the big waters of the Susitna. Shirley did not want to attend the graveside service, deciding instead to attend the memorial service at the Salmon Episcopal Church set a few days later.

The 20 attendees gathered around the grave, standing close to one another, watching as the body was lowered by ropes into the six-foot hole. Wildflowers were thrown into the grave, and the kayak paddles were used to scoop dirt over the body. The short service included a reading of the 23rd Psalm and the singing of a few stanzas of "He's Got the Whole World in His Hands." John Blackadar lit a candle in a tin can, the same kind of candle lantern used by his mother on a backyard camp out with John and Walt nearly half a century earlier. As the candle was passed from one to another, each person could, if so moved, say a few words.

It had been a cool day with overcast skies, and, as the service wound down around 7 in the evening, the clouds had thinned some, allowing a brief illumination of the surrounding hillsides in a diffused evening light before the coming night.

Downhill from the small cemetery, across a flat and out of the sight of the small group, the river flowed by. There are no big rapids in this part of the South Fork, no ominous roar of water plunging over boulders, just a few rocks and ripples, an easy run in a kayak, and the calm, whispering assurance of a flowing stream, flowing on, ever on, as endlessly as time itself.

XIV
Epilogue

IT DIDN'T TAKE LONG for the kayaking world to react to Blackadar's death. Words of praise were profuse: "The paddling world lost one of its most enthusiastic devotees"; "Blackadar was whitewater sport's most famous personality"; "He always had time to phone or write to our [club members] when they needed help or advice...he treated [us] as equals and as long lost friends"; "Adventurous, amazing, admirable may be words to describe him, but all words are inadequate and will not do him justice."

Barbara Wright wrote in *Canoe* that "few men will be missed as much as Walt, by so many people. Although he left us too young, he could never have grown old." Don Wilson's profile, written while Blackadar was still alive, portrayed him as one who could focus the sum of physical and mental energies in a match against the great power of water. If sometimes he was overpowered, he kept fighting, learning from mistakes, and trying again. "He does not take the risk so much as he takes the kayaking—and in drinking the last of the good wine, he is prepared to taste the bitter lees in the bottom of the glass."

Much good wine remained to be poured from the glass after

his death. Among the eulogies, the one prepared for national airing by *American Sportsman* in June of 1978 would have pleased Blackadar the most. It consisted of a series of segments taken from previous programs, showing him flirting with the monstrous waves of the Colorado and the Susitna. The idea to do a tribute to Walt Blackadar originated with ABC Sports staff members who had come to greatly admire the gutsy and charismatic 55-year-old doctor.

"Walt Blackadar was truly alive," narrates Curt Gowdy in the *American Sportsman's* tribute, "a man who knew how to live with determination and courage and boundless uninhibited joy. Especially at moments like this . . . ". As Gowdy's voice trails off, the scene shows Blackadar in slow motion edging towards a wall of whitewater, spitting and curling over on top of him and consuming him in froth and foam. At the end of the moving tribute, Gowdy says, "Walt Blackadar drew tremendous life from the water and shared it with us. He met its unrelenting force head-on and gave his own life back to it."

Of all the unrelenting forces he faced in his odyssey, the Alsek River remained his great triumph. Three months after Blackadar's death, Klaus Streckman and Kay Swanson organized an expeditionary trip down the Alsek, taking with them a paddle painted with a silhouette of Blackadar's face. The memorial paddle to Blackadar's achievement was left with a copy of Blackadar's diary of his solo run, some matches, and a candle in a cairn at the entrance of Turnback Canyon.

After toasting Blackadar with drinks of Everclear, Streckman and Swanson, unable to portage Turnback Canyon because of the surging Tweedsmuir Glacier, lined their boats upstream to Range Creek. At Range Creek, they laboriously dragged their boats up the shallow creek, crossed over a divide and dragged their boats down another drainage, eventually reaching the Tatshenshini River. One month after they started their arduous journey, the tired party arrived successfully at Dry Bay.

Streckman's efforts to commemorate his old friend didn't

end with the Alsek-Tatshenshini trek. Shortly after Streckman returned to his home in Vancouver, he began working with the Ministry of the Environment in British Columbia to have the mountain at the entrance of Turnback Canyon named for Blackadar. With the support of the British Columbia Whitewater Canoeing Association, the name Mt. Blackadar was officially accepted before the year's end.*

❋   ❋

WHILE Streckman prepared for his commemorative Alsek trip, the initial jolt of Walt Blackadar's death in Salmon had passed, and the topic of local conversations turned to news of the Middle Fork of the Salmon. President Jimmy Carter, a whitewater buff, and Cecil Andrus, now his Secretary of Interior, planned a float trip through the Idaho Primitive Area.

The national publicity generated from Carter's trip would give Salmon's recreation economy a big boost. Even so, Carter didn't win any popularity contests among the community who had voted overwhelmingly for Gerald Ford in 1976. The late Dr. Blackadar's fellow Chamber members were unhappy about Carter's plans to protect wilderness in central Idaho. The Chamber had long since distanced itself from Blackadar's stances on wilderness and supported Gordon Crupper and the timber industry's position. A petition drive, in which Crupper participated, was launched to collect names on a statement opposed to any further wilderness. The petition with 942 signatures was flown into Indian Creek and presented to Carter before he began his float trip.

Statewide and nationally, however, the cry for protection of wild lands had grown louder. Central Idaho, which harbors the clear streams of the Salmon River system, diverse wildlife and

---

*On August 18, 1983, Bob Blackadar became the first person to stand on the summit of the glaciated peak named in his father's honor. Other members of the first ascent party included James Brock, Jerry Dixon, Mike Dixon, and Ron Watters.

untrammeled natural beauty, and places like it had become valuable national treasures by virtue of their rarity. Bob and Sue Blackadar took up their father's fight, and both worked actively for the protection of central Idaho. Finally, in the summer of 1980, Carter signed a bill creating a 2.2-million-acre River of No Return Wilderness in central Idaho.

Starting from a pile of maps on Blackadar's living room floor, the River of No Return Wilderness proposal had been a compromise. But Blackadar and his friends hoped that the power of a reasonable bill would attract public and political support. With the help of Frank Church, their hard work paid off.

Blackadar's role in the creation of the River of No Return Wilderness was a small one, but his marks are in the final legislation. Three of his key fears were addressed. The bill stopped the logging of Clear Creek, it prevented dredge mining on the Middle Fork and its tributaries, and it classified the 79 miles of the Salmon River as a wild river.

Of all his life's contributions, the River of No Return Wilderness may be his greatest legacy. In this wilderness, a remnant of the western frontier was saved, a frontier which he had eagerly sought by coming to Salmon in 1949. It was wild, untamed country which had nurtured him and shaped his life. Others will follow to face their own challenges and will find something that only wilderness can provide. "Thousands of tired, nerve-shaken, over civilized people," wrote John Muir, whom Blackadar quoted, "are beginning to find out that going to the mountains is going home; that wildness is necessity; and that mountain parks and reservations are useful not only as fountains of timber and irrigating rivers, but as fountains of life."

The River of No Return, the largest wilderness in the 48 states, is also a fountain of wealth for the small town that had meant so much to Blackadar. He had said as much in 1965. A few years later, he said, "Outdoor recreation is one of our most important uses. It will perhaps bring the greatest long-term good & dollars to our area." Since then, an industry built around

wilderness has prospered. Because Blackadar and his conservation friends had the foresight to work against the dismantling of
the central Idaho wilderness, backcountry recreation now brings
in millions of dollars to central Idaho communities.

*   *

IN the years following Blackadar's death, the town of Salmon
has continued its slow evolution, which had started with a few
tents along the banks of the river. Although growing, it is still
very much a small, friendly western town. Controversies come
and go. The battle to protect the River of No Return is now long
over, but skirmishes over other isolated tracts of wilderness near
Salmon flare up. Gordon Crupper, however, is no longer a
spokesman for the logging industry. He retired in 1985 and
moved away. The mill he managed was shut down earlier that
year when it could no longer be run profitably by its new owner,
Champion, a multi-national firm based in Connecticut.

Most of Blackadar's old hunting friends, such as Joe
Nebeker, Jim Caples and Jack Nancolas, have retired, but they
remained in the Salmon area, continuing to enjoy hunting, fishing, and the benefits and comforts of a small-town atmosphere.

Bill Baker, the Lemhi County sheriff who watched
Blackadar's frightening swim in Dagger Falls, has retired from
law enforcement. He enjoys his privacy at his home on Poison
Creek and keeps it that way by not having a telephone.

Karyn Prestwich, the little girl mistakenly shot by a hunter,
is no longer a little girl. Doc Blackadar, who had worked against
terrible odds that morning in 1970, would be pleased seeing her
now. She has finished her education degree and gets along just
fine, working and staying fit by skiing and playing tennis.

Blackadar's good friend and his first rafting companion on
the Salmon River, Eddie Linck, had passed away years before
Walt's accident on the South Fork. Linck, who was very much
like Blackadar, short, gutsy and powerfully built, died of cancer.

But cancer was probably far from their minds as they made their way down the river in spring of 1953. For Blackadar, it was the first of many delightful and satisfying trips on the Salmon.

Of all the rivers he had run in his life, he knew the Salmon River the best. He returned many times to run the 100-mile stretch through the wilderness of central Idaho. On the Salmon, he could leave roads and life's responsibilities behind him. On the Salmon, Walt Blackadar was free. The scene was much the same each time he started a journey down the river: the last-minute loading and tying of gear in boats, the hurried talk of rapids below, and the celebratory shouts as the boats were finally launched.

Watching from shore, we imagine him leaving on one of these trips. As his boat drifts away from shore, it is caught by the current and carried downstream, appearing smaller as it moves farther away. Then, in the distance, the tiny dot of the boat rounds a corner, and he disappears from our sight, blending into the mountains and deep recesses of the River of No Return Wilderness.

Acknowledgements

It was only natural to expect that when writing about someone like Walt Blackadar, I would find among his acquaintances both supporters and detractors—and all shades in between. In trying to paint an accurate picture of his life, I sought out views from all sides, and I have many people to thank for their thoughts, time, and candor.

First and foremost, I want to thank the Blackadar family who allowed me access to the doctor's files and correspondence. I can't express my gratitude and admiration enough. They were articulate, insightful, and candid. Never once did they try to limit access or attach strings to my research. No author has been treated better. My sincere thanks goes out to Walt's four daughters, Ruth Blackadar, Lois Blackadar, Nan Bryant and Sue Blackadar for all of their help. Walt's brother, John, and his wife Phyllis were gracious hosts, taking time from their busy schedules to show me around Watchung, New Jersey, and the old family home. Gordon (Walt's other brother) and his wife Virginia were equally generous, taking my wife Kathy and me by boat from Mortimer's Landing to the family cabin on an island on Muskoka Lake in Canada. It was here, on rivers winding through dense forests of the Muskoka area, that Walt Blackadar got his first taste of whitewater.

Of all the family members, I owe my greatest debt of gratitude to Bob Blackadar, Walt's son, who spent many hours with me, looking up his father's old acquaintances, sifting through manuscript materials, and shuttling me around Salmon. In 1983, with Bob's assistance, an expedition was mounted to the Alsek River, in part to gather data for this book, and to make an attempt to climb the mountain named in honor of Blackadar's achievements there.

During the expedition, Dr. Jim Brock, a river ecologist from the Idaho State University Biology Department, provided important clues on Walt Blackadar's famous run of Turnback Canyon by taking some of the first rough measurements of water flows. Besides Jim, other members of the party included Kathy Daly, and D'Arcy, Jerry and Mike Dixon. An early pre-trip flyover of Turnback Canyon was made by Jim Brock and Kathy Daly in a plane piloted by the indomitable Layton Bennett, who had flown Walt Blackadar over the canyon before his descent of the river. It was a remarkable adventure in one of the wildest, most capricious places that I have ever seen, and it was a journey none of us will ever forget. For Bob, it was a particularly unforgettable experience. During the expedition, he became the first person ever to stand on the summit of his father's mountain, Mt. Blackadar.

I want to thank Father Dick Tero of Anchorage for his assistance in providing materials on the Alsek and Susitna Rivers. An Alsek adventurer in his own right, he was kind enough to provide me with a place to stay during my trips to Alaska to do research. Ron Chambers of the Kluane National Park in Canada was another important source of information on the Alsek River, and I greatly appreciate his assistance in obtaining historical river running information and photos of Turnback Canyon.

Another individual who deserves my thanks is Andrew Embick, a well-known Alaskan climber and river runner, who sent me portions of his extensively researched manuscript on the rivers of Alaska. The sections prepared on the Alsek were especially valuable. On the same topic, Rob Lesser and Klaus Streckman, both kayakers who number among the select few that have successfully run Turnback Canyon, were of immeasurable assistance in identifying the rapids in the canyon and clarifying parts of Blackadar's Alsek diary entries. Lesser's perspective from that as a world-class expeditionary kayaker was crucial and provided an objective view of the importance of Blackadar's journey down the Alsek.

During the research stages of this project, I received a great amount of assistance from Roger Brown of Summit Films. He sent me transcribed copies of wild track recordings made on films which featured Blackadar. Of the many sources of information, the transcriptions were some of the most beneficial since they contained direct quotes made by Blackadar in an informal setting along a river.

Space limits me from detailing the contributions made by the many people that I interviewed, but I owe all of them my gratitude and sincere thanks for their time and help. They include: Fletcher Anderson, William Baker, Al Beam, Berniece Benedict, Jeff Bevan, Janice Blackadar, Nellie Bunce, Jerry Butler, Jim Caples, Phyllis Caples, Dr. Tullio Celano, Ken Collins, Cary Cook, Cort Conley, Francis Crawshaw, Dr. Dee Crouch, Pat Davis, Hazel Dean, Joy Dean, John Dondero, Helen Durand, Lloyd Edwards, Cully Erdman, Eric Evans, Jill Frye, Ron Frye, Stacy Gebhards, William Goetz, Barney Griffith, Dick Griffith, Betsy Hazelwood, Roger Hazelwood, Jack Hession, Gene Hussy, Evelyn Jardine, Jackie Johnson, Al Lowande, Ted Maestretti, Lynn McAdams, Woo McLean, Jack Nancolas, Joe Nebeker, Tim Nettleton, Tom Patterson, Don Prestwich, Marsha Prestwich, Clem Rawert, Dr. Dick Roberts, Muff Roberts, Dr. Boyd Simmons, Dr. Richard Smith, Jill Smith, John Spencer, Heidi Stolp, Dr. Kay Swanson, Margaret Taylor Sutherland, Dawn Taylor, Dr. Keith Taylor, Jean Tomita, Dr. George Wade, Doug Wheat, Dr. Barbara Wright, and Gary Young.

Acknowledgements

I wish to also thank the staffs of the Watchung and Plainfield Libraries in New Jersey, Anchorage Public Library, Salmon Public Library, and the Idaho State University Library. Gladys Swanson of the Lemhi County Museum and Nancy Anthony of the Interlibrary loan department at Idaho State deserve to be singled out for their kindness and helpfulness. I am indebted to Dave Meyers and Susan Duncan of the Idaho State Photography Department for their meticulous work in restoring and converting old color prints and slides into usable black and white photos. A special thank you is due to my supervisors in the Student Affairs Department at Idaho State University, Tony Barone, Greg Anderson, and Dr. Jan Anderson, for seeing the value of this project and supporting my request for leave to finish the work. I want to acknowledge my technical reviewers, including my companion of many wilderness journeys, Jerry Dixon of Seward, Alaska, and international kayak adventurer, Liam Guilar of Australia. They were both good enough friends to be frank with me and wisely encouraged me to take a very close and serious look at the lengthy first version. Thanks to their suggestions, the final version has been vastly improved.

I also want to recognize and thank my editor, Tracy Montgomery, who smoothed out the manuscript's rough edges and whose understanding of the book aided me in keeping my bearings. The final manuscript also greatly benefited by the proofreading talents of Elizabeth Neuhoff and Jo Parris, who painstakingly scoured it for blemishes. And most particularly, I want to thank Kathy for always being there and never doubting that it was all worthwhile.

Source Notes

CHAPTER I: SALMON CITY

8 "best place to live in the U.S.A.": W. L. Blackadar, Letter to Charles B. Everitt, *circa* 1-73.

8 Eastern medical friends warned him: Personal interview with John Blackadar, 8-10-85.

8 The new 18-by-18-foot surgical room: *Recorder Herald*, 2-23-50.

8 "real eastern lady": Personal interview with Lois Blackadar, 5-24-84.

9 "She was no milk toast": Telephone interview with Evelyn Jardine, 10-12-85.

9 "You won't be happy": Personal interview with Helen Durand, 6-29-84.

9 1948 Chevrolet sedan: *Recorder Herald*, 9-29-49.

9 luggage tied to the roof: Durand interview, 6-29-84.

9 he had his choice of Fords: *Recorder Herald*, 11-24-49.

10 Two or three log cabins: *Recorder Herald*, 7-15-54.

10 "completely modern home": Ads in fall, 1949 issues of *Recorder Herald*.

11 three prisoners sawed through: *Recorder Herald*, 9-29-49.

11 dynamiting his father-in-law's house: Personal interview with Bill Baker, Lemhi County Sheriff.

12 Ashbaugh was caught: *Recorder Herald*, 9-29-49, 10-6-49 and 10-27-49.

12 county records show: *Annual Report, Division of Vital Statistics* (Boise, Idaho: Idaho Department of Public Health, Division of Vital Statistics, 1953).

13 the bus en route from Pocatello: *Recorder Herald*, 2-17-49.

13 the flowers on Durand's: Durand interview, 6-29-84.

13 The disastrous winter: *Recorder Herald*, 9-13-49.

13 Once there Blackadar gave: Personal interview with Jim Caples, 5-23-84.

14 grows to an average 10 pounds: Anthony Newboy, *The Columbia River Salmon and Steelhead Trout, Their Fight for Survival* (Seattle: University of Washington, 1980), p. 42.

14 Some of summer run: Don Corley, "Steelheading on the Salmon River," *Idaho Wildlife Review*, September-October, 1971, pp. 3-4. Corley does a fine job of describing steelhead fishing in this article. Blackadar, Durand, and his friends dressed just as Corley described.

14 It comes as no surprise: Caples interview.

14 Like most steelhead fishermen: Corley, p. 3.

15 "He hated to be from there": Personal interview with Nel Bunce, 5-25-84.

15 "Walt was trying to be": Personal interview with Jean Tomita, 5-24-84.

15 "Alone against the wilderness,": Robert V. Hine, *The American West, An Interpretive History* (Boston: Little and Brown, 1973), p. 270.

16 Roy Durand could empathize: Durand interview.

16 Although Lloyd worked: John Blackadar interview. Additional information on Blackadar's childhood was provided by Gordon Blackadar, Joy Dean and Margaret Taylor Sutherland.

17 When Sam Popejoy was shot: *Recorder Herald*, 7-5-51.

18 Blackadar took a more ambitious: *Recorder Herald*, 10-18-51.

18 At the southern edge: Personal interview with Robert Blackadar, 5-24-84.

19 Ginger was an example: Unattributed anecdotal material from here to the end of the chapter is from a personal interview with Joe Nebeker, 5-25-84.

CHAPTER II: THE MIDDLE AND THE MAIN

24 Geologically, here the river has eroded: Terry Maley, *Exploring Idaho Geology* (Boise, Idaho: Mineral Land Publications, 1987), pp. 7, 64.

24 "Deciding there was no time": *Recorder Herald,* 4-2-53.

24 "one of those guys who'd be the first": Telephone interview with Lloyd Edwards, 8-22-87.

24 "fit into the time of the 1800s": Telephone interview with Helen Shelby, 10-10-87.

25 Jim Caples recalled: This and other anecdotal material about Main Salmon trips are from a personal interview with Jim Caples, 5-23-84.

28 "watching hundreds of huge salmon": Walt Blackadar, "Ordeal at Dagger Falls," unpublished TS., nd., p. 3.

29 "Gibson suddenly dropped" and related information: *Recorder Herald,* 7-9-53 and 7-23-53.

30 "Looks like he's": Personal interview with Robert Blackadar, 5-24-84.

30 in a record 19 hours: *Recorder Herald,* 7-23-53.

30 next Middle Fork trip came in 1954: Personal interview with Jerry Butler, 8-22-84. Jerry Butler could not be certain whether this first trip took place in 1953 or 1954. Because the Spaulding-Blackadar trip, reported by the *Recorder Herald*, took place in July of 1953, it is most likely that the trip with Butler occurred in 1954. It is, however, difficult to confirm the date since many of the principals are dead.

31 "You know what that little guy did": Butler interview.

32 "Below the two water segments": This and all subsequent quotes concerning Blackadar's near death at Dagger Falls come from Walt Blackadar, "Ordeal at Dagger Falls," unpublished TS., nd.

35 "a rite of initiation": Evan S. Connell, *Son of the Morning Star* (San Francisco: North Point Press, 1984), p. 266.

CHAPTER III: ESQUIMAUTAGE

37 "No wet suits": Walt Blackadar, "Kayak Technique" in *The All-purpose Guide to Paddling*, ed. Dean Norman (Matteson, Illinois: Great Lakes Living Press, 1976), pp. 14-15. Both the final edited version and the unedited ms. of Blackadar's early kayak attempt on the Salmon were utilized in introduction of this chapter.

39 As agreed, the group presented: *Recorder Herald,* 7-26-66.

39 Using the description: John T. Urban, *A White Water Handbook for Canoe and Kayak* (Boston: Appalachian Mountain Club, 1965), pp. 16-21.

39 "I had learned": Blackadar, *All Purpose*, p. 14.

40 by 1967 she remained undefeated: Bill Reynolds, "Interview: Barbara Wright," *Down River*, June, 1976, p. 11.

40 she wrote an article: Barbara Wright, "Esquimautage Sans Paddle," *American White Water*, Winter, 1964-65, pp. 14-15.

41 "He had been a rafter": Personal interview with Barbara Wright, 5-2-84.

42 Blackadar had arranged for Bill Guth: *Recorder Herald,* 7-18-68.

Source Notes

42   "more bounce to the ounce": Dave Binger, "Easterners on the Middle Fork," *American Whitewater*, Summer, 1968, p. 9.

42   "I would love": Blackadar, *All Purpose*, original ms., p. 5.

43   "Watching them": Binger, p. 10.

44   Klaus Streckman watched Blackadar: Personal interview with Klaus Streckman, 8-5-84.

45   "all lounging around": Binger, p. 11.

47   "Blackadar was drinking": Personal interview with Lynn McAdams, 5-22-84.

49   "After three pleasant days": *Recorder Herald*, 7-18-68.

49   "My helmet was sucked": Binger, p. 13.

49   On March 16, 1960: *United States Federal Power Commission Reports: Opinions, Decisions, and Orders*. Vol. 31, January 1, 1964 - June 30, 1964 (Washington: USGPO, 1967), p. 250.

50   Already, three dams: *Columbia River Fish Runs and Fisheries, 1957-1977* (Oregon Fish and Wildlife Commission and Washington Department of Fisheries), Vol. 2., no. 3, December 1978, p. 32.

50   Research biologists were finding: Anthony Newboy, *The Columbia River Salmon and Steelhead Trout, Their Fight for Survival* (Seattle: University of Washington Press, 1980), pp. 95-101.

50   according to a U.S. Geological report: L.L. Young and J.L. Colbert, "Water Power Resources of Idaho," *U.S. Geological Survey Open-file Report 1965*, pp. 131-156.

51   In 1964 and 1965, rapidly melting snow: A major climatic event, the "Christmas Flood of 1964," which caused severe erosion, is described in James M. Hockaday, *History of the Payette National Forest* (McCall, Idaho: Payette National Forest, 1968), pp. 49-50. Additional climatic events are described in Jerry Dixon, *The South Fork of the Salmon: Wild and Free*, np, McCall, Idaho, 1979, pp. 13-14.

51   The gravel of one famous hole: Stacy Gebhards, "The Vanishing Stream," *Idaho Wildlife Review,* March-April, 1970, p. 5.

51   The salmon declined dramatically: Jerry Mallet, "Long Range Planning for Salmon and Steelhead in Idaho, Inventory of Salmon and Steelhead Resources, Habitat, Use and Demands," Job Performance Report, Project F-58-R-1 (Boise, Idaho: Idaho Fish and Game Department, November, 1974), p. 121.

51   10,000 angler days: Mallet, p. 121.

51   3,927 of the big fish: David W. Ortmann, "Test to Evaluate Methods of Estimating Anadromous Fish Sport Harvests and Escapements," *Annual Progress Report, Salmon and Steelhead Investigations* (Boise, Idaho: Idaho Fish and Game Department, December, 1965), p. 17.

51   The Idaho Fish and Game Department had: David Ortmann, "Problems and Progress in Salmon Research," *Idaho Wildlife Review*, July-August, 1967, p. 8.

52   The first records of large fish kills: William S. Platts, Susan B. Martin, Edward R.J. Primbs, "Water Quality in an Idaho Stream Degraded by Acid Mine Waters," *USDA Forest Service General Technical Report INT-67* (Ogden, Utah: U.S. Department of Agriculture Forest Service Intermountain Forest and Range Experiment Station, 1979), p. 4.

52   Blackadar wrote to Stewart Udall: W.L. Blackadar, Letter to Stewart Udall, Secretary of the Interior, Washington, D.C., 4-2-65.

271

NEVER TURN BACK

CHAPTER IV: EMERGENCY CALL FROM NORTH FORK

55 The following spring, Dick Roberts: Personal interview with Dick Roberts, 8-24-84 and Al Beam, 8-25-84.

55 a descent of the wild Bruneau: In the first printing of this book, it was noted that Blackadar's party made the first kayak descent of the river. That is incorrect. The first known kayak descent was made in 1964 by Tom Steinburn and Cecil Oulette.

56 "He may be the only man": "Bruneau River Excursion Achieved By Local Trio," *Times-News*, Sunday, June 15, 1969.

56 Dave Binger's article: Dave Binger, "Easterners on the Middle Fork," *American White Water*, Summer, 1968, p. 9.

56 "one of the most experienced authorities": "Bruneau," *Times-News*.

57 The 80,000-acre roadless area: Ron Watters, "Clear Creek: Home for Big Game," *The Idaho Citizen*, April-May, 1978, p. 19.

57 The five family-owned mills: *Recorder Herald*, 7-29-65, 8-12-65 and 8-19-65.

57 The company grew exponentially: *Recorder Herald*, 8-19-65.

58 timber industry pushed for larger cuts: *Recorder Herald*, 8-27-64.

58 both were fellow Chamber members: *Recorder Herald*, 1-18-68.

58 Crupper steadfastly supported Republicans: *Recorder Herald*, 8-22-68.

58 estimated to be 72 million board feet: *Recorder Herald*, 4-13-67.

58 moved to obtain a right of way: *Recorder Herald*, 4-15-65.

58 They were held up: *Recorder Herald*, 4-13-67.

59 The Clear Creek hearing: *Recorder Herald*, 3-12-70.

60 Swelling the total: *Recorder Herald*, 4-2-70.

60 "Students had hoped": *Recorder Herald*, 4-23-70.

61 A dentist from California: Personal interview with Dick Smith, 8-22-84.

61 he said in a guest editorial: *Recorder Herald*, 8-13-70.

61 In a virulent opposing guest article: *Recorder Herald*, 8-27-70.

62 "bird-watching squirrel chasers": *Recorder Herald*, 3-26-70.

62 "I talked to some kid": Personal interview with Tullio Celano, 5-26-84.

62 Hazelwood and Celano: Personal interview with Roger Hazelwood, 5-15-84.

64 "I decided": Personal interview with Al Beam, 8-25-84.

64 "Home safe . . . .": W.L. Blackadar, Letter to Al Beam, 5-8-70.

65 Blackadar had interested Boyd Simmons: Personal interview with Dr. Boyd Simmons, 5-23-84.

65 "I spent 10 years": W.L. Blackadar, Letter to Charles B. Everitt, Little Brown & Co., *circa* 1-73.

66 Smith built a platform: *Recorder Herald*, 6-18-70.

66 "No, boys": Al Beam interview.

67 He complained in his letter: W.L. Blackadar, Letter to John R. Woodworth, Director, Idaho Fish and Game Department, 7-23-70.

68 Woodworth politely replied: J.R. Woodworth, Letter to W.L. Blackadar, 8-20-70.

68 He had sent out letters: W.L. Blackadar, Letter to Barb Wright, 10-18-69.

69 Smith insisted: W.L. Blackadar, Letter to Grand Canyon participants, 12-29-69.

69 In the end, 27 kayaks: Roger Parsons, "Grand Canyon By Canoe and Kayak," TS., nd., p. 1.

69 "harder to paddle in": W.L. Blackadar, Letter to Grand Canyon participants, 5-14-70.

70 "Next morning we arose": Parsons, p. 2.

71 "It looks like we're incompetent": Streckman interview.

71 "was stood on its broken end": Parsons, p. 2.

72 "was a top quality big river": Personal interview with Lynn McAdams, 5-22-84.

72   The race began heating up: Sydney Duncombe and Boyd A. Martin, *Recent Elections in Idaho (1964-1970)* (Moscow, Idaho: Bureau of Public Affairs Research, 1972), p. 21.

73   American Smelting and Refining Company: *Recorder Herald*, 9-19-68.

73   At the hearings: Boyd Norton, *Snake Wilderness* (San Francisco: Sierra Club, 1972), p. 75.

73   "The natural resources of Custer County": *Recorder Herald*, 6-12-69.

73   "The Good Lord": "Governor, Congress Aspirants' Points of View," *The Idaho Statesman*, Sunday, November 1, 1970, p. 8-B.

74   "a natural resource": *Statesman*, p. 8-B.

74   Samuelson had garnered: *Recorder Herald*, 11-5-70.

74   The election had been won: "In Idaho, A Life-Style Choice," *The Post-Register*, November 5, 1970, p. 2A.

74   *Time* magazine agreed: *Time*, November 16, 1970, p. 27.

74   Roy Wells of Torrance, California: *Recorder Herald*, 11-12-70.

74   6-year old Karyn Prestwich: Personal interview with Marsha and Don Prestwich, 1-10-86.

CHAPTER V: A LOOK IN THE MIRROR

79   A palpable air: This and other descriptions of the Alsek country from author's observations, Alsek-Mt. Blackadar Memorial Expedition, August 19, 1983.

80   more than half of the park: *Kluane National Park* (Ottawa: Parks Canada, 1980).

80   Within its icy boundaries: Robert A. Henning, Barbara Olds and Penny Rennick, *Wrangell-Saint Elias: International Mountain Wilderness* (Anchorage, Alaska: Alaska Geographic, 1981), p. 15.

80   The canyon's name: L.M. Sebert, Chief Technical Information Office, Department of Energy, Mines and Resources, Letter to Mr. Richard Tero, 12-1-71; and Alfred H. Brooks, "The Geography and Geology of Alaska," *U.S. Geological Survey, Professional Paper No. 45*, Washington, 1906, pp. 53-54.

81   The first known descent: Telephone interview with Clem Rawert, 6-22-87.

81   By late December: *Recorder Herald*, 12-31-70.

81   Temperatures in town dropped: *Recorder Herald*, 1-7-71.

82   Blackadar was taking advantage: Blackadar Family Christmas letter, 1970.

82   During Lloyd's lingering bout: Personal interviews with Joy Dean, 3-24-86, Lois Blackadar, 5-24-84, and Jean Tomita, 5-24-84.

82   "Hi, 'Wild Al.'": W.L. Blackadar, Letter to Al Beam, 2-4-70.

82   "Al has finally gotten": W.L. Blackadar, Letter to Barbara Wright, 4-7-70.

82   Blackadar was also pleased: Personal interview with Al Beam, 8-25-84.

83   In mid-February: W.L. Blackadar to Klaus Streckman, 2-26-71; and Kay Swanson interview, 5-21-84.

83   As the winter progressed": *Recorder Herald*, 12-24-70, 12-31-70, 7-22-71.

83   the appeal was denied: *Recorder Herald*, 12-16-71.

84   "The Alsek River is a major stream": Richard D. Tero, "Running the Alsek," *Alaska*, March, 1971, p. 36.

84   "Exploring was handicapped": Tero, "Running," pp. 39, 49.

85   On February 26, he wrote: W.L. Blackadar, Letter to Klaus Streckman, 2-26-71.

85   "Sounds like a fun trip": W.L. Blackadar, Letter to Barbara Wright, 2-26-71.

86   "I have been very intrigued": W.L. Blackadar, Letter to Richard Tero, 4-9-71.

86   Tero immediately replied: Personal interview with Richard Tero, 8-11-84.

86   Telephone interview with Clem Rawert, 6-22-87.

86   "I repeated it again": Telephone interview with Dee Crouch, 6-24-87.

87   The heavy snow knocked out: *Recorder Herald*, 4-29-71.

87   Blackadar and his other son-in-law: Blackadar Family Christmas letter, 1970.

88   Late in April he went: Robert O. Collins and Roderick Nash, *The Big Drops* (San Francisco: Sierra Club Books, 1978), p. 154.

88   "washer and dishwasher busy": Blackadar Family Christmas letter 1970.

88   the Alsek country was making news: "38 Days In the Wilderness," *Anchorage Daily Times*, August 2, 1971, p. 1.

89   "ill-prepared": Al Beam interview.

89   "I cancelled plans": W.L. Blackadar, Letter to Richard Tero, nd (*circa* September, 1971).

90   "My birthday!": W.L. Blackadar, Original Alsek Diary(OAD), entry for 8-13-71. This excerpt is from a typescript copy of the most original version of the diary that has survived.

90   "did not want to urge [them]": W.L. Blackadar, OAD, entry for 8-19-71.

90   Barb Wright believes: Personal interview with Barb Wright, 5-22-84.

90   "I'm not suicidal": Walt Blackadar, "Caught Up in a Hell of White Water," *Sports Illustrated*, August 14, 1972, p. 43.

91   "I lost a good patient": Jackie Johnson, "Whitewater Surgeon," *Down River*, March, 1977, pp. 27-28.

91   it had been a particularly bad year: *Recorder Herald*, 12-24-70, 8-19-71 and 12-9-71.

91   Type T's are driven psychologically: John Leo, "Looking for a Life of Thrills," *Time*, April 15, 1985, p. 92; and work by Marvin Zuckerman: *Sensation Seeking: Beyond the Optimal Level of Arousal* (Hillsdale, New Jersey: Lawrence Elbaum Associates, 1979); "Sensation Seeking and Sports," *Personality and Individual Differences*, Vol. 4, no. 3, 1983; "Sensation Seeking and Risk Taking," in *Emotions in Personality and Psychopathology*, ed. Carroll E. Izard (New York, Plenum Press, 1979).

92   "He had a super big ego": Personal interview with Dr. Boyd Simmons, 5-23-84.

92   "a screw-ball whitewater kayaker": W.L. Blackadar, Letter to Robert Shalton, n.d.

92   "If my boat is found swamped": W.L. Blackadar, OAD, entry for 8-20-70.

92   He called Barb Wright: Barbara Wright interview.

93   "pretty damn scary": Personal interview with Lynn McAdams, 5-22-84.

94   "I wondered if the guy": Author's conversations with Layton Bennett, 8-13-83.

94   "wingtips nearly touching": W.L. Blackadar, *Sports Illustrated*, p. 43.

94   "Several very impressive boiling pots": Unattributed quotes from here to end of chapter are from W.L. Blackadar's Original Alsek Diary.

CHAPTER VI: "IN THE GORGE AND STRANDED"

97   "Lowell Glacier, off to the right": Walt Blackadar, "Caught Up in a Hell of White Water," *Sports Illustrated*, August 14, 1972, p. 44.

97   From the ice wall at the river: William O. Fields, ed. *Mountain Glaciers of the Northern Hemisphere*, Volume 2, Hanover, New Hampshire, June 1975, p. 206.

98   "two-thirds the size of a football field": This and other short unatttributed quotes in the chapter are from Blackadar, "Caught Up," p. 44-45.

98   "became lost in the floating ice": "Alsek River: Excerpts From My Diary," second surviving version of Blackadar's Alsek diary, entry for 8-24-71.

Source Notes

98   One glacier in the St. Elias: Robert A. Henning, Barbara Olds, Penny Rennick, *Wrangle-Saint Elias: International Mountain Wilderness* (Anchorage, Alaska: Alaska Geographic, 1981), p. 63.

98   River temperature readings: James T. Brock, unpublished research notes, August, 1983.

99   "It's ice and brown": W.L. Blackadar, Original Alsek Diary(OAD), TS, entry for 8-24-71.

99   After the second rapid, the Alsek: Author's Observations, Alsek-Mt. Blackadar Memorial Expedition, August, 1983.

99   In 1961, Clem Rawert: Telephone interview with Clem Rawert, 6-22-87.

100   Before leaving for the Alsek: Telephone interview with Dee Crouch, 6-24-87.

100   To other friends he once explained: Personal interview with Gary Young, 10-6-85.

100   "The amazing thing was that Walt": Personal interview with Richard D. Tero, 8-11-84.

101   "I will wait until the next day": Blackadar, OAD, entry for 8-24-71.

101   "Rescue by another boater": "Alsek River: Excerpts From My Diary," entry for 8-24-71.

101   The 40-mile-long glacier: Bradford Washburn, Letter to Richard D. Tero, 5-18-71.

101   the Tweedsmuir was beginning to surge: Canadian Ministry of Environment, Ottawa, Press Release, October, 1973.

102   During this time river flows exceed: James T. Brock, "Discharge Estimate—Alsek River, Below Turnback Opposite Tweedsmuir Glacier," unpublished, 8-21-83.

103   "tossed it some distance": W.L. Blackadar, Letter to Barb Wright, nd. *circa* September, 1971).

104   "I tried & tried to regain my paddle": Blackadar to Wright, 1971.

104   The rapid, now called the S-turns: Identification of rapids described by Blackadar is based on aerial photographs taken by the U.S. Geological Survey, Glaciology Project, Tacoma, WA, specifically, photo # F7-61-171 on which Rob Lesser marked Turnback's rapids after his two runs through the canyon. Additional assistance was rendered by a drawing prepared by Klaus Streckman and his interview on 8-5-84. And lastly, during the Alsek-Mt. Blackadar Memorial Expedition, the author made several trips through the canyon in a helicopter and scouted two of the major rapids from the ground.

104   "A huge 45-degree drop": Blackadar, "Caught Up," p. 49.

105   His planned portage route led: Blackadar to Wright, 1971.

106   "Suddenly, I was in a frothy mess": Blackadar, "Caught Up," p. 49.

106   Referring to the wave as the "roller": Blackadar, OAD, entry for 8-25-71. From this point on it becomes more difficult to identify the rapids described in Blackadar's diary. Rob Lesser and Klaus Streckman both believe that Blackadar's Roller is likely what Lesser called at the time of their descent, "Percolator." Blackadar said he spent the night just below the roller across from a waterfall, which would verify Lesser's hunch, since a large zigzagging waterfall descends from the left side of the canyon here. Streckman concurs, feeling the waterfall is significant and uses it as a canyon landmark. Lesser named the area directly opposite the waterfall, appropriately, Walt's Refuge.

107   "I was sure the roller": Blackadar to Wright, 1971.

107   "After scouting": Blackadar to Wright, 1971.

107   "in the middle of the river": Blackadar, "Caught Up," p. 49.

107   For an hour, he surveyed: Blackadar to Wright, 1971.

108   "[I] could feel the tug of war": Blackadar to Wright, 1971.

108   "I forced myself not to swim": Jackie Johnson, "Whitewater Surgeon," *Down River*, March 1977, p. 28.

108   "I got scrubbed": Blackadar, "Caught Up," p. 49-50.

109   "In the gorge and stranded!": Blackadar, OAD, entry for 8-25-71.

109 "one huge horrendous mile": Blackadar, "Caught Up," p. 49.

109 Blackadar's piece on the Alsek is the best: Tero interview.

110 He was on the left bank: Blackadar, OAD, entry for 8-25-71.

110 "I slipped by the edge": Blackadar, "Caught Up," p. 50.

110 "Now relaxing": Blackadar, OAD, entry for 8-26-71.

111 "woozy, shaken": Andrew Embick, "Alsek River," unpublished ms., 1987, p. 16.

CHAPTER VII: THE BIG SU

114 Jones' major achievement: Mike Jones, *Canoeing Down Everest* (London: Hodder and Stoughton, 1979).

115 Rob Lesser, who has built: Personal interview with Rob Lesser, 8-7-84.

116 "I'll agree it was a crazy trip": W.L. Blackadar, Letter to Barbara Wright, nd. (*circa* September, 1971).

116 "If they don't give encouragement": Copy of Blackadar's correspondence with *Reader's Digest* sent to Barbara Wright with additional notes by Blackadar, 9-30-71.

116 "Thanks for letting us see": Ed Fortnier, Executive Editor, *Alaska*, Letter to W.L. Blackadar, 12-28-71.

117 "Before, I had just a hint": Pat Ryan, Text Department Editor, *Sports Illustrated* to W.L. Blackadar, 1-31-72.

117 Indeed, within a few months: W.L. Blackadar, Letter to Barbara Wright, *circa* September, 1971.

117 "Part of living": Jackie Johnson, "Whitewater Surgeon," *Down River*, March, 1977, p. 27.

118 Logging in itself he accepted: Personal interview with Robert Blackadar, 1-10-88.

118 "We cannot desecrate": *Recorder Herald*, 3-23-72.

119 "a continuing threat": *Recorder Herald*, 12-9-71.

119 "I could hear wind": Personal interview with Cary Cook, 8-24-84.

120 "He stunned us": Personal interview with Richard Tero, 8-11-84, and Dee Crouch, 6-24-87.

121 Just above the entrance: Telephone interview with Jack Hession, 3-29-88.

122 "We made a pact": Personal interview with Roger Hazelwood, 5-15-84.

122 "Walt was in the lead": Personal interview with John Dondero, 8-25-84.

122 "Then I ran it": Tullio Celano, "Notes," 1972.

123 "Malone was sitting": Personal interview with Al Beam, 8-25-84.

125 To the Upper Inlet Athapaskans: James Kari, "Dena'ina Place Names in and Adjacent to the Talkeetna Study Area," *Cultural Resources Assessment, Lower Susitna River Basin*, U.S. Department of Agriculture, Soil Conservation Service, January, 1983, p. 48.

125 The most precipitous part: "Upper Susitna River, Alaska, An Inventory and Evaluation of the Environmental Aesthetics and Recreational Resources," Jones & Jones/Alaska District of Corps of Engineers, March, 1975, p. 291.

125 Susitnu, or syitnu: Kari, p. 48.

126 "[A]fter hearing these fearsome stories": This and all other unattributed quotes are from W.L. Blackadar, "The Susitna," TS, nd, *circa* 1972.

126 "Hey," Blackadar said: Tero interview.

127 "We began to feel tense": C.H. Swanson, Jr., "Eaten by an Alaskan Devil River," TS, *circa* 1973. This is the unedited version used in the *Relax* article.

128 "If you guys want to run that": This and related quotes from Hazelwood interview.

129   "Walt was having a hard time": This and related "spoken" quotes from personal interview with Kay Swanson, 5-21-84.

131   "We couldn't see into it": This and related "written" quotes from Kay Swanson, "Alaska's Devil River," *Relax*, September, 1973, p 34.

132   "Walt, look, we saw": Swanson interview.

CHAPTER VIII: TRAGEDY ON THE WEST FORK

139   "I truly enjoyed paddling": Julie Wilson, Letter to W.L. Blackadar, July 10, 1973.

140   She confided to him: Julie Wilson, Letter to W.L. Blackadar, October 25, 1973.

140   "I've never felt so comfortable": Julie Wilson, Letter to W.L. Blackadar, September 25, 1973.

140   She also reported: Wilson, July 10, 1973.

140   "I've finally made my decision": Julie Wilson, Letter to W.L. Blackadar, December 17, 1973.

141   "[I] cancelled": Walt Blackadar, "Julie Wilson Falls," TS, *circa* 1974, p. 1.

141   several inches of snow covered the ground: Telephone interview with Ken Collins, 11-3-87.

141   overall difficulty was not nearly as hard: Walt Blackadar, "It Didn't Have to Happen," *Down River Magazine*, September, 1974, p. 22.

142   The group talked: Collins interview.

142   "After a hearty steak breakfast": Walt Blackadar, "Julie Wilson Falls," *American Whitewater*, July-August, 1974, p. 117.

142   "We slowly and carefully worked": Blackadar, "Julie Wilson," *AWA*, p. 118.

143   "We relaxed a bit": Blackadar, "Julie Wilson," *AWA*, p. 118.

145   "I had to wait forever": Blackadar, "Julie Wilson," *AWA*, p. 119.

145   Collins also found himself swept: This and material on pages 145-148 from Collins interview.

148   "I ran up to the bank": Ken Collins, "West Fork Ordeal," ms., 1974.

149   Pointing their lights: Collins interview.

149   "When you get back down": This conversation (pages 149-150), related by Collins in his interview, differs some from his notes of the accident. In his notes he says that Blackadar gave this information to Stapleman and Jones. Since Collins has such a vivid memory of the conversation and it seems to accurately reflect Blackadar's reasons for continuing on alone, it has been included in the text.

151   Nettleton was visibly angered: Rodger Losier, sworn statement concerning events after death of Julie Wilson, *circa* September, 1974.

151   "Sad as this experience has been": Ross Wilson, Letter to W.L. Blackadar, May 2, 1974.

152   "We hereby constitute": Ross Wilson and Elizabeth Osborne Wilson, "Power of Attorney," May 3, 1974.

152   The arrangement was formalized: Personal interview with Nancy Bryant, 5-23-84.

152   "Shirl Darling": W.L. Blackadar, Letter to Shirley Blackadar, 5-3-74.

153   Blackadar, his daughter, Nan: Bryant interview.

154   flew the river once with Dick Roberts: Personal interview with Dick Roberts, 8-24-84.

154   "We managed": Losier and JoAnne Comins, sworn statements concerning burial of Julie Wilson, September 26, 1974.

CHAPTER IX: THE BIGGEST RIDE

157   "Enclosed is the": Elizabeth Wilson, Letter to W.L. Blackadar, 6-2-74.
157   "We are truly grateful to you": Ross Wilson, Letter to W.L. Blackadar, 5-31-74.
158   going as high as an unusual 103 degrees: *Recorder Herald*, 6-20-74.
158   "He was a man": Personal interview with Marsha Prestwich, 1-10-86; and *Recorder Herald*, 6-20-74.
158   The Salmon River claimed more: Personal interview with Al Beam, 8-25-84.
159   "For the first 10 days": Walt Blackadar, "Julie Wilson Falls," *American White Water*, July-August, 1974, p. 120.
159   "he was devastated": Personal interview with Lois Blackadar, 5-24-84.
159   "He was crying": Personal interview with Dr. Boyd Simmons, 5-23-84.
159   He wrote to Barb Wright: W.L. Blackadar, Letter to Barbara Wright, 5-6-74.
159   After Julie's death: Telephone interview with Ken Collins, 11-3-87.
159   "Please publish the paper": Dr. Donald H. Wilson, Letter to W.L. Blackadar, May 21, 1974.
160   "I was her": Blackadar, "Julie Wilson," *AWA*, p. 117.
160   In the article he detailed: Blackadar, "Julie Wilson," *AWA*, pp. 120-121.
161   Driving at his usual pace: Personal interview with Nancy Bryant, 5-23-84.
163   "I heard it was great": W.L. Blackadar, Letter to Barbara Wright, 4-12-72.
164   He wanted a mixed group: Glenn Giere, ABC Sports, Letter to "Those Concerned" (W.L. Blackadar, et. al.), 7-16-74.
164   Dondero had recently started: Personal interview with John Dondero, 8-25-84.
165   "We have a very good group": *ABC American Sportsman*, "Colorado River Kayak Trip," filmed in 1974, appeared on national television January, 1975.
165   John Dondero, eager to help: Dondero interview.
166   At Lava Falls, the ABC crew: *ABC American Sportsman*, "Colorado River Kayak Trip."
168   According to the Twin Falls *Times-News*: "Grave Opened in Owyhee," *Times-News*, Sunday, September 22, 1974, p. 1
169   When asked by reporters: *Owyhee Chronicle*, 10-31-74.
169   "He [Nettleton] wanted to get me": Telephone interview with William Goetz, 3-9-88.
170   In the *Statesman* article: "Leader of Kayak Trip Assails Exhuming of Bruneau Victim," *The Idaho Statesman*, October 19, 1974, p. 15.
170   "show their support": W.L. Blackadar, Letter to newspapers, 10-15-74.
170   When the all county election returns: *The Owyhee Chronicle*, 11-7-74.
171   When interviewed later: Telephone interview with Tim Nettleton, Sheriff, Owyhee County, 3-16-88.
172   In late September after he had learned: Sworn statements by JoAnne Comins, Vane Jones, and Merlin Stapleman are all dated at the end of September, 1974.
173   "could very well be the best": Ted Trueblood, "Can Idaho's River of No Return Wilderness be Saved?" *Idaho Environmental Issues* (Boise, Idaho Wildlife Federation, nd), p. 7.
173   "To win": W.L. Blackadar, Letter to "Friends" (kayakers), *circa* late 1973.
173   "An analysis of the responses": U.S. Department of Agriculture, *A Proposal: Salmon River Wilderness and Idaho Wilderness*, 1974, pp. 23-24.
174   was linked by conservationists to a meeting: "A Primitive Decision" in *Lewiston Morning Tribune*, December 8, 1974, p. 4A.

Source Notes

CHAPTER X: ON THE EDGE

177   The red, white and blue rocket: Robert F. Jones, "'We Shoulda Run One More Test,'" *Sports Illustrated*, September 16, 1974, pp. 26, 28, 29.

178   The wave of bodies pounds: Cricket Bird, "Fence, Guards, Psychology Protect Snake Rim," *Times-News*, Thursday, September 5, 1974, p. 1.

178   Part of the crowd breaks through: "Security Plan Fails," *Times-News*, Monday, September 9, 1974, p. 1.

178   "I knew": Walt Blackadar, "Evel Landed in My Lap," unedited MS, *circa* September, 1974, p. 1.

178   "The Tweedsmuir": Personal interview with Klaus Streckman, 8-5-84.

179   Their escape from the canyon: Dee Crouch, "Alsek Revisited," unpublished diary, 1974, pp. 8-13.

179   His daughter, Lois, noticing the same: Personal interview with Lois Blackadar, 5-24-84.

180   The canyon is not nearly: Robert F. Jones, "Make it or Break it," *Sports Illustrated*, September 2, 1974, p. 61.

181   Knievel would be strapped: Jones, "Make it," p. 58.

181   That night, Dee Crouch drove in: Telephone interview with Dee Crouch, 6-24-87.

182   "The rocket then careened down": W.L. Blackadar, "Evel's Rescue," *Sports Illustrated*, September 23, 1974, p. 78.

183   "Well, so am I, sonny": Author's conversations with W.L. Blackadar.

184   "He is a braggart": Blackadar, "Evel Landed," pp. 2-3.

184   Margaret Meagher, Knievel's secretary: Margaret C. Meagher, Letter to W.L. Blackadar, May 5, 1975.

184   The film was conceived: Roger C. Brown, "Filming Along 'The Edge' Between Great Joy and Possible Death," *American Cinematographer*, August, 1975, p. 940.

185   "I was really forced": Telephone interview with Roger Brown, 11-3-87.

186   "At that time both Walt and I": This and subsequent quotes from telephone interview with Fletcher Anderson, 11-3-87.

187   Nan had heard: Personal interview with Nan Bryant 5-23-84.

190   His daughter, Sue: Personal interview with Sue Blackadar, 6-27-82.

190   Three cameramen were positioned: Herb A. Lightman, "Plunging over Lava Falls with Kayak and Camera," *American Cinematographer*, August, 1975, p. 966.

190   "I knew behind me": Transcripts of "wild track" recordings for *The Edge*, May, 1975, Summit Films, Gypsum, Colorado.

192   Blackadar sent invitations: W.L. Blackadar, Letters to Al Beam, Dr. Keith Taylor, Roger Hazelwood, Dr. Tullio Celano, and Ron Watters.

192   The word had gotten around: Author's observations, March 12, 1976.

193   At a showing in his own town: W.L. Blackadar, Letter to Roger Brown and Barry Corbet, 3-31-76.

193   "We feel that because of his": Roger C. Brown, "Walt Blackadar: Doctor, Boater, and Frontiersman," unpublished ms., nd., p. 3.

194   That night while his wife: Author's observations.

195   Over fillet of sole: Roger C. Brown, "Filming along the Susitna: Kayaking's Everest," *American Cinematographer*, September, 1978, p. 902.

195   "It makes Lava Falls look": W.L. Blackadar, "Proposal for Filming Kayak Run Through the Susitna River Including Devil's Gorge in Central Alaska," nd, p. 1.

196   Blackadar went to work: W.L. Blackadar, Letter to Dr. Barb Freemont-Smith (Wright), April 23, 1976.

196   He chose John Dondero: W.L. Blackadar, Letter to John Wasson, June 11, 1976.

197   "Getting a lot of inquiries": W.L. Blackadar, Letter to Roger Brown, June 29, 1976.

197   Lori Kincaid in Anchorage: Lori Kincaid, Letter to W.L. Blackadar, June 12, 1976.

197   "Have lined up": Lori Kincaid, Letter to W.L. Blackadar, June 19, 1976.

197   "To Whom It May Concern": William Baker, Sheriff, Lemhi County, July 13, 1976.

198   "It's all falling into place": W.L. Blackadar, Letter to Roger Brown, nd, *circa* July, 1976.

CHAPTER XI: I'LL BE BACK

199   One morning in late May: Personal interview with Joe Nebeker, 5-25-84.

200   for some time he fed himself: Personal interview with Ruth Blackadar, 6-27-82.

200   Hazel Dean, his nurse: Personal interview with Hazel Dean, 8-24-84.

200   Sue Blackadar remembers: Personal interview with Sue Blackadar, 5-16-84.

200   To help correct the problem: On the "Medical Examiner's Report" for the Equitable Life Assurance Society, 3-1-69, Blackadar attributes his problem known as shoulder outlet syndrome to the two clavicle surgeries. According to medical records provided by Bob Blackadar, the first corrective surgery on the left shoulder took place in 1965 or 1966, and the second on both shoulders in early 1974.

200   Devil Creek Rapids is a powerful stretch: Author's notes, 8-8-84 and 8-9-84.

202   There was no room: Personal interview with John Dondero, 8-25-84.

202   Although Dick Griffith: Personal interview with Dick Griffith, 8-12-84.

202   "an excellent boater": Walt Blackadar, "Before you go to Hell . . . Paddle the Devil," TS, nd, p. 7.

203   "Barney," Spencer said jokingly: Personal interview with John Spencer, 3-25-85.

203   The film crew and boaters: Roger C. Brown, "Filming along the Susitna: Kayaking's Everest," *American Cinematographer*, September, 1978, p. 910.

203   Additional food, alcohol, and supplies: Fletcher Anderson, "Keeping the Donkey's Attention: A First Descent on Daytime T.V.," TS, nd., pp. 2-4.

204   Walt, I am up at High Lake: Brown, "Filming," p. 913.

204   Blackadar was angered: Telephone interview with Roger Brown, 11-3-87.

204   Part of the attraction of the film: Walt Blackadar, M.D., "My Race with the Devil," *Medical Economics*, August 8, 1977, p. 248.

204   "I had a long serious discussion": Brown interview.

204   "Join us—Land upriver": Note, dated August 3, 1976, in possession of Dick Griffith, Anchorage, Alaska.

205   "Barney was in for": John Dondero interview.

205   "In one way it was": Personal interview with Barney Griffith, 3-25-85.

205   "A common adversary": Brown, "Filming," p. 913.

205   "You probably heard": Telephone interview with Fletcher Anderson, 11-3-87.

205   When Anderson wrote about his impressions: Anderson, "Donkey's Attention," p. 17.

205   Hazelwood didn't like the atmosphere: Personal interview with Roger Hazelwood, 5-26-84.

206   Blackadar called Hazelwood's decision: Blackadar, "Before you go to Hell," p. 8.

206   "Even more perhaps than the others": Blackadar, "Before you go to Hell," pp. 6, 8. Other subsequent unreferenced quotes to Blackadar are from this TS.

206   "His boat was tiny in the big river": Brown, "Filming," p. 914. Other subsequent unreferenced quotes by Brown are from this article.

Source Notes

206 "A piece of driftwood": Personal interview with Keith Taylor, 5-26-84.

207 Blackadar rose up toward the top: "Alaska Kayaking," a filmed segment in *American Sportsman*, American Broadcasting Company, first aired February 1977.

207 "I tried every roll I had": Dialog from above film.

208 John Dondero ran next: Dondero interview.

209 Concerned about Barney's safety: Brown interview.

210 "When I got out of that water": Dialog.

210 The next day, the weather: Personal interview with Bob Blackadar, 5-24-84.

212 The weakness in his technique: Personal interview with Barb Wright, 5-22-84.

212 He does not allow his hips: Author's observations and telephone interview with Rob Lesser, 12-2-87.

212 Cully Erdman also tried: Personal interview with Cully Erdman, 10-5-85.

213 Their run, though not without: Bob Blackadar interview.

213 "I had lost my self-confidence": Transcripts of "wild track" recordings for *The Edge*, May, 1975, Summit Films, Gypsum, Colorado.

214 "Let's go get him": Dondero interview.

214 Hazelwood tried to paddle: Hazelwood interview.

215 "Walt said it was big": Barney Griffith interview.

215 "It was some of the biggest": Erdman interview.

215 "I'll never forget it": Dondero interview.

215 Sometime after the Susitna: Erdman interview

215 Brown replied that it sounded: Roger Brown, Letter to W.L. Blackadar, November 8, 1976.

216 In February of 1977: Bob Nixon, Talent Coordinator, *American Sportsman*, ABC Sports, Letter to W.L. Blackadar, February 18, 1977.

216 "All of us were very chagrined": W.L. Blackadar, Letter to Ms. Donna Berglund, March 14, 1977.

216 "It was a team effort": W.L. Blackadar, Letter to Dr. Dee Crouch, 1-11-77 (sic, probably 2-11-77).

216 "You don't want a whole bunch": Lesser interview.

CHAPTER XII: THROUGH THE NIGHT

219 During the first part of 1977: W.L. Blackadar, Letter to Donna Berglund, 2-14-77.

220 Blackadar's third journey down: This and related unattributed quotes from telephone interview with Rob Lesser, 12-2-87.

221 One stretch of rapids: Kay Swanson, Letter to W.L. Blackadar, 8-24-73.

221 "The more I think about": W.L. Blackadar, Letter to Klaus Streckman, 6-7-77.

221 "He took the Susitna": This and related unattributed quotes from telephone interview with Ron Frye, 12-2-87.

222 Some of his hunting friends: Personal interview with Ted Maestretti, 8-21-84.

222 When he visited his daughter: Personal interview with Ruth Blackadar, 6-27-82.

222 "It was almost like he": This and related unattributed quotes from telephone interview with Al Lowandi, 12-2-87.

229 "We are now contemplating": W.L. Blackadar, Letter to Doug Wheat, 3-14-77.

230 "Walt was indignant": This and subsequent unattributed quotes from telephone interview with Doug Wheat, 12-7-87.

230 "If you guys need anything": This and related unattributed quotes from personal interview with Gary Young, 10-6-85.

230 "I had no affection": Tom Johnson, Diary of Tatshenshini Trip, August 7-25, 1977.

231 "I'm having a blast": Wheat interview.

232 The fishermen working: Johnson, Diary.

234 Approaching Lituya Bay: Wheat interview. Blackadar, in later correspondence to Rod Nash, 9-12-77, referred to encountering 30-foot swells during the motoring out trip.

234 Lituya Bay's narrow 1,000-foot entrance: Don J. Miller, "Giant Waves in Lituya Bay Alaska," *Geological Survey Professional Paper 354-C* (Washington: USGPO, 1960), pp. 51, 53, 56, 57-59.

234 "We were perhaps two swells away": This and related unattributed quotes from personal interview with Klaus Streckman, 8-5-84.

235 "No problem": Young interview.

235 Blackadar called Idaho: Johnson, Diary.

236 "We were getting tired": Personal interview with Keith Taylor, 5-26-84.

236 "Let's go boating": Author's observations.

236 Snowfall on Lost Trail Pass: *Recorder Herald*, 12-28-78.

236 "It was a heavy snowstorm": Wheat interview.

236 That January temperatures: *Recorder Herald*, 12-28-78.

237 Outside the Idaho Falls workshop: *Idaho Environmental Council Newsletter*, August, 1977, p. 6.

237 In February of 1978, Frank Church: *Idaho Environmental Council Newsletter*, February-March, 1978, p. 2.

237 The new library: *Recorder Herald*, 6-16-77.

237 Construction on a badly-needed: *Recorder Herald*, 4-6-78, 12-28-78.

238 He wrote back: W.L. Blackadar, Letters to Pamela A. Miller, *River World*, 2-8-78, and to Peter Skinner, American Whitewater Affiliation, 2-8-78.

238 Don Wilson, his kayaking friend: Donald H. Wilson, Letter to W.L. Blackadar, 4-24-78.

238 "Saw you . . .": Andrew A. Westerhaus, Burnsville, Minnesota, Letter to W.L. Blackadar, 3-21-77.

238 "a terrific boater": A.C. Freemen, Pine Bluff, Arkansas, Letter to W.L. Blackadar, 3-7-77.

238 "[you give] me motivation": Terry Goss, Letter to W. L. Blackadar, *circa* late 1975.

238 "You might be the answer": Shirley Haycock, Helper, Utah, Letter to W.L. Blackadar, 2-27-77.

238 "I'd like to get you down here": David Sumner, Letter to W.L. Blackadar, 5-4-77.

238 "Sounds like fun": W.L. Blackadar, Letter to David Sumner, 3-29-77.

238 Sumner, because of marital problems: David Sumner, Letter to W.L. Blackadar, 5-4-77.

239 To approach kayaking: Telephone interview with Roger Brown, 11-3-87.

CHAPTER XIII: RIVER OF NO RETURN

241 During the winter he had slipped: Telephone interview with Rob Lesser, 12-2-87.

241 By now both Boyd Simmons: Personal interviews with Keith Taylor, 5-26-84 and Boyd Simmons, 5-23-84.

241 For the pain: Personal interview with Hazel Dean, 8-24-84.

241 He had hoped to join: W.L. Blackadar, Letter to Dr. and Mrs. Richard Furman, 5-4-77, and Letter of Dr. Myron Schultz, Center for Disease Control, 6-7-77.

241 He also continued his interest: W.L. Blackadar, Letter to John C. Bangeman, 3-14-77. His continuing interest in the Stikine is revealed in a letter to Roderick Nash, 9-12-77.

242 He started on a fitness regimen: Personal interview with Lois Blackadar, 5-24-84.

242 Instead, to his alarm: Personal interview with Woo McLean, 7-1-84.

243 "The stories I'd heard of him": Eric Evans, "Rx for the American Sportsman," *Canoe*, July, 1978, p. 16.

243 What Evans found: Telephone interview with Eric Evans, 12-2-87.

244 At one point when the kayakers: Lesser interview.

244 "The water was a good Class IV": Evans, "Rx," p. 16.

244 "It was obvious": Lesser interview.

245 "He said his roll was terrible": Personal interview with Barb Wright, 5-22-84.

245 "I did get to Boston": W.L. Blackadar, Letter to Dr. Don Wilson, 5-11-78.

245 "I will admit": Wright interview.

245 To Joe Nebeker: Personal interview with Joe Nebeker, 5-25-84.

246 He and Doug Wheat: Telephone interview with Doug Wheat, 12-7-87.

246 He was lining up: W.L. Blackadar, Letter to Dr. Don Wilson, 5-11-78.

246 In a letter to a film producer: W.L. Blackadar, Letter to Bob Greenaway, 4-14-78.

246 "there was probably a mental aspect": Lesser interview.

247 For a couple of weeks: Lois Blackadar interview.

247 "I could see": Personal interview with Berniece Benedict, 8-22-84.

247 "He'd come cruising in": Personal interview with Jeff Bevan, 1-11-86.

248 "Honey": Personal interview with Sue Blackadar, 5-16-84.

248 Blackadar had also phoned: Personal interview with Keith Taylor, 5-26-84.

249 "Look, you've got": Bevan interview.

250 "It's paddleable": Bevan interview.

253 "I've spent a long time thinking": Personal interview with John Dondero, 8-25-84.

254 "Jeff called": Personal interview with Bob Blackadar, 8-24-84.

254 After hearing of the accident: Personal interview with Tullio Celano, 5-26-84.

255 Early the second morning: Personal interview with John Blackadar, 8-10-85.

CHAPTER XIV: EPILOGUE

259 "The paddling world lost": Kenneth H. McAmis, "Dr. Walt Blackadar," *Georgia Canoe Association Newsletter*.

259 "Blackadar was whitewater sport's": "Obituaries," *American Whitewater*, May-June, 1978, p. 93.

259 "He always had time": John Shannon, *Basic Canoe Club Newsletter*, Henderson, Nevada.

259 "Adventurous, amazing, admirable": Klaus Streckman, "Farewell to a Fine Friend," *BC Whitewater*, June, 1978, p. 11.

259 "few men will be missed": Barbara Wright, "Epitaph for a Friend," *Canoe*, November, 1978, p. 69.

259 "He does not take the risk": Don Wilson, "A Personal Look at Walt Blackadar," *River World*, September, 1978, p. 70.

260 The idea to do a tribute: Telephone interview with Roger Brown, 11-3-87.

260 "Walt Blackadar was truly alive": *ABC American Sportsman,* "Tribute to Walt Blackadar," aired June, 1978.

260 Of all the unrelenting forces: Personal interview with Klaus Streckman, 8-5-84.

260　Streckman's efforts to commemorate: Klaus Streckman, Letter to Mr. D. F. Pearson, B.C. Representative on Canadian Permanent Committee on Geographical Names, Ministry of Environment, September 27, 1978, and D.F. Pearson, Letter to Mrs. Shirley C. Blackadar, February 2, 1979.

261　Even so, Carter didn't win: *Recorder Herald*, 11-4-76.

261　A petition drive: *Recorder Herald*, 8-24-78.

262　"Thousands of tired, nerve-shaken": John Muir, "The Wild Parks and Forest Reservations of the West," *Atlantic Monthly*, Vol. 18, January, 1898, p. 15.

262　He had said as much in 1965: W.L. Blackadar, Letter to Stewart Udall, Secretary of the Interior, Washington, D.C., 4-2-65.

262　"Outdoor Recreation is one": W.L. Blackadar, untitled testimony presented at Salmon National Forest Service hearing on roadless lands, nd.

263　He retired in 1985: Bob Johnson, "Two Retire from Sawmill in Salmon," *Idaho State Journal*, September 5, 1985, p. 6B.

263　Bill Baker, the Lemhi County sheriff: "Salmon's Sheriff Mixes Poetry with Old Time Justice," *Idaho State Journal*, March 23, 1987, p. 2A.

Index

About the Author

Ron Watters is the author of *Ski Trails and Old-Timers' Tales*, *The Whitewater River Book*, *Ski Camping: A Guide to the Delights of Backcountry Skiing,* and *The Outdoor Programming Handbook*. An active kayaker and rafter, he has run rivers in the Alps, Norway, Australia, Alaska, and throughout the western United States and Canada. As part of the research for this book, he and Bob Blackadar organized an expedition down the Alsek River. It was on this expedition that the first successful ascent of Mt. Blackadar was made. He has climbed in the Himalayas and has made several long backcountry ski journeys, including the first ski traverse of the River of No Return Wilderness in central Idaho. Watters is the Director of the Idaho State University Outdoor Program and a proponent of outdoor recreational programming for people with disabilities.

Also Available

For the visually impaired, *Never Turn Back* is available from The Great Rift Press on computer disk or audio cassette tape. Additionally, an unabridged volume of Walt Blackadar's life will be released soon for readers and researchers who are interested in more details of his life, river running, Idaho conservation issues, or history of the Salmon area. Also available from The Great Rift Press are Ron Watters' popular book, *Ski Camping: A Guide to the Delights of Backcountry Skiing*, and RACEAID, an IBM compatible computer program for the scoring of marathons, road races, bicycle races, cross-country running meets, and triathlons. For more information, contact The Great Rift Press, 1135 East Bonneville, Pocatello, ID 83201; or call (208) 232-6857.